Curriculum Design
in a Changing Society

Curriculum Design in a Changing Society

Richard W. Burns
and
Gary D. Brooks

The University of Texas at El Paso

Editors

Preface by Robert M. Gagné
Epilogue by John I. Goodlad

Educational Technology Publications / Englewood Cliffs, New Jersey

Printed in the United States of America.

Library of Congress Catalog Card Number: 75-122811

International Standard Book Number: 0-87778-003-X

First Printing

Preface

The writers of the chapters in this volume share in common the belief that educational improvement is critically needed, and needs to be approached by way of revisions in the curriculum. They agree that needs for change in the schools involving administrative structure, teacher roles, staffing patterns, building characteristics and other considerations of this general nature are overshadowed in importance by the pressing nature of the requirement to attend to what students learn and how they learn. In fact, by implication at least, they are agreed that the physical and administrative structure of the system of education should be derived from a prior determination of what is to be done about the curriculum, rather than the other way around.

It may be readily perceived, also, that these writers are generally of the opinion that whatever changes in curriculum may have been wrought in recent years, they are not sufficiently fundamental. The curriculum reforms which have been brought about in the 1960's, in science, mathematics, social studies and in other subjects, are of unquestioned value. Perhaps they have

v

helped in no small measure to set the stage for the more comprehensive view of the curriculum problem that is reflected in these chapters. These now familiar "new" curricula have been, with few exceptions, intra-disciplinary in their orientation and execution. The writers of these papers, however, appear to be saying that bringing school subjects into line with the modern structure of the disciplines is not enough.

Many signs point to the need for curriculum reform: the changing nature of our society, the startling increase in our rate of accumulation of new knowledge, the national dedication to equal educational opportunity for all segments of our school population, the need for relevance of educational pursuits to individual goals, the apparent erosion of a shared set of values pertaining to human interaction, and the diminution of expected standards of competence in basic skills throughout a broad sector of our population. A valuable perspective on the history of curriculum change and curriculum reform is given in this book. However, an understanding of past events is not likely to alter the impression that powerful social forces of the present day are at work in pressing for fundamental alterations in our approach to the enterprise of education.

Many diverse views are presented in these chapters, and an almost equal number of proposed solutions to the problem of curriculum revision. Some authors are concerned with what appear to be missing pieces, such as a humanistic emphasis, education in early childhood, the instruction of children of the poor. A good many emphasize the need for improvement in conditions of instruction, in any and all subjects, by application of knowledge of the learning process, by the employment of techniques made possible by new media, and by the systematic design of instructional systems to promote effective learning. Some of the most challenging ideas are those which suggest that educational goals and objectives need to be planned anew, from the ground up, on the basis of a careful analysis of individual and societal needs.

Certain common themes can be derived by implication from the diversity of approaches described. First is the idea that a modern educational system probably needs to have a great deal of diversity in itself, and to avoid the restraining influence of a single educational model. Just as there apparently need to be special kinds of schools for children of the inner city, probably also there need to be special kinds of schools for people of different interests and life goals — for example, for those who wish to become artists, or scientists, or public servants. Perhaps it is not too soon to think of differentiated curricula, in which the learning of a common core of basic skills in the early years is followed by a pluralistic variety of educational choices.

A second implication of differing curriculum approaches deserves special mention. Some writers today emphasize the kinds of educational outcomes that are readily specifiable and closely related to practical performances: reading, writing, reasoning and computation with numbers, and the like. Others emphasize goals partaking of imagination, creativity, independent thinking, which tend to be more remote as observable outcomes of any single course of study. Furthermore, these two kinds of aims are often sharply contrasted, as if the attainment of one kind actually precluded the attainment of the other. This kind of argument seems based on a gross misconception of what the human being is like and of how he learns. The fact is that school learning has two perspectives, and both are necessary for effective human development. On the one hand, one cannot confine instruction to the learning of basic intellectual skills, since these amount to little unless they are used in a great variety of problem solving situations requiring imagination and inventiveness. On the other hand, one cannot adequately design opportunities for creative thought for students who do not possess the basic intellectual skills necessary for effective functioning. It is ridiculous to claim that such skills are simply "picked up," or learned incidentally, without some systematic study on the part of the student. A well-designed curriculum must surely include both perspectives — competence and independent thought — if it is going to serve the needs of students with a broad range of innate capacities.

Robert M. Gagné
Florida State University

Contents

x *Contents*

Curriculum Design in a Changing Society

1

The Need for
Curriculum Reform

Richard W. Burns and Gary D. Brooks

School curricula at all levels of education need to be critically
reviewed in the light of present cultural needs, global pressures
and technological innovations. In the papers which follow, significant curricular problems are discussed, recommendations are
offered, and several areas of import, such as minority education
and implications of computer usage are explored.

The problems and pressures — the cries for change — have
received almost continuous recognition in the educational literature of this century. The pressures for change and the calls for a
new curriculum are mounting.

What are these pressures? What are the needs for curricular
reform? Perhaps two other questions should be asked first: Have

RICHARD W. BURNS is professor of education at the University of Texas
at El Paso. GARY D. BROOKS is director of the Office of Institutional
Studies at the University of Texas at El Paso.

3

there been changes in our curricula? Aren't we currently experiencing reform within our schools?

Yes, there have been changes in our curricula, but most of the major changes are historical. The last major change of great significance at the secondary level was the addition of vocational education in the early years of this century. Virtually all the subjects taught now in elementary and secondary schools were taught in 1920.

Are we currently experiencing a reform movement? Programmed instruction (PI), computer assisted instruction (CAI), team teaching, micro teaching, educational television (ETV), desegregation, the development of special minority education programs and many more innovations indicate a rather widespread recognition of the need for change. However, some of these innovations have not been of great *curricular* significance — just technological improvements in methods and hardware.

Technological innovations should be exploited more thoroughly. *Of particular import is the development of curriculum designs worthy of modern technology.*

Basic curricular reform must deal with *content* first. We can expect even greater ingenuity in devising new systems for education incorporating radical designs for information storage, information retrieval, content presentation to learners and achievement analysis; but *such changes do not strike at the heart of the problem.* The central problem is the curricular content, which is not much different today from what existed in the schools of the 1800's. *What is needed is a thorough revision of curricular content.*

Since 1950, various individuals, groups and organizations have sensed the need for changes in our curricula. As a result, improvements have been made, especially in mathematics, biology, physics, chemistry, English and foreign languages at the high school level. To a lesser degree, reforms have been made in high school music, economics and geography. Elementary education, preschool education, reading, mathematics and special education have experienced some reform. Unfortunately, *none of the reforms have gone far enough to produce the curricula needed for today's education.*

Science instruction today is leading the way in recognizing the *process deficiency in education*. Learners need to know more than mere information — they need to know how information is gathered, identified and transformed; in short, they need to know how information is *used*. Learning must involve more than the mere memorization of facts and principles. Learning must involve an understanding of the methods by which fields of knowledge have been constructed. Learners should know the "hows" and "whys" — the whole structure of the sciences, mathematics and social sciences. Learners must develop skill in using the same processes that physicists, historians, zoologists, economists and others use to study and pry information out of our natural and social environment. Learners need to know the methods, the ways — *the processes* — by which factual information, once gained, is transformed into generalizations, concepts, principles and laws. Learners need to know how to learn, how to use what they have learned and how to communicate about what they have learned.

Fourteen reasons why our curricula need changing are identified and outlined below. No order of importance is intended.

1. We are living in a global society.
2. We are living in a rapidly changing world.
3. Our culture is experiencing an information explosion.
4. Present curricula are information oriented rather than process oriented.
5. There is a lack of relevancy between in-school education and out-of-school life.
6. There is a prohibitive time lag in education between the discovery of new techniques and the incorporation of these techniques into educational practice.
7. General education and core curricula are presently too survey oriented.
8. There are new technical innovations for which new curricular patterns can be designed.
9. Urban living, a decreasing emphasis on family structure, and the increasing mobility of the population demand greater individual responsibility.

10. There is an increased recognition of the needs of minority groups and minority group problems.
11. Our knowledge of what is true is constantly changing.
12. There is an increased understanding of how people learn.
13. The behavioral definition of learning products has revealed deficiencies in our present curricula.
14. Productivity has released men from the necessity of long labor.

(1) A Global Society

People use the expression "my world" to mean the environment in which they operate. For many people, the world in which they live is extremely small and isolated. In times past what people did in other "worlds" had little effect on people in their "world." Provincialism and isolationism are rapidly becoming dead ideologies. Events in Egypt, Japan, Vietnam, Peru and hundreds of other places directly or indirectly affect "home." War, atomic energy, space travel, germ warfare, communications satellites and dozens of other phenomena eventually affect the welfare of each individual on this planet. The effects of global pollution of atmosphere and water are influencing every living thing on earth. The problems which face society now and in the future will not be solved from a state of ignorance. The population explosion, for example, can only be solved by the intelligent behavior of every adult the world over.

(2) A Rapidly Changing World

Perhaps ninety percent of all scientists who have ever lived are now alive. What will future generations call this age? Whatever the designation, it will imply "change." Within the life span of many individuals, our society has progressed from the horse-and-buggy to Apollo spacecraft, and Apollo is only the beginning. Scientists and engineers have changed and are changing our world far beyond the wildest futuristic dreams of the individual citizen.

Change is a difficult phenomenon to accept and even more difficult to prepare for. How do we educate for change? Logically the answer lies in (1) the efficient learning of basic materials which will have wide transfer value and (2) acquiring ability to learn independently, outside the classroom. In a changing world, the curriculum can afford few frills; it must be flexible; it must be constantly changed and augmented; and it must prepare the learner for *change*. It may well be that the test of an educated person in the near future will be his or her ability to adapt to change.

What is needed are curricula designed not as collections of independent bits of knowledge, not as isolated and static subjects learned in a vacuum. Instead, our curricula must reflect the complex interrelationships and processes inherent in the many problems facing our society. Knowledge, understanding, skills, attitudes, appreciations, interests and processes should be studied as integrated units in curricular designs which reflect the rapidly changing aspects of our society. Learners must *think;* that is, use all of the mental processes implied in problem solving, instead of merely *remembering,* as they are currently required to do in recalling information.

Another aspect of change relating to curricula is the effect change has on increasing obsolescence. Curricular materials (texts, maps, charts, diagrams, films, filmstrips, microfilm and other learning resources) will need updating or replacing much more rapidly in response to the speed with which information is discovered and to the degree that our knowledge of what is *true* is altered. Changes in learning theory, modes of communication, methods of communication, and methods of instruction will also produce early obsolescence in instructional materials of all kinds.

(3) The Information Explosion

The world is currently experiencing an information explosion, the import of which we are just beginning to realize. Knowledge is increasing at a geometric ratio. Thus, it is inconceivable that learners can be educated by the daily feeding (in most states, 180 days) of *bits* of information. The role of information and its relationship to education should be intensively re-examined. There is no intent to exclude information; in fact, much more information is going to be needed and utilized by learners. The bulk of this information, however, will not be stored in the minds of learners but rather in computers or comparable devices. Modern information storage and retrieval systems will make it possible for learners to have at their fingertips an infinite amount of information which can be utilized in problem solving. Information *usage* must be emphasized in the curriculum, rather than the mass acquisition of information. This shift in emphasis will not only radically affect the learner but also will result in a redefinition of the role of the teacher. Teachers will no longer *tell,* lecture and present lessons, but will assume roles akin to counseling, consulting and guiding.

New curricular designs should be developed utilizing the technological capacities of devices which can store and instantly retreive information. Such devices, with the proper curricula, will enable students to define problems, gather data, suggest hypotheses, generalize, propose novel solutions and reach conclusions — all based on their own "research." Such problem solving skills can and should be developed in all subject areas through the use of special curricular designs in the early grades.

(4) Information Orientation of Curricula

Present curricula and present teaching methods emphasize *information* learning rather than discovery, problem solving, data analysis, data gathering and related activities. Textbook learning, teacher telling, lectures and factual achievement tests all indicate the overwhelming emphasis placed on the mastery of information in our present system. The complex nature of today's world demands the acquisition of behaviors other than those classified as *knowledge.* Learners also need to develop understandings, motor skills, processes (mental skills) and affective traits — attitudes, interests and appreciations. It has already been observed that learners need to be prepared for "change" in a rapidly changing world. It is no longer conceivable that learning (and getting an education) can be pinpointed to the acquiring of a specific set of finite behaviors containing the exact amount of information which will serve the learner to meet his present and future needs.

(5) Lack of Relevancy

Many teachers hate to admit it, and school administrators frequently act as if they had never thought of the problem, but a little soul-searching will force almost all educators to realize that the content taught in most classrooms is not relevant to the lives of the learners. The more "different" the student, the greater this problem becomes and the easier it is to see.

It is fairly easy to see, for example, that a young Huk child in the Philippines or a Montagnard youngster in the mountains of Vietnam would have little use for a lesson in literary criticism of *Beowolf,* a laboratory exercise in disecting crayfish, or a mathematics lesson dealing with the relative rates of two trains traveling between Chicago and New York. It is more difficult to admit that a Navaho learner in Utah or Arizona might not profit from *The Scarlet Letter* or need to know how to draw the pores on a starfish. Minority education in a Los Angeles slum district just might be conceived as having to be different from the equivalent grade level education needed in Winnebago, Iowa. Once we accept the idea that an education might necessarily be different if the pupils are to profit from their learning, we must come to an attack on the problem of relevancy. Learning, to be relevant, must deal with those interests, problems, frustrations, yearnings, aspirations, feelings, struggles, cravings and dilemmas *within each learner.* Hunger is not appeased by pursuing Shakespeare, disease is not avoided by memorizing the names of the bones of the body, and poverty is not overcome by memorizing the first ten articles of the Constitution. The content of any curriculum must consider the realities of the environment, be it island, slum, mountain, or desert. Topics germane to the actual problems of nutrition, disease, sanitation, water supply, family size, personal income, job security, entertainment, crime, drug use, health insurance and dozens of other problems should certainly be the first bases for curricular content in preference to topics unrelated to life.

It does not follow that all instruction must be confined to these problems, nor must the instruction deal only with "what is" rather than "what should be." However, instruction must begin where the student *is* if it is to make much sense to the learner. Hopefully, the learner will be carried beyond the present — that is, all learners should be inspired to attain the highest levels of vocation and avocation possible.

(6) The Time Lag

There are so many reports of the time lag between discovery and application, all of them negative, that one is hard pressed to decide if twenty or one hundred years is the proper descriptive term. In education, competent observers report that the time lag is even more serious than in other segments of society.

Curricula must be updated and integrated with methods which will maximize learning. Materials for learning should be empirically designed, behaviorally oriented, up-to-date, intensive, adapted to the learner, and relevant to his environment. Multi-sensory approaches should be used — students should work with things, instruction should be based on reality, and the classroom and environment should be brought closer together.

Perhaps all of this demands new approaches to teacher training and certainly some system of inservice retraining of teachers and administrators. If financial obstacles prevent schools from utilizing proper methods and instructional materials, then some basis for financial assistance to school districts must be initiated. Cost-effectiveness studies of many of the new materials and much of the new equipment for instruction indicate that the initial outlay is frequently no more, and sometimes less, than materials and equipment currently in use.

Tradition plays an influential role in educational practice. Perhaps this is because our schools have been largely controlled, staffed and designed for a conservative, middle-class type of education. It is not our intent to raise *value* issues — but rather to point out that tradition is a poor excuse for continuing outmoded and detrimental practices. The same people who fail to sense the need to update schools are often the first to initiate new business and agricultural practices where financial profit is the incentive. Perhaps this is the key to the problem: Where is the incentive to improve education — to bring it up-to-date? One incentive which might be suggested is human survival!

(7) Survey Orientation of General Education and Core Curricula

Pursuing a general education degree should not imply the learning of a little bit about a lot of things. A general education should develop behavior competencies just as well as does its opposite, special or technical education. The difference in behaviors is one of kind and not degree.

Many courses of study for survey, core, introductory, orientation and general courses reflect a "let's cover the whole thing" type of organization. The result is that the "learner knows a lot about nothing." This expression implies that the learning is too shallow to be functional. Survey, core, orientation, introductory and general courses need to cover fewer topics—and cover them well. The topics covered should reflect the "core," "general," or "survey" title. That is, the topics should be basic, fundamental and representative of a broad area. The topics studied should be carefully selected and then studied as intensively as topics in other courses. The behavioral outcomes should be functional and useful. For instance, a course in "Survey of Literature" need not attempt to cover all literature. Rather, the selections should be carefully selected; they could be representative of various literary types or styles. Each selection should be studied in depth, with behavioral goals reflecting the acquiring of a general literary criticism ability. Poorly organized core and general courses waste many hours of valuable learning time; those responsible for their presence at all levels of education should hasten to revise them.

In this same sense, a general education should result in *useful* behaviors. The title "general" applies to the fact that the behaviors acquired have general application to some restricted area of learning. An educated person in the general sense should study broad problems — serious problems — and study them intensively. The general education major should concentrate on goals like communication — speech, writing and languages. Acquiring a general education does not imply speaking four languages poorly but rather four languages well. A general education through high school, as opposed to a vocational or college preparatory education, should certainly have as its goal the development of independence in the pursuit of knowledge. This type of program along with other types should develop problem solving skills — in other words, *processes*. The problems studied should be more general; in fact, they could be extremely significant global problems, such as conservation of wildlife, conservation of water resources, atomic war, air pollution, or overpopulation. Thinking generally and broadly does not mean shallow thinking.

(8) New Curricular Patterns for Technical Innovations

Many of the possibilities for new curricular patterns can barely be imagined, since only meager beginnings have been made. However, there are four major ways in which technology can directly affect curricula. First, technology can be a tool used to improve the design and organization of curricula. For example, PI and CAI are tools which can be used to locate stimuli which will elicit desired responses, help establish hierarchies of proper steps in learning high order principles, record student responses to locate weak spots in learning sets, and tailor-make curricula to the needs of individual learners. Second, technology can be an area of study in itself, thus adding to what is to be learned in a given curriculum. Third, technology can provide new sources of materials, making it possible to devise curricular problems either currently superficially studied or altogether absent from the curriculum. CAI provides a good illustration of how a technological innovation can be harnessed to facilitate problem solving. With the tremendous storage and retrieval capacities of computers, learning can be increased in both breadth and depth. Information pertaining to any given problem can be more readily obtained in a greater quantity if a computer library is available. With a computer library at one's fingertips, and an index guide, any problem solver can locate all that is currently known about a given topic and bring it to bear on his problem. Fourth, technology can provide "on the spot" coverage of history in the making, thus eliminating both the time lag and inaccuracies which are often characteristic of historical reporting. The most dramatic examples of this point were the TV and radio coverage of the Apollo 11 and Apollo 12 flights to the moon. Years from now learners won't have to imagine or guess about what happened nor depend on second-hand reports of historic events. Learners will be able to see and hear exactly what took place.

All of these major influences of technology on curricula should be fully exploited. Learners should be brought into visual and audio contact with government, business, religious, social and military leaders. The environment of far-away places should be brought into the classroom. Efficient learning materials must be designed that are guaranteed to result in learning *if used properly*. Children should be trained in computer language, computer skills and similar functions so that they can use technological aids in learning.

(9) Urban Living, Family Structure, Mobility and Individual Responsibility

Should schools stress individuality and individual freedom, or should they train individuals to become effective members of groups — such as families, communities, states and nations? *They should do both.* Should schools educate students to develop their personal role, their unique talents, or should schools develop good citizens, with a high degree of interest and responsibility in public affairs? *They should do both.*

Urban living, giant industries, huge federal programs, increased mobility of the population, large tax burdens, military service and changing moral values cause individuals to become lost, isolated and alienated.

(10) Minority Group Needs and Problems

One important aspect of the subgroups within any culture is their tendency to develop unique communication systems. This phenomenon results in isolation of the groups from outsiders. Any one individual may be a member of several such groups and must master several communication systems. An individual belonging to several groups may be frustrated by attempting to identify with conflicting group goals. On the other hand, he may be denied membership in a group because he has failed to master the correct communication system. Schools are faced with a substantial dilemma when the communication system of the school differs radically from the system(s) needed by the learners in their extra-school life.

Our nation's schools are faced with the problem of training individuals to acquire an appreciation of other cultures, to become tolerant of people who are different from them, and to understand the concept of the brotherhood of man.

Minority education poses an additional problem because content needs differ from group to group. To the degree that groups differ, so must their education differ.

An additional problem is one of the proper curricular design for disadvantaged learners. Educators have observed the obvious deficiencies in both traditional methods and curricula. Current practices are producing failures, underachievers and school dropouts, all of whom by definition are unfit to play a normal role in our culture.

(11) Truth Is Changing

Our understanding of what is *true* is constantly undergoing change as new information is discovered. Constant revision and updating of curricular content is required if learners are to "know the truth." As examples, we *used to believe:*

1. The earth was round
2. The atom was indivisible
3. Wet feet caused colds
4. The earth was approximately two billion years old

5. Permissiveness was the key to child rearing
6. The American Indian was a blood-thirsty savage
7. Infants thrived best on regular feeding schedules
8. It would be difficult to walk on the moon

Some measure of the degree of this problem, especially with textbook centered learning, is provided by the realization that curricular materials are frequently out-of-date. We are led to believe that in any decade man discovers as much or progresses as far as from the beginning of man up to the initial year of the decade. If this is true, and it requires two years to develop a textbook, a third year to get it commonly accepted in the market, and schools use the book for an additional five years (a common practice), then as much as forty percent of what we might know about a topic could be excluded from the learning at the eighth year. *Textbook learning is outdated learning;* good teaching practices have long recognized this problem. Teachers have struggled to update and thereby upgrade curricula by bringing into the classroom recent content provided by magazines, journals, newspapers, etc.

Technology should be adapted to this *dating* problem. Source materials should be continuously updated and made available through microfilm, computer techniques, or by comparable means.

(12) An Increased Understanding of How People Learn

Significant advances have been made in learning theory—which have *not* been applied to classroom practices to any significant degree. A good illustration is furnished by the concept of individual learning. Even though individualized instruction is commonly recognized as a valid *principle,* very little has been accomplished by way of making it a classroom *practice.* Numerous techniques and innovations, including tutoring, pupil-pupil assistance, teacher aides, the contract method, supplementary assignments, individualized lesson assignments, flexible scheduling, programmed instruction, television and data retrieval systems are available as ways of implementing individualized learning. What is holding us back?

Other profitable outgrowths of studying how people learn have shown the value of relevancy of psychologically structured learning, discovery methods, student sequenced subject matter, reinforcement, stimulus control, diagnostic techniques, learning hierarchies, feedback, multisensory methods, cueing and instruction in processes. It appears that little progress has been made on any of these factors, although the presence of all of them can be detected by observing many different teachers in the classroom. Learning theorists must be brought into closer working relationship with those responsible for the production of instructional materials.

In addition, empirical methods should be employed to develop learning models, learning strategies, hierarchies of concept formation, job and task behaviors, efficient examples and sensory stimuli which will prove effective in promoting individualized learning. It is apparent that there is a serious time lag (see No. 6) between research identification and practical application in the area of learning theory.

(13) Behavioral Objectives and Curricular Deficiencies

The analysis of learning in terms of changes in behavior has progressed remarkably in the past decade. The best instructional materials now on the market are a result of the careful delineation of the terminal behaviors, or specific objectives expected to be achieved by the learners.

In the past, educators, especially teachers, have tended to rely on broad, vague and general statements of goals. The reasons for this dependence on the more or less useless, general statements about learning stem from ignorance of how to develop specific objectives, general satisfaction with present accomplishments, a vague feeling that being "pinned down" would disclose deficiences, and a hazy notion that general goals provide room for "on the spot" adjustments which are necessary in light of learner interests and learner contributions. General satisfaction with present student accomplishment stems from those learners who exhibit a natural inclination toward the academics — the above average learners.

In the development of PI, it was quickly discovered that the brighter students should not be used to test the adequacy and effectiveness of the materials being developed, for almost *any* method, *any* material, *any* sequence would "work" with these students. Rather, average and below average learners should be utilized to empirically test new methods and materials. To design learning sequences which "work" with those who learn with difficulty has proven to be a real challenge to program writers. There has been less perceived need to develop behavioral objectives for higher education, since college level students are generally a select group. In addition, the teaching ranks at colleges and universities are more jealous and protective of their private "expertise;" to expect agreement on "what should be taught" for any course at any level is perceived as akin to interference with academic freedom. Most professors are adamant that what they teach is vital, necessary and of such a nature that probably it should be "required." But they are not willing to specify *exactly what is to be learned.*

The lack of stated goals for any course of instruction can only mean that the learner has a fuzzy notion of what is to be accomplished. This undoubtedly accounts for some of the student unrest which impinges upon the educational process. Many students are confused about what they are to learn — in fact, students have often been observed leaving final exams and remarking to each other, "Did you know what he wanted?" or "So *that's* what he wanted!"

The percentage of college level students who are doing unsatisfactory work, "D" and "F," has some relationship to this problem. The challenge should be to educate learners and not to fail them. Admittedly, all students who attend college may not be blameless where unsatisfactory achievement is concerned, but it is also incorrect to consign to them total responsibility for failure. A recent, unpublished analysis of the grades assigned at several colleges and universities revealed a high proportion of non-success. One university with twenty-eight academic departments revealed six departments where the total of

"D"and "F" grades assigned reached 30% or higher.

Educational writers, teachers, program developers and technologists who have attempted and frequently accomplished the task of developing specific objectives are unanimous in reporting that it is in itself an "educational experience." It is highly probable that every teacher who undergoes this experience has, as a result, become a better teacher. The experience can be shocking and even traumatic — it inevitably reveals teaching deficiencies. But in the end it is one of the most rewarding experiences within the profession, except for observing learners realizing their achievement capabilities.

Educators not familiar with developing specific objectives are urged to acquire the appropriate understanding and skill.

Present and past educational reforms in courses, curricula, methods and testing will never achieve the desired and necessary changes until specific objectives are carefully defined.

(14) Increased Leisure

Science and technology have contributed to the increased productivity of man to a degree which presently affords the individual in our culture the prospect of eventually being free of drudgery. During the 1970's, the average worker will probably spend less than forty hours gainfully pursuing a living. Many people already have achieved relative independence from the time clock. Each person, to the degree that he is free from work, needs recreational skills; especially leisure time skills of a creative nature. This demand leads to two curricular needs; first, a curriculum designed to develop specific skills which the individual can use immediately upon leaving school, and second, a general orientation of the curriculum away from viewing it solely as a means where the learner prepares himself only for productive *work*. Again, it must be emphasized that the curriculum should reflect the culture. If our culture is increasingly to allow for leisure, then our schools must prepare individuals to use that time wisely. Some educators view this problem as solely the province of "adult" education, but this is a very limited viewpoint.

2

Cultural Change and the Curriculum: 1970-2000 A.D.

June Grant Shane and Harold G. Shane

One of the popular radio and comic strips which originated in the 1930's was built around the adventures of a muscular character somewhat anachronistically named Buck Rogers. Some of the wonders that his creator, Dick Calkins, envisioned for Captain Rogers included: space ships and interplanetary travel; jumping belts; video telephones; electronic beams for medical and defense purposes; and food in pill form. Mr. Calkin's prescience was not limited to technological developments! He also forecast the mini-skirt and women's high boot fashions of today when he created a wardrobe for Wilma Deering, Buck's presumably platonic lady friend on various intersteller voyages.

Interestingly, most of the changes that Calkins projected

JUNE GRANT SHANE is professor of education at Indiana University. HAROLD G. SHANE is university professor of education at Indiana University.

did not occur in the twenty-fifth century but in the twentieth century — not in six hundred years but in approximately thirty years. In other words, these developments were a part of the experiences of many people living today; people whose experiences have carried them from the horse-and-buggy life of the early part of the century to the electrical, nuclear energy and space travel world of the seventies. How many of these people would have dreamed that most of the fantasies depicted in the science fiction of the last hundred years would be less amazing than the realities of 1970?

Our present century is viewed by Kenneth Boulding,[1] the economist, as the middle period of a great transition in the history of the human race. Within this period and within the memory of living people is a kind of dividing point or watershed that separates the history of man into two parts. During the first part man moved from a "pre-civilized" to a "civilized" society. At present he is involved in a second great transition — one moving from a "civilized" to a "post-civilized"[2] society. Unfortunately, we seem to be both unknowing participants in an intermediate state of civilization and inadvertent midwives for the birth of a new era. For many of the participants in such midwifery, this is a strenuous, uncomfortable, and frequently disconcerting experience. According to Sir George Thompson,[3] the closest historical analogy, although an inadequate one, would be the permanent changes created by the invention of agriculture during the neolithic age. Even this explanation does not always help us to accommodate ourselves to the rapid acceleration in man's ability to make material progress and to his remarkable increasing powers over his environment.

The Impact of Tomorrow

The deranging influence of future-shock. Alvin Toffler[4] has used the term "future-shock" to identify a condition which has begun to affect many persons in the U.S.; a condition that he predicts might be one of tomorrow's most important "psychological diseases." Toffler describes "future-shock" as a time-change phenomenon resulting from rapid socio-technical developments which have carried us from familiar yesterdays to unknown tomorrows. He describes it as "culture shock in one's own society"[5] and feels that its permeating quality is often more disorienting to people than is the culture shock which a traveler experiences in visiting countries where the customs and cues as to ways of living are radically different from his own. The impact of future-shock, however, is greater than *culture* shock because the visitor to a foreign country always can comfort himself with the thought that he may return to the familiar environs of his own land.[6]

This is not possible for the sufferer of future-shock. He cannot look homeward and feel secure knowing that he may once again function in easily recognizable situations with his old patterns of behavior. For him, the changes that have deranged his once-familiar environment are irrevocable. One cannot "return home" to yesterday.

We are now rapidly approaching the time depicted by George Orwell — the fateful year 1984. In fact, so near is this date that children enrolled in our elementary schools will be young adults and of voting age when Orwell's mystical date becomes a reality. Sixteen years thereafter we confront the beginning of the third millenium — the year 2000.

What will this new millenium be like? Will it be a chiliastic era — one of "great happiness, perfect government, and freedom from imperfections in human existence?"[7] Or will it be one beginning in chaos and leading to a new dark age? What will the *degree* of change and the rate of change do to people? Surely, it will affect our conceptions of ourselves, our work, leisure, social living — indeed, every aspect of human endeavor.

The Curriculum Worker and "Information Overload"

Among the many agents of educational change, the school curriculum specialist should be especially aware of developments that may affect man's future. As a professionally trained person, he is committed to facilitating the individual student's development of his potential. Because he carries this responsibility, there are many components to the curriculum planner's role. He must be concerned with (1) the integrity and dignity of the individual; (2) the dynamics of group behavior; (3) the learning process and qualities in the home and school environment that help mediate experience; (4) social trends that influence a student's present world and the world he will enter; and (5) the economic, political and technological developments that help shape people's lives, their work and their leisure activities. All of these dimensions of the curriculum developer's responsibilities are appreciably influenced or tempered by our rapid movement from yesterday to tomorrow.

Curriculum development and coordination, for example, are complicated by the uneasiness of teachers and students who fear change. Such persons are not reassured by being told that change is inevitable. They resist change because they feel that the stability of the known is threatened by the insecurities of the unknown, and many of them simply are not sufficiently appraised of the importance of socio-technical developments in their lifetimes. Again, there are school workers and students who are unaware of what change demands. Both of these extremes can become severe problems.

At the same time, the curriculum developer's colleagues and their students can not entirely be blamed for their apprehensions or for their blind spots. The rapid changes have been too extensive for some people to assimilate. In the words of James R. Platt, "If the two billion years of life are represented by a 200 foot height . . . the 20,000 years of agriculture make a thick postage stamp . . . [and] the 400 years of science make the ink."[8] Because these changes are such recent ones, we are burdened with what may be called an "information overload." Indeed, one might say that almost without our understanding it, this overload is pressuring us into a very different view of life.

The nature of "information overload." Let us examine briefly some aspects of information overload. Television has exposed us to a broad spectrum of human transactions that have lost their familiar territorial limits of 50 — or even 15 — years ago. At the same time, large numbers of people all over the world have become aware of tangible goods and privileges that often are the possessions of a minority of people.[9] This diffusion of knowledge with respect to the goods and privileges of the few represents a powerful source of discontent and a goading motivation for have-not members of the world's cultures—including that of the U.S. No longer can the individual wants and needs of the have-nots be ignored, nor can any one particular segment of any of the world's populations exist in isolation from the rest. A greater, more coordinated mankind seems all but inevitable as we move along in the "film of moisture on top of the ink on the postage stamp."[10]

This seems to imply that we must search with vision and compassion into ways in which communities of men — hopefully through improved education—may arrive at wise decisions. This will not be an easy goal to reach. As the world is learning, it is far less difficult to use the products of technology — the wonder drugs, paper clothing, computers, frozen foods, and the like — than to relinquish methods of thinking and ideas that have become obsolete in recent years. According to Irwin Bross,[11] this delay in the transmission of ideas is one of the factors which led our world civilizations to their present crises. Lawrence Frank, in a 1965 meeting, also emphasized the importance of ideas when he said, "My historical understanding indicates that ideas have been the most effective agent of change."[12]

Under the circumstances, one of the curriculum specialist's most important tasks becomes that of helping students have experiences that permit them to work with ideas — both in terms of understanding and of anticipating change. Perhaps nothing is more likely to stimulate the learner's thinking about man's personal involvement in planning tomorrow today than his participatory experimentation with ideas. As Bertrand de Jouvenel reminds us, "Obviously, we cannot affect the past, or that present moment which is now passing away; but only what is not yet; the future alone is sensitive to our actions."[13]

Generating the habit of forward looking encourages man to think explicitly about what he cannot avoid doing implicitly — conjecturing about the future.[14]

When startling and often irreversible changes occur rapidly, familiar psychological clues tend to be lost and people find themselves groping for ways in which they may function effectively in what seems to be a strange and incomprehensible world. It becomes difficult to comprehend how the people we know — those who have lived beside us for many years — were ever involved in shaping this disconcerting future. The frequent use of such expressions as: "What is the world coming to?" "Things were never like this in my time," or "We never seemed to have so many problems!" attest to widespread reactions to time-change phenomena that occasionally beset even the most stable and thoughtful among us.

As we generate a habit of looking forward, we should also stimulate man's more effective use of one of his most tremendous abilities, one that decidedly distinguishes him and sets him apart from other forms of life — his ability to function as a decision-maker and shaper of his own life and future. The success of his journey into possible tomorrows is dependent both upon his use of contemporary technological and sociological knowledge (or neglect of it) in considering alternatives when planning future environmental designs. As we learn how to mediate future possibilities, courses of actions actually can be planned so that they do not lead to unalterable and disastrous consequences. And this probably can be accomplished through more provocative, socially relevant education.

The curriculum planner today needs to serve as a catalyst influencing change as well as being helpful in the transmission of ideas. It is essential that he encourage our youth to acquire the habit of anticipating tomorrow's changes intelligently. This habit is difficult to imprint on the young since the information with which they are loaded is approaching a circuit-breaking point. Confusion is increased in many instances because we have looked upon our present "concept map" of our environment as if it were an unchanging one, and therefore a valid map for use in the future. Actually, our present knowledge depreciates rapidly, has very short validity, and must be corrected by careful and continuing speculation about our role in an emergent world.[15]

Educational Cartography for an Unfamiliar Socioeducational Terrain

Maps for educational futures. How does one draw a map for tomorrow? Predictions, speculations and forecasts about the future have fascinated humans throughout the centuries as man searched for solutions to his problems. At Delphi, for example, the garbled and cryptic phrases and sometimes incomprehensible sounds emanating from the priestess of Apollo were used to sway public opinion with respect to politics, economics and religion in early Greek times as the purported words of the sun god were interpreted to the people by priests. During the sixteenth century, Nostradamus used verse as a vehicle for expressing his cryptic prophecies. Although the prophecies were vague and obscure and could be interpreted in many ways, even as late as the 1930's the old writings of Nostradamus were consulted. Feeling that he had predicted the rise of Hitler, some people consulted his *Centuries* for future gleanings.

Moving from oracles and prophecies, one learns that the idea of "reasoned conjectures" was used as long ago as 1773 when J. L. Favier prepared a report for Louis XV about foreseeable (i.e., probable) changes in the European system of power alliances. Favier's approach to studying possible developments has found a new currency among today's futurists.[16]

In our own recent past, pollsters like George Gallup and Elmo Roper used short-term forecasts in a pre-computerized era when attempting to assess public opinion. These forecasts, as did those of the Delphic oracle in ancient Greece, influenced American political and social thought and action.

Today, people seem to be either uneasy or intrigued by the advent of imaginative and usually scientifically oriented people who are employed to peer into the future where foresight blends with fantasy.[17] These scientific seers who might in the past have been considered either visionaries or crackpots are now recognized as able to perform a significant role in helping military, corporate and technological America move into the future with greater prescience and perhaps even to shape the possible future which lies before us. Indeed, as far back as the mid-1950's

General Electric Company established a long-range planning corps to anticipate the potential shape of the future and its possible implications for the corporation.[18]

In addition to foundations and industry, government and scientific organizations both in the United States and in Europe were widely engaged in some form of future planning enterprises by 1970. Among participants in these groups are serious scholars who are carefully projecting trends (and their possible consequences) into the future so that we can learn to cope with and to benefit from technological advances and the need for innovations which they imply in the social, cultural, political, moral and spiritual dimensions of our lives. We will be able to look confidently into the future as computers *support* rather than *direct* our thinking. As this occurs we will have the opportunity of participating in one of the more important events in evolution. This is what Platt calls "the step to man." We have been *men,* he tells us. We can emerge into *man.*[19]

Some Educational Implications of Social Change

Overspill from the future: some implications for curriculum development. Both the field of curriculum planning and the work of the curriculum coordinator are going to be modified appreciably by elements in the discernible future that will create new opportunities, increase his responsibilities, and eventuate in important changes both in his role and in his preparation for service.

Until recently it was reasonable and proper to think of the past fading into the present and of the present flowing into the future. Now we find, in an unprecedented reverse of the tide, that the future has become so jammed with potential and variables that there is an *overspill from the future that is pouring into the present.* So rapid is change that half-formed developments are now mediating our present activities and plans to such an extent that even many highly literate Americans have yet to recognize them.

Let us now consider ten developments as envisioned by

scholars in various disciplines that already are either theoretically feasible or in their early ascent stages and that seem to have a direct or oblique bearing on the curriculum change.

• *The education of very young children will be emphasized and priorities established for it.* Not too long ago, anyone who suggested that intelligence might be other than fixed and unchangeable was frequently classified as a crackpot by his colleagues. Now, as new data are collected and organized, concepts and meanings as to the nature of the child and of man have changed. With increased insights into the modifiability of human development through experience, the early years of childhood are considered so critical that suggestions have been offered that education should be methodically planned by society to begin at about the one-year-old level.

To take advantage of these years when children learn so rapidly and effectively, proposals have varied from the use of "professional mothers" to a *kibbutzim* type of communal living arrangement.[20] These are suggestions for radically different patterns of family living since they deal with the years when children in our society usually have been most closely associated with their parents. Nevertheless, some writers contend and predict that changes of this nature will occur as the importance of early environmental influence continues to be stressed and as new ways are devised to stimulate the child's intellect. A few seers have gone so far as to argue that education of this nature is inevitable if a society with discord and discrimination eliminated is ever to be achieved.

Many questions regarding childhood in the future come to mind. Who helps plan the educational programs so that the numbers of failures in both human and educational enterprises are drastically reduced? What can be done now for young children to encourage the greater development and use of human potential and reduce the numbers needing remedial assistance during their pre-adolescent, adolescent and adult years?

• *Population trend estimates suggest that some 14 million persons will be enrolled in higher education in 25 to 30 years.* Students presently studying in our colleges have increased from approximately 14 percent of our secondary school graduates in 1939 to 42 percent in 1966. Over two-thirds of the youth in our population are expected to complete a college education within the next 25 to 30 year period. Also, more and more persons are making claims against the world of higher education as employment continues its demands for high level technical and professional skills. It seems likely that our present institutions of higher learning will be significantly altered in the years ahead as people who have either been ignored by the educational system or who have neglected to take advantage of it knock on the school house door.[21]

Flexibility may prove to be the key to improved educational enterprises as resources are combined to lessen the gap between the "have" and "have-not" schools. Certainly the curriculum planner will attempt to provide both for quality and equality in meeting the learner's educational, vocational and personal-social needs. Technological advances almost certainly will make it operationally and economically feasible for students and faculty to pursue both individual *and* coordinated group programs of study and research. Large educational compounds may emerge combining the resources of universities, museums, theaters, libraries, research institutes, hospital and other public and private institutions to create a highly varied responsive environment for education, health and leisure for people of all ages. Education — operating within the ivory tower with its formal lectures, class assignments and removal from many of the reality aspects of life — could disappear as the interrelatedness and interdependence of varied educational resources are recognized as being more important than any single organization operating separately.

• *Education will almost inevitably become continuous; some persons may prepare for a second or third career in their middle years.* The expansion of knowledge, the increasing amount of leisure time, and the socially portentous technological changes that occur as a predominantly product society transforms into a primarily service society will require that people refresh and expand their knowledge, adapt, or replace their skills several times during their working careers, and constantly reformulate their conceptualization of education, work and leisure. Particularly, as technological advances alter concepts of "time-worthiness," personal fulfillment through *education* could be considered as essential to physical and spiritual welfare just as the *work ethic* has been stressed in the past. The curriculum developer is likely to find that helping to increase people's educational potential for moving from one occupation to another with ease and pleasurable anticipation can become as important to society as the less complex task of simply creating in the learner the ability to cope with new jobs.

In the discernible future the inhabitants of our large educational compounds probably will no longer be a predominantly selected group of adolescents and young adults. People of different ages will flow in and out of many different institutions at different periods in their lives. The idea of one university providing for most of an individual's continuing educational needs will diminish as new, cooperative and diversified inter-institutional relationships develop both here and in other countries. This seems wholesome since community concerns, educational concerns, national goals and interests, and international dimensions of trade and politics are more clearly understood by a more coordinated mankind.

• *Life spans will increase appreciably; old age will be postponed and eased as it begins to be treated more as a wasting disease than as an unavoidable fate at three-score and ten.* Before long the chemistry of aging and knowledge of how to postpone it may be partially grasped, and man will need to give more thought as to what to do with his additional years of life. Determining who receives this added longevity has already raised ethical questions. Who, for example, will be among the first beneficiaries of the new machines and medicines devised to fight disease when at a given time not enough equipment and medications are available to meet all persons' needs?

As more effective ways of delaying death extend our life expectancy, they also place humans on the verge of a new way of life which promises to transform both our familiar institutions and our human interactions. The population explosion, for example, has already generated world concern over the problems of food and space. As human life is extended, radical changes also could occur in our social structure. In the past the number of young persons has always exceeded the number of old people. With the same number being born in a decade that die in a decade, major social transformations could occur 20 or more years hence if the number of persons within each age-stage is comparable to that of all other age groups.

• *Leisure, once a wistful dream for nearly all the world's peoples, can (beginning in the USA) become first a bore and then a problem — if not an actual danger.* As man's life divides itself into one-third education, one-third productive activity, and one-third enjoyment of an interim of active retirement, the matter of making "worthy use of leisure time" may prove difficult.

Men may be at home or at least "around the house" for much longer periods of time. As more part-time jobs become available and as the workweek shortens, more women will be seeking opportunities for self-fulfillment away from the confines of the kitchen. They are likely to achieve them, too, since many home responsibilities will be eased or eliminated by new products. All the same, there remains the matter of determining who does what in planning and organizing for earning the family income, for home maintenance and child rearing. The decisions reached may well result in some novel reversals or changes with educational consequences in our present organization of home living and of male and female roles.

Some occupations and professions, as we know them, will vanish; others will continue to exist as new ones emerge. As affluence and leisure increase, it may also mean that some people literally will never engage in a paid form of work. What then happens to man; who, particularly in American society, has long used productive work as an actualizing factor in his life? As work becomes less important and less central an activity than it is now, what changes will govern the values which determine a man's contribution to society and the esteem in which we hold him? These developments pose interesting questions for both marriage and family relationships and suggest that the curriculum of the future may be designed to help people attain a balance between the pleasure of self-cultivation through leisure and the threat of tedium from too much surplus time.

• *Extensive supplementary schooling may be carried on at home through personalized self-instructional material. Schools, as a concomitant development should have less formal class work and may become more like reference and social experience centers.* Computer-based instruction already is offering the teaching profession an important although as yet largely unexploited array of tools for recognizing significant individual differences and helping to carry us more rapidly toward the goal of realizing the learning potential of children more fully. As computers become located in more and more educational enterpises, they also will move into our homes, transforming the family or recreation rooms into centers for private business, education and recreation. They will offer important assistance in practical home and business problems, such as those required for managing a home and earning a living as well as offering appreciable intellectual and professional assistance. Rapid transmission of facsimile material will permit print-outs of library resources, as well as mail, newspapers and commercial materials — all tailored to individual specifications.

As it becomes possible to store millions of books within the confines of one small room, vast amounts of material become more rapidly and readily available. Our present library problems related to storage and circulation should diminish and our present library facilities may well become as anachronistic as the pyramids for storing the effects of the past. Three-dimensional television, 3-D photography and movies as well as other types of illustrations are likely to bring into every home the wealth of cultural experiences now enjoyed by only a limited number of people.

Furthermore, technology promises to provide men with the means of sharing in both past and present events and decisions to an extent that was not possible in previous generations.

As this occurs, schools will become learning centers rather than mere repositories for past knowledge. In such centers people would no longer be passive recipients of information doled out by the teacher but will become active respondents in appraisals, discussions, interactions and transactions that have a bearing on learning.[22]

• *Nationwide personal information data banks are likely, their records beginning with one's birth certificate. Automation will permeate and expedite nearly all forms of record keeping. Privacy could well be threatened both by the increase in population and by diverse electronic-listening-viewing devices.* More and more automatic information processing devices become available for both extensive and intensive centralization of information. This clearly suggests that all kinds of information — both personal and business — both private and public — can be easily and rapidly stored and retrieved. As this takes place, massive quantities of information can be assembled speedily without a great deal of effort and without an individual even aware that data are being obtained. Educational data, medical histories, financial and adult records, credit assets and liabilities, traffic violations, recreational pursuits, vocational experiences, military records, personality profiles, and the like, were once housed in separate places. Now it is becoming possible to collect these bits and pieces of data and compile them to present a comprehensive picture of an individual's past personal history.

The danger of violating what is considered "personal privacy" has been noted, and warnings sounded lest additional pressures be placed upon people to contribute more and more personal information. As computers collect and collate information, record systems could become an alarming force for keeping men under Orwellian surveillance throughout their lifetimes. On the other hand, with wisdom, great good could come from information banks in speeding up business, in rapid diagnoses in case of illness, in identifications, and in educational practice. The question is, will society move soon enough so that traditional democratic principles are not jeopardized?

• *Personality will be modified appreciably by drugs. The im-*

provement of learning and memory will be induced through chemical and electronic means. The transfer of experience may become possible. The possibilities of manipulating human behavior and modifying personality have moved from the realm of the possible to the realm of the probable not only through the use of drugs but through systematic stimulus control and neurosurgical intervention. In the near future experimental drugs are likely to be perfected so as to control perception, mood, fatigue, alertness, relaxation and fantasy as well as for more radical personality changes. As necessitated by personal problems, "artificial" relaxation therapy will be used to relieve tension when harmful levels are reached. For various medical reasons, human beings also might choose to hibernate for indeterminate periods of time, reviving at a time, say, when a cure has been found for a fatal disease or malignant condition.

Breakthroughs in the use of drugs to enhance the efficiency of learning have already achieved limited success along with chemical controls for some mental illness and certain aspects of senility. Current projections also include the possibilities of chemical and electronic means to raise the level of intelligence. It is also forecast that the brain can be electronically linked to computers to increase the application of the human intellect to problem solving and lead more or less directly to the improvement of human analytical ability. In light of past developments, these techniques should grow more efficient each year, promising to offer valuable help for normal learners, for the treatment of criminals, for the mentally retarded, and for the mentally ill. They also could threaten both individuals and society, since the effects of faulty human experimentation are sometimes irreversible.

Limited evidence, by 1970, also was available to suggest that knowledge and experiences might be transferred from one organism to another. Although successful with simple multicellular creatures and apparently with mice, the implications and uses of mental "molecule" transfers are not as yet clear where higher life forms are concerned.

• *Many individuals who are now well-nigh physically helpless will have their handicaps reduced or eliminated by human organ transplants, plastic or electronic implants, and improved therapy and surgery.* Promising medical research and experimentation is contributing to our understanding of immunology which are almost certain to result in the transplanting of healthy organs to supplant those of the individual's that have been ravaged by disease or injured through accident. The 1967 pioneering heart transplant in South Africa is a recent major illustration of further achievements to be anticipated in the 1970's. Eventually, some organs undoubtedly will be replaced by mechanical substitutes. When this is accomplished, then we have the prospect of the advent of the *cyborg* — a coined term that comes from cybernetic and organic — or a human body that is a mixture of organic and inorganic parts.

Other predictions include the possibility of biochemically assisted growth of new organs and limbs. As these probabilities become realities, what will their effect be on man's perennial self-concept questions: "Who am I?" "Where am I going?" "What am I doing?" What will happen to man as his body changes — as he is part himself — part a stranger — or part a machine? How will our conceptions of ourselves be changed?
• *Genetic controls of birth defects and hereditary factors influencing the general physical nature of the child as well as prenatal selection of the sex of the unborn infant are likely in the next decades.* Permanent and quite extensive "natural," prenatal or pre-conception changes can almost certainly be made (at the option of the parent) in his child's sex, coloration, height, weight, physique, hair growth, features and other biophysical attributes. We are only beginning to understand how our biological potentialities can be improved, varied and more fully utilized. While plant and animal studies have been carried on for a long time, the possibilitiy of reshaping the human organism to insure a better start, rather than a focus on the "repair" aspects of a faulty product or unsatisfactory part at a later date, was not considered seriously. Recently, it was suggested that we are no further now from partial synthesis of human life than we were from the release of nuclear energy in 1920. Indeed, artificial life at the virus level was produced three years ago! Also in

prospect is the control of hereditary defects by altering genes and modifying the genetic code.[23]

There is at least the theoretical prospect that man can escape damage from many diseases, avoid permanent incapacity from many accidents, and even alter the "biological housing" in which he exists. Man may become more sound in body and find himself raised above some of the more unkind vagaries of heredity — less the product of accident or change and more the product of careful, thoughtful human choice.

Conclusion

This preview of the world of 1975 to 1999 has presented some of the implications of the sudden "collision with tomorrow" which has taken place during the lifetime of most adults who came of age prior to the 1960's. Changes transpiring with great rapidity have thrown some of us out of phase with an era and also placed us on our mettle to face tomorrow with vision, with courage leavened with optimism, and with confidence in the future.

In curriculum development, which is a profession intimately linked to human development and its unbounded potentialities, there is particular reason to participate in this speculative process, to peer into the future, and to help turn possible problems into promising possibilities. This will require persistent thought and effort — but seldom in the history of man could such effort count for more. This *is* an era of superlatives — one unique in intellectual, technical and social potential. This *is* a time for men to participate in shaping a world of new promise. In the process we should remember that our knowledge determines the limits of our vision, and that the limits of our vision are the only boundaries of the world of the future that wise curriculum planning can help create.

REFERENCES

1. Kenneth Boulding. The Meaning of the Twentieth Century. In Ruth Nanda Anshen (Ed.) *World Perspective,* Vol. 34, New York: Harper and Row, 1964.

2. Boulding also suggests the use of "technological" or "developed" society if the word "post-civilization" seems objectionable.

3. Sir George Thompson. *The Foreseeable Future*. Cambridge, London: The Syndics of the Cambridge University Press, 1960. Sir George is a British physicist and holder of the Nobel Laureate.

4. Alvin Toffler. The Future as a Way of Life. *Horizons,* Summer, 1965, pp. 109-115.

5. *Ibid.,* p. 109.

6. Also cf. Harold G. Shane. Future-Shock and the Curriculum, *Phi Delta Kappan, 49*:67-70. October, 1967.

7. The definition of millenium is taken from *Webster's Seventh New Collegiate Dictionary*. Springfield, Massachusetts: G. and C. Merriam Co., 1961, p. 538.

8. James R. Platt. The Step to Man. *Science,* 149:613, August 6, 1965.

9. Daniel Bell. The Year 2000—The Trajectory of an Idea. Toward the Year 2000: Work in Progress. *Daedalus*. Vol. 96, No. 3, Boston, Massachusetts: The American Academy of Arts and Science, 1967, p. 643.

10. Platt, *op. cit.,* p. 613.

11. Irwin D. Bross. *Design for Decision*. New York: The Free Press, 1965, The Macmillan Co., 1953, p. 3.

12. *Daedalus, op. cit.,* p. 664.

13. Bertrand de Jouvenel. Political Science and Prevision. *American Political Science Review,* 5:29, 1965.

14. Statement by Bertrand de Jouvenel in a lecture delivered to RAND's Interdepartmental Seminar on November 30, 1964.

15. *Ibid.,* p. 4.

16. Bertrand de Jouvenel. *The Art of Conjecture*. New York: Basic Books, Inc., 1967, p. 21.

17. Tom Alexander. The Wild Birds Find a Corporate Roof. *Fortune,* August, 1964, p. 130.

18. Brownlee Haydon. The Year 2000. Paper read at Wayne State University, March, 1967, p. 5 of typescript.

19. Platt, *op cit.,* p. 613.

20. For a current view on the "kibbutzim kids," cf. Urie Bronfenbrenner, The Dream of the Kibbutz, *Saturday Review, 52*:72-73; 83-85, September 20, 1969.

21. cf. Alvin C. Eurich (Ed.) *Campus 1980*. New York: Delacorte Press, 1968.

22. Even before 1970, experimentation in public education conducted *without a school plant* was underway. The community environment itself was the "school."

23. R. Michael Davidson. Man's Participating Evolution. *Current, 105*:4-10, March, 1969.

3

Behavioral Objectives and the Curriculum Processor

Philip G. Kapfer

A new breed of teacher is developing in American education. He cannot be distinguished from other teachers by age, sex, experience, dedication, or level of militancy. He can be distinguished, however, by the type of educational tasks he performs and by the orientation which he brings to those tasks. His role eventually will be recognized by school boards and administrators through some form of differentiated staffing. If he were given a title, it might be "curriculum processor."

He is involved with students in developing a more humanized school atmosphere, one based on mutual trust and respect. He believes in the *heretical assumptions* that learning is a natural human enterprise, that students want to learn, and that they will learn voluntarily and efficiently when given opportunities to

---

PHILIP G. KAPFER is associate professor, Bureau of Educational Research, University of Utah.

become responsibly involved in determining the character of their learning experiences.

Not every teacher is capable of or interested in being a curriculum processor, although most teachers can be trained by such a person to use the products he develops. The teacher functioning as a curriculum processor believes that behavioral objectives are one of the tools which he uses in curriculum development — so that students can be freed from their traditional dependence on teachers. In essence, the role of the curriculum processor involves translating school district curriculum guides or other curricular sources into desired teacher and student behaviors, by developing and implementing individualized learning materials.

The title of this paper indicates a two-fold focus — on behavioral objectives in the curriculum and on the new role of the teacher as curriculum processor. Concentrating on these two facets of the school necessitates distinguishing between *curriculum* theory and *instructional* theory.

Curriculum theory, as the term is used here, relates to the derivation, specification, selection, mediation and assessment of behavioral objectives. These topics represent the structure around which this paper is built. Skills in these areas are essential if the curriculum processor is to prepare behaviorally oriented learning materials for use by individual students and small learning teams.

Instructional theory, on the other hand, is concerned with the environmental conditions which are necessary both for the student to acquire the desired behaviors and for him to develop positive attitudes toward learning and toward himself as a learner. Instructional theory is discussed herein whenever its inclusion serves to strengthen the case being made for the use of behavioral objectives in the *curriculum*. Thus, instructional theory is the fabric which covers the framework of curriculum theory and enables the work of the curriculum processor to achieve its fullest potential in the classroom.

Who Needs Behavioral Objectives?

Much of the literature on writing behavioral objectives is focused on the function of such objectives in curriculum construction and instructional sequencing. Similarly, much of the criticism of behavioral objectives deals with limitations of the function they serve in curriculum theory. Although discourse in these two areas is important, it is not nearly as critical to the training of the teacher as curriculum processor as an examination of *who* needs behavioral objectives. Only through such a discussion can behavioral objectives be placed in the proper perspective so that their limitations in curriculum theory can be overcome in instructional theory and practice.

A good example of the limitation of behavioral objectives in curriculum theory can be seen in many school districts. Despite the serious efforts of school district central office curriculum specialists to promote the use of behavioral objectives, few teachers and building administrators take them (either curriculum specialists or behavioral objectives) seriously. For example, curriculum guides containing behavioral objectives at varying levels of specificity are often ignored by teachers and building administrators, rather than used for school-level curriculum construction.

In fact, in a paper pointing out the limitations of behavioral objectives, Eisner went so far as to say that "if educational objectives were really useful tools, teachers, I submit, would use them. If they do not, perhaps it is not because there is something wrong with the teachers but because there might be something wrong with the theory."[1] However, what is "wrong with the theory" has more to do with the theory of instruction than with the theory of curriculum. In those cases in which behavioral objectives are not "really useful tools" for teachers, the problems most often relate to undeveloped systems of instructional implementation rather than to the inadequacy of the objectives.

There are many roadblocks to providing students with adequate behavioral objectives. The most critical one has to do with the philosophy and instructional theory undergirding the operations of many of our schools. In too many schools (with the exception of some in which teachers *are* functioning as curriculum processors) "it seems obvious that our traditional curricula — our time-honored notions about the structure and sequence of content; our preference for seated, indoor, verbal learning activities; our defensive notions about control; our limited respect for the human potential; our undemocratic manipulation of other people's choices; our procedures for being helpful; our concept of the teacher's role"[2] — all these represent untenable positions concerning the conditions under which positive attitudes toward learning develop.

To put it bluntly, we do not trust children, adolescents, young adults, or even mature adults *whenever they are placed in school-type situations*. For this reason, we do not permit them to make choices concerning what, when, how and where they will learn. If they do not want to learn what *we* want them to learn, we make life so miserable for them that they have only three available choices. They can knuckle under and either lose their own identity or learn how to beat the system; they can become in-school dropouts; or they can become out-of-school dropouts. According to Clark and Beatty,

> At no time in history have we tried wholeheartedly to foster individuality, to open choice-making, to support the uniqueness of becoming effective, to demonstrate real faith in the potential of humanity. We have accomplished something of these all along because the strength of individuals found effectiveness, but development has been haphazard, by chance and good luck, and in spite of many blocks to learning set up by schools. Even now we could not be altogether successful immediately, but we do know enough about the learning process and how to establish helping relations between people to make a good start.[3]

It is only too obvious that in the many decades general (non-behavioral) objectives have been used in curriculum construction, students have not been given many choices — except to *do* or *not to do* what the teacher directed. When students have been given choices while still maintaining the same old curriculum (such as occurred when students were given independent study time and a choice of places to go in "flexibly scheduled" secondary schools), abortive, laissez-faire conditions frequently developed *for which students were unprepared by earlier experiences.* However, teachers functioning as curriculum processors are able to guide students, through properly constructed lessons, into successful choices in the area where it really counts — in the curriculum.

Who needs behavioral objectives? Students. Behavioral objectives are a tool which lets students know where they are going so that they can then make intelligent choices concerning how they will get there. Curriculum processors who are constructing individualized curricula in the form of *student* lesson plans containing behavioral objectives are opening up one avenue for choice-making by providing media-and-method alternatives from which students can select. In a few curricular areas, notably science and social studies, teachers are even encouraging students to select and sequence the lessons they desire. Thus, the behavioral objectives the students will achieve have been opened to choice. Where such choices have been provided, students are beginning to make the further step of determining their own behavioral objectives.

If we can keep in mind *who* needs behavioral objectives and *why,* in the ultimate sense, as we are involved in preparing teachers to be curriculum processors, we can avoid many of the problems inherent in the behavioral approach. The choice is ours. We can predetermine all of the subject matter content which everyone must learn (because the teacher knows best!) and force everyone through a single sequence designed to result in the desired behaviors. Or, we can encourage curriculum processors to trust in each student's drive for finding his own effectiveness as a human being. As a result of the latter approach, the curriculum processor can provide the student with alternatives (including the student's as well as the teacher's objectives) through which students can exercise their own individuality and uniqueness in the continuous process of becoming effective.

Formulating Behavioral Objectives

The formulation of behavioral objectives can be divided into two distinct stages. The first stage, *derivation,* refers to the data sources which are employed for locating and developing objectives. The second stage, *specification,* deals with the ways in which behavioral objectives are stated for the user.

Derivation

McNeil,[4] in a discussion of forces influencing curriculum, provides a convenient classification of data sources for deriving objectives. The first data source, *subject matter,* has given us a basically verbal curriculum. This source is exemplified in Bruner's *The Process of Education.* Bruner's emphasis on the "structure of the disciplines" has provided much support for developing conceptual and skill verbalizations (typically abstractions) organized in hierarchies, to serve as the basis for writing behavioral objectives.

The second data source, society, is founded on the assumption that what goes on in schools should be directly transferable to the student's behavior in situations remote from the classroom. According to Woodruff, although "the bodies of verbal information that fill our books and lectures are related to the environment," and thus relevant in that sense, verbal information "is almost completely nontransferable" to in-life behavioral problems.[5] For this reason, the use of society as a data source would require the associated development of a "phenomenalized" subject matter as opposed to subject matter based on verbal abstractions.

The third data source is the *learner* himself. It is concerned with his needs, wants, interests and concerns. Woodruff's model for an in-life internship curriculum takes into account the learner as a data source through the development of "projects for the production of some object or other form of satisfier the learner wants enough to motivate him to work for it."[6] Those concepts and skills (in phenomenal rather than verbal forms) which are necessary for accomplishing projects would then be associated with the projects, thus making the projects serve as carriers for concept and skill learnings (hence the term "carrier projects").

Additional comment concerning the use of verbal subject matter as a data source is not necessary. This has traditionally been our most common source for deriving behavioral objectives, and should remain so in those courses (primarily at the university upper division and graduate levels) which are designed to prepare academic scholars to extend the frontiers of a discipline. However, a great deal of work, with massive funding, is needed to develop phenomenalized subject matter sources as well as pervasive societal and learner data sources upon which behavioral objectives can be formulated. But even without such input, the training of curriculum specialists and processors must encourage greater sensitivity toward a creative synthesis of all three of these data sources for the derivation of objectives.

Specification

Many articles have appeared in the professional literature concerning the specification of behavioral objectives since Mager's book, *Preparing Instructional Objectives,* was published. Most of the articles refer to Mager and identify the following three components that should be included in objectives: (1) *an action* — what the student is supposed to be able to do when he is evaluated — which is communicated by means of action words such as identify, write, list and contrast; (2) *a context or signal* — the conditions under which the student will be evaluated — which might be implied or stated in a phrase frequently beginning with the word "given;" and (3) *a criterion* — the level of performance expected of the student — in which quality and/or quantity expectations are stated.

A word of caution is needed, however, in preparing curriculum processors to write behavioral objectives for use by students. When constructing the criterion portion of the objective, care must be taken to avoid specifying quantitative expectations that might be inappropriate for individual students. In fact, such quantitative specifications might well be omitted from such objectives when preparing student lessons. Qualitative criteria against which the student's performance will be evaluated are much less of a problem. Although there is still a danger of overwhelming the student, the potential for student failure is greatly reduced through provision of a qualitative criterion.

The most important structural part of a behavioral objective is the action term. Sullivan's[7] synthesis of basic action terms is a very useful point of departure for the curriculum processor. Sullivan distilled the somewhat overlapping AAAS *(Science — A Process Approach)* action words into the following six terms: identify, name, describe, construct, order and demonstrate. The six Sullivan terms, together with equivalent terms, in the continuum given below will help the curriculum processor write behavioral objectives in all curriculum areas. The continuum also includes an explanation of the meaning of each behavior.

(1) IDENTIFY (equivalent terms and phrases — choose, compare, discriminate between or among, distinguish between or among, indicate, mark, match, select):

The learner indicates whether or not specified phenomena (objects, events, or behaviors) are members of a class when the name of the class is given.

(2) NAME (equivalent terms — designate, label, list, state):

The learner supplies the correct verbal label (orally or in writing) for one or more phenomena (objects, events, or behaviors) when the name is not given.

(3) DESCRIBE (equivalent terms and phrases — analyze, characterize, define, diagram, explain, replicate, report, represent, reproduce, tell how, tell what happens when):

The learner represents by words (a) the structure and qualities of the objects or (b) the processes and consequences of events and behaviors.

(4) CONSTRUCT (equivalent terms — build, draw, formulate, make, prepare, synthesize):

The learner puts together the parts (objects, events, or behaviors) making up a concept. Thus, he builds or produces a product such as a drawing, article of clothing or furniture, a map, or an essay. The product itself is evaluated.

(5) ORDER (equivalent terms and phrases—arrange in a pattern, arrange in order, catalog, categorize, classify, list in order, outline, rank, relate, sequence): The learner arranges two or more phenomena (objects, events, or behaviors) in a specified order. He may be given the names of the objects, events, or behaviors which he must order, he may be asked to name them himself as well as order them, or he may be asked to order them without having to provide verbal labels.

(6) DEMONSTRATE (equivalent terms and phrases — perform an experiment, perform the steps, role play, show the procedure, show your work, simulate):

The learner performs a task according to pre-established or given specifications. The task may involve a number of behaviors including identifying, naming, describing, constructing and ordering (or combinations of these). The procedures the learner follows in performing the task are of greater concern than the product which may result from those procedures.

By using the above terms, variety and increasingly sophisticated levels of performance can be introduced into the lessons being prepared. Students who do not do well at such verbal behaviors as identifying, naming and describing can still have successful experiences by selecting lessons which focus on the potentially non-verbal behaviors of constructing, ordering and demonstrating. At the same time, terminal performances so frequently equated with paper-pencil testing can be substituted by the curriculum processor with a larger proportion of en route behavioral expectations.

Implementing Behavioral Objectives

The implementation of behavioral objectives is a three-stage process. The first stage, *selection,* is concerned with how the user (i.e., both the curriculum processor and the student) can be made aware of the alternatives available for choice. The second step, *mediation,* includes both media and methodology choices which are available to assist the student in achieving the behavioral objectives. The third stage, *assessment,* includes both student and curricular evaluation.

Selection

Mager stated that the "selection of objectives may be made in the presence or absence of information or wisdom, in the presence or absence of clearly specified alternatives, and in the presence or absence of information about implications associated with the selection."[8] This statement holds true both for the curriculum processor and for the student. The curriculum processor's work is greatly facilitated when catalogs of behavioral objectives (e.g., curriculum guides) are available which include (1) the data sources from which the objectives were derived, (2) clearly stated behavioral objectives and (3) media and methodology suggestions and facilities requirements. Even in those cases where the data sources are primarily of the verbal subject matter variety, the curriculum processor can develop lessons which provide many alternatives for students.

Mediation

The key word, again, is *choice.* The curriculum processor, through his activities in the development of individualized student lessons, can provide the student with alternative media of all types, including book, non-book, and human resources. Library card catalog entry words also can be provided so that students can locate additional multi-media resources which have not been suggested or which become available subsequent to the lesson's development. There is no question but that "given an objective derived and selected by fair means or foul, it is possible to select ways [note the plural] of achieving it."9

The problem which remains, of course, has to do with instructional theory. *Schools must be organized so that the alternatives are honestly available to students.* This is difficult to do in schools which are built and organized like prisons, are overcrowded and oversized, and which are managed as though students should be dependent on the teacher for making most, if not all, of the decisions. Elementary schools across the country either do not contain multi-media libraries or do not make such facilities and equipment available for continuous student use. Many secondary school libraries function almost solely as study halls for doing textbook assignments. Getting teachers involved as curriculum processors can be the first giant step toward correcting such conditions.

Assessment

The curriculum processor's first assessment task, upon completion of the student's lesson plans, is to examine those lessons for internal consistency. The following questions should be answered:

(1) Do the objectives describe behaviors which might be expected to result from internationalization of what is to be learned?

(2) Is the student able to practice behaviors which are identical, and also perhaps analogous, to those described in the objective by selecting media and methodology alternatives singly and/or in combination?

(3) Is student evaluation strictly congruent with the behaviors and conditions described in the objectives?

Teachers functioning as curriculum processors frequently have the most difficulty with the third question. Part of the problem is the tendency to employ terminal assessment even though an objective may call for en route assessment. The greatest difficulty, at least initially, relates to the need to rework tests in which the specified evaluation behaviors bear little relationship to the behaviors described in the objectives.

The second assessment task for the curriculum processor

occurs during pilot testing and full-scale use of the individualized lessons. Were the students able to achieve the objectives? If not, were the lessons at fault? Were the prerequisite behaviors inaccurately specified or assessed? Were indicators of the achievement of the desired terminal behaviors genuinely assessable? Were students interested in the lessons? That is, did students find the lessons appropriate for accomplishing *their own objectives* as well as the teacher's? These and similar questions can be used to guide the curriculum processor in his ongoing assessment tasks.

Conclusions

Behavioral objectives are a potent weapon either for controlling human behavior or for fostering the full human potential to strive for *individual* effectiveness. We will not be successful in promoting teacher use of behavioral objectives unless we are personally committed to and therefore emphasize the *second* of these alternatives. But who knows? The choice may not be ours. "Perhaps this time it could happen to all of us," say Clark and Beatty, "for it may be that we know enough about manipulating learning to destroy the full realization of human potential."[10]

It is for this reason that a concerted effort is long overdue to develop a large number of curriculum processors at the school level. Such teachers can go far in implementing a behaviorally oriented curriculum theory which is imbedded in a humanistically oriented instructional theory.

REFERENCES

1. Elliot W. Eisner. Educational Objectives: Help or Hindrance? *The School Review, 75,* Autumn, 1967, pp. 250-260.
2. Rodney A. Clark & Walcott H. Beatty. Learning and Evaluation. *Evaluation As Feedback and Guide* (Ed. Fred T. Wilhelms). Washington, D.C.: Association for Supervision and Curriculum Development, 1967, p. 65.
3. *Ibid.,* p. 66.
4. John D. McNeil. Forces Influencing Curriculum. *Review of Educational Research, 39,* June, 1969, pp. 293-318.

5. Asahel D. Woodruff. Untitled manuscript delivered at the tenth Annual Phi Delta Kappa Research Symposium, Salt Lake City, 1969, p. 3. (Mimeo.)
6. *Ibid.*, p. 7.
7. Howard J. Sullivan. Improving Learner Achievement Through Evaluation by Objectives. Inglewood, California: Southwest Regional Laboratory for Educational Research and Development, undated, pp. 15-17. (Mimeo.)
8. Robert F. Mager. Deriving Objectives for the High School Curriculum. *NSPI Journal, 7,* March, 1968, pp. 7-14.
9. *Loc. Cit.*
10. Clark and Beatty, *op. cit.,* p. 66.

4

Processes, Problem Solving and Curriculum Reform

Richard W. Burns and Gary D. Brooks

What are *processes?* What role should they play in education? How are they related to problem solving and other terms used with them? How can they influence curriculum reform at all levels of education?

Processes belong to a type of objective differing from the cognitive entities (knowledges, understandings and skills), the affective entities (attitudes, interests and appreciations) and heuristic entities (strategies). Processes, as a type of objective, are specific mental skills which are any of a set of actions, changes, treatments, or transformations of cognitive or affective entities used in a strategy in a special order to achieve the solu-

The material presented in the first two sections of this paper is taken largely from an article by the authors titled "What Are Educational Processes?," which appeared in the February, 1970 issue of *Science Teacher*.

tion of a problem associated with the learning act, the use of learning products, or the communication of things learned. Processes are, more simply, *transformational entities.*

Processes are not new — they are the skills that learners have utilized since learning first occurred. Being a type of objective or end-product, it is inaccurate to view them singly or collectively as a "method of instruction." Processes are complex skills which learners use in transforming knowledges and understandings in order to effect solutions to problems. They could also be called "problem solving skills." Processes are the mental skills needed in any problem solving situation associated with learning, using what has been learned, or communicating about things learned.

Examples of process terms are abundant. It is difficult, however, to be sure that a listing of processes is complete and that each process identified is "pure" (without overlap with another process). Much further research is needed to compile a comprehensive, valid and clearly defined list of processes. The following list of terms is not comprehensive, but typifies what is meant by processes:

1. Abstracting
2. Analyzing
3. Classifying
4. Equating
5. Evaluating
6. Generalizing
7. Inferring
8. Sequencing
9. Simulating
10. Synthesizing
11. Theorizing
12. Translating

Each of these process terms is in reality a category name for a subgroup of synoptic or highly correlated terms. For example, *simulating* is also affecting, assuming, copying, counterfeiting, faking, imitating, making believe, mocking, pretending and shaming.

To describe each process in detail and to list behaviors associated with each is beyond the scope of this essay. However, *translating* will be explained as an example.

Most behaviors associated with translating can be either oral or written; and the majority are also reversible. The outline below lists the main transformations a learner could make in translating. The term "symbol" refers to any character other than a word, and the term "verbal" refers to word symbols.

I. Verbal to Verbal
   A. One language to the same language
      1. Rewording—finding a synonym
      2. Converting to another form—poetry to prose
      3. Rewording—idiom to general language
      4. Rewording—simile to general language
      5. Rewording—metaphor to general language
      6. Abstracting (outlining)—lengthy to brief
      7. Abstracting—concrete to abstract
      8. Rephrasing—general language to general language
      9. Substituting—example one to example two
   B. One language to another language
      1. Rewording—finding synonym
      2. Converting to another form—poetry to prose
      3. Rewording—idiom to general language
      4. Rewording—simile to general language
      5. Rewording—metaphor to general language
      6. Abstracting (outlining)—lengthy to brief
      7. Abstracting—concrete to abstract

II. Symbolic to Verbal
   A. Symbol to word
      1. Converting—number to word
      2. Converting—abbreviations to words
      3. Converting—technical symbols to words
   B. Illustrations (two dimensional) to words
      1. Converting—drawings to words
      2. Converting—paintings to words
      3. Converting—photographs to words
      4. Converting—graphs to words
   C. Realia (three dimensional) to words
      1. Converting—object to words
      2. Converting—object system to words

III. Symbolic to Symbolic
   A. Technical symbol to technical symbol

      1. Converting—number to number
      2. Converting—letter to letter
      3. Converting—color to number
  B. Symbolic to Illustration
      1. Graphing—number to drawing

IV. Symbolic to Performance
  A. Illustration (two dimensional) to performance
      1. Constructing—drawing (plan) to scale model
      2. Constructing—drawing (plan) to real object
      3. Converting—music to playing

V. Verbal to Performance
  A. Words or letters to performance
      1. Converting—words to hand signals
      2. Interpreting—words to actions

How do processes relate to other educational end-products?[1] If one refers to the cognitive entities as Type I objectives and the affective entities as Type II objectives, then processes are transformational entities, or Type III objectives. A fourth type of objective, heuristic entities, are called strategies. Processes are mental skills used in handling, dealing with, or transforming information, using the term broadly. Type I and Type II objectives are learned behaviors which can be thought of as input in a computer analogy, while the *processes* are the separate treatments applied to the input by the computer. The specific sequence of treatments is the program or the *strategy*. The output is the solution of the problem.

Information as knowledges (facts, dates, names, events, laws, low order principles) and understandings (high order principles, relationships, classifications, functions, etc.) are the major sources of input, but these are essentially sterile bits of information unless they can be related, compared, equated, generalized, ordered and in other ways treated or transformed in what is generally called thinking or problem solving.

Expressions such as "he knows a lot but can't apply it," "he is smart enough but a poor teacher," "he knows it but can't explain it," indicate a common notion that learning can be less than functional. An interesting hypothesis is that the fault lies in the learner's failure to master process goals. Data, to be functional, must be manipulated and transformed by the thought processes previously listed as examples.

Processes and Strategies

Strategies should not be confused with processes. Strategies are high order heuristic principles which are used in devising or applying specific processes in a plan (used in a special order) to achieve a definable goal, such as in problem solving. Although strategies are learned and necessary in problem solving, which makes them important goals in education, it remains doubtful that they should be taught as such in the classroom. Learners in problem solving situations will automatically learn strategies. Generally, strategies will be highly individualized. In devising plans for use in problem solving, each learner will find unique procedures which are effective. Uniqueness may be the result of trial and error, past learnings, lack of identifying an alternative, prior exposure to a particular method, habits, or other factors. Most problems do not have just one method of solution. Two individuals faced with the same problem, with access to identical data, and using the same material facilities, may reach identical conclusions by utilizing different strategies.

Formalized strategies occur with some frequency in mathematics. These strategies are taught and learned directly as objectives. In this same sense a computer program, after it is devised, becomes a formal strategy. The scientific method is merely a condensed and loose description of a general way of thinking; and, in practice, the method varies greatly with the problem to be solved and the human problem-solver.

The term "process method" has no meaning, as processes are used in all strategies of problem solving. Gagné[2] describes the relationship between problem solving and discovery as one involving the presence or absence of a "verbally stated solution." Both problem solving without discovery (principle learning) and problem solving with discovery entail the use of instructions (aids to the learner). The difference lies in the fact that in principle learning the solution to the problem is given verbally, while in discovery learning the solution is never given verbally. In other words, problem solving and discovery are the same when a verbal solution is not given and the learner solves the problem by discovering.

Are processes and the teaching of processes the sole property of science education? Obviously not, as processes are used whenever and wherever problems are solved. Any curriculum and any subject learning can be process oriented.[3]

In summary, processes are learned, transformational entities which are used in learning and problem solving — regardless of the methods used and subject matter considered. Using one or more processes in any order to solve a problem results in a strategy. Strategies may or may not be direct educational goals, due to their variety and uniqueness to the individual learner who applies them. A great deal more research is needed to validate processes and to define their total role in learning.

The Process Approach and Information Orientation

The first paper in this collection, "The Need for Curriculum Reform," detailed the futility of conceiving new curricula based on the traditional approach, which is essentially one of *information orientation*. Information oriented curricula should be extensively re-evaluated in the light of current social-cultural trends and new insight into how people think and learn.

What is information orientation and why are curricula so oriented? Information orientation quite simply refers to subject matter content dealing with topics which are presented in such a way that learning becomes primarily a memorization process. Learners acquire *bits of information,* such as names of authors, painters, composers and inventors; assorted dates associated with discoveries, financial transactions, court rulings and battles; the names of the parts of animals, plants, machinery, grammar and speech; and thousands of other assorted facts. Currently students are being educated as if each was a type of memory drum — they are expected to store hundreds of thousands of bits of information in the fond hope that they will both need and recall such information at later times.

The effect of the modern "information explosion" has been to outmode any type of education conceived on the basis of information needed to effectively master "a single subject." Each historical subject is now more likely a field of study. For example, chemistry has grown from a single subject to several large fields of concentration, including physical chemistry, bio-chemistry, nuclear chemistry and petroleum chemistry, each of which is a specialized area demanding several years of concentrated study.

Perhaps the very broad goals of education haven't changed. These broad goals generally refer to the learner acquiring behaviors that will insure his becoming an effective, productive member of a family unit and an effective member of the society in which he lives. However, to achieve these goals today requires a new approach to education. No one operating in a complex social structure can be effective in that culture by merely attempting to assimilate facts.

An Alternative — A Process Oriented Curriculum

What is it that a person must do beyond acquiring information? The most obvious answer to this question is, "the person must think."

Today's living calls for problem solving skills, concept formation skills, data processing skills, the ability to make judgments and discriminate, the ability to relate causes to effects, the ability to analyze, the ability to summarize, and the ability to form valid conclusions. The cultivation of these general abilities is not and never will be the result of curricula which are solely information oriented. To develop behaviors associated with these abilities requires curricula which are specifically designed to achieve such ends. Curricula must be process oriented if the learners are to develop processing behaviors.

On the surface, it may appear that present-day curricula do teach thinking and problem solving. Many educators, especially school administrators, claim goals, aims and objectives for school systems that in actual practice are not being achieved. High-sounding terms such as effective citizenship, the scientific method, creativity and problem solving are prominently displayed in lists of educational goals. Actually, the behaviors required of students are those that are measured in unit, semester, or final examinations. A recent analysis of 50 such tests in science and history reveals the true nature of what is often being expected of learners at the high school level. Each item on the teacher-made examinations was analyzed as to the type of objective it measured. A summary of the results revealed that 1,620 of 2,010 items (81%) were classified as measuring "knowledges" (facts and low order information) exclusively. "Understanding" accounted for 219 items (11%) and 164 items (8%) were classified as measuring "skills." Less than 1% (7 items) were designed to measure "processes" or high order mental skills. However, the goals reported by the teachers for the subjects covered by the fifty tests included research skills, problem solving skills, reasoning, logical thinking, appreciations, and interpretation of research data.[4] It is extremely doubtful that these exemplary goals were being accomplished.

Further studies should be initiated comparing the actual achievement of learners with the types of objectives that can realistically be achieved.

Information would not be excluded from the new curriculum, but the *amount* would be reduced. Whereas information is now both the means and the end of instruction, it would in most instances be reduced to the role of means only. Information would provide the basic input — the grist — for the development of problem solving skills. Problem solving, with and without discovery, would demand that learners develop skill in each of the processes named. These processes, in turn, when applied to further learning, using what has already been learned, and in communicating about things learned would result in the learners' acquiring useful strategies.

Processes are extensively used in problem solving, and therefore it is reasonable to assume that one of the primary ways processes are acquired, developed and become functional is through learning to solve problems.

What Is Problem Solving?

A problem exists for any learner when his present knowledges, understandings, skills, attitudes, appreciations and interests are such that his behavior repertoire (what he can do) is incapable of finding a solution. If a problem exists, it may or may not be capable of being solved. If the learner has the appropriate, recallable knowledges, rules, concepts and principles needed for the solution then it is highly likely that he can succeed. So, problem solving is in some sense having the appropriate background. This implies that a state of readiness is a necessary prerequisite. Problem solving implies that as the learner solves a problem he acquires a new behavior, which he adds to his behavior repertoire. In other words, at the end of the problem solving sequence, the learner can do something he couldn't do before. Problem solving results in learning, and it is not merely a mechanical process. Some types of classroom activities are inappropriately called problem solving. Problem solving, in the sense used here, means that the learner acquires some new knowledge, rule, concept, or principle or that some new relationship between previously learned entities is discovered which allows him to demonstrate a terminal behavior that he did not have when he entered the problem solving situation. *Unless learning occurs, there is no problem solving.*

Steps in Problem Solving

In problem solving, the first step can be described as *problem recognition,* which is marked by behaviors that are goal oriented. If the learner is motivated to solve problems, his behavior will be sustained until a solution is found. In the classroom, problem solving is rarely associated with the reduction of primary drives (acquisition of food, water, air, physical security, sex). Most human motives are social in origin; and some, such as competition, vary in strength from one culture to another. Problem solving is therefore associated with social drives, such as success (achievement), mastery (excelling), approval (recognition, acceptance), and curiosity (excitement, adventure).

There is no absolute need that problems possess social usefulness, but the problems posed will more likely be solved if they are perceived as useful by the learner. By useful is meant relevant to the life of the learner, sensible and logical, and of immediate satisfaction. If problems meet these criteria, there is no guarantee that each learner will recognize the problem for what it is. Some needs may have to be developed by the learner prior to his being able to perceive or conceptualize the problem as one worthy of his consideration and effort.

Some problems may have high intrinsic interest, especially to learners who have developed motives associated with "learning for learning's sake." These students are definitely in the minority, but, because of their excellent learning skill, the problems they work on should be associated with individualized instruction in preference to their being offered to all groups. Other pupils may undertake the solution of problems merely for the sake of pleasing the teacher or to avoid adult disapproval and censure. Problems of this type — that have no other appeal —should be eliminated from curricular designs.

Problems, then, are perceived by individual learners generally to the degree that they appear to be significant. Problems perceived by teachers as having social utility may be rejected by learners because there is no immediate indication of a personal need — no immediate payoff. Teachers may pose problems for students as opposed to having students locate and identify them, but the problems so posed should be relevant to the students' lives, or possess high intrinsic interest to individual learners.

Finally, when are learners ready to work on a problem? A handy proof of readiness is the learner's ability to express the problem in his own terms. Failure to express a problem verbally or in writing indicates the learner's need for direction, which may be given by the teacher. Directions may aid the learner in locating, perceiving and conceptualizing cues, and verbalizing the statement of the problem.

The second step in problem solving is *conceptualizing the solution*. This step may be imperfectly formed, but the intended solution must be a reasonable enough model so that when solution occurs it is recognized as fulfilling the criteria for solution as posed by the problem. Gagné suggests that instructions as an external condition to learning may be given to inform the problem solver of the criteria for solution. In a sense, the problem solver conceptualizes a solution model, which he carries with him until the solution is accomplished.

The third step in problem solving is *recall and selection of related information*. No learner solves problems without first securing (learning) those rules, principles, concepts and knowledges necessary for a problem's solution. This step in a sense is twofold: (1) recalling of information and (2) selecting those bits of information pertinent to the problem. These functions do not necessarily occur contiguously, nor completely. Recall and selection may continue throughout the problem solving process, but obviously occur prior to the solution. Again, instructions may be given by the teacher to help direct the problem solver to recall or select relevant information.[5]

The fourth step in problem solving is *hypothesis formulation*. At this step the learner combines the rules, principles, concepts and information which he selected in the third step. Obviously, many combinations are possible, and the learner does not always select the correct combination. In this sense, the hypothesis or hypotheses are only tentative. Effective problem solving quickly narrows the possible combinations down to one. Again, external instruction may be used which in effect both narrow the search for highly probable combinations and reduce the search time.[6]

The fifth step in problem solving is the *formation and matching of the tentative solution*. In the fourth step, the search for a tentative solution narrows the search until a highly probable combination of information is devised which will apparently fit the problem. In the fifth step, the tentative solution is then matched with the conceptualized solution from step two, which is recalled for the matching. If it appears that the tentative solution matches the conceptualized solution model, then the learner is ready to begin verification.

The sixth step is *verification*. At this point in problem solving, the learner applies the tentative solution from the fourth step to a problem instance (real example). Sometimes several examples are verified to be sure the solution "works." Should the solution not appear applicable, the learner generally returns to the fourth step, and selects another highly probable combination from the information he has recalled, enabling him to form a new tentative hypothesis concerning the solution. If the verification process is successful, then the solution has been validated.

Summary

In summary, present day education places too much emphasis on the learner's memorization of information. Problem solving skills are neglected and the processes needed for problem solving are not receiving direct instructional attention. Curriculum reform efforts need to consider the inclusion of materials and activities associated with processes and aimed at learning objectives related to learners' abilities to solve problems, think and become independent in the pursuit of "understanding the world about them."

REFERENCES

1. Richard W. Burns. The Theory of Expressing Objectives. *Educational Technology, 7,* October 30, 1967.
2. Robert M. Gagné. *The Conditions of Learning.* New York: Holt, Rinehart and Winston, Inc., 1966.
3. Richard W. Burns. The Process Approach to Software Development. *Educational Technology, 9,* May, 1969.
4. Richard W. Burns. Objectives and Content Validity of Tests. *Educational Technology, 8,* 23, pp. 17-18.
5. Benjamin Klinemuntz. *Problem Solving: Research Method and Theory.* New York: John Wiley and Sons, Inc., 1966, p. 36.
6. *Ibid.,* p. 141.

5

Toward Improved Rigor in the Design of Curricula

G. L. Oliver

The general goals of this essay are (1) to improve the rigor and forecasting* power of curriculum design and (2) to aid in the development of a set of basic notions or commonplaces for a technologically based conceptual structure for the field of curriculum design. Its specific objective is to examine some of the implications of technological methodology as the most appropriate source or means to achieve these goals. In the course of

---

*Finan's (1963) notion of technological forecasting is a useful one for describing in basic terms what technologists do. Finan describes technological forecasting as the process by which the technologist indicates in advance the extent to which a specific set of dependent events (i.e., the goals and objectives of the technologist) can be anticipated by means of some set of independently selected variables (i.e., the technical activities specified by the technologist).

G. L. OLIVER is a research assistant at the Department of Curriculum at the Ontario Institute for Studies in Education.

meeting this objective, some of the historical attributes of curriculum design as well as some of the recent innovations in the field are examined. In order to bring out certain implications for improving the rigor of curriculum design, its present mode of functioning is then contrasted with that suggested by technology as a generalized mode of functioning.

The need for increased rigor in the planning and design of curricula is acute and generally well recognized. The rationales for the planning and design of curricula have historically dealt with the development of surveys intended to identify, describe, analyze and order the opinions of experts in fields of general societal needs, occupational and/or disciplinary needs, and the needs of learners themselves.

These rationales and related techniques have, however, drawn a good deal of criticism, for the following reasons: They are, at best, based on unrelatable and value-laden statements of the beliefs and attitudes of a limited number of experts in a given subject matter field. In many instances, they are based entirely on rationally derived rather than hard empirical data. Parochial in their preoccupation with specific occupational or disciplinary issues, these rationales and techniques fail to generalize to the needs of the curriculum field as a whole. They are not subjected to rigorous programs of diagnosis and assessment, designed to establish their empirical validity. They lack descriptive and analytical sophistication in the manner in which their various dimensions are identified, analyzed and ordered. And, most important, they are not, in general, based on any comprehensive theoretical position as to the nature of education, training, curricula, or instruction. The result, especially of this latter condition, has been the proliferation of a number of unrelated and unrelatable rationales and techniques — that have left the field without a viable conceptual structure upon which it can build.

Curriculum Design as a Crude Technology

Fortunately, during the last decade a number of rationales and related sets of techniques have been developed which have helped to move the field of curriculum design away from this outmoded position.

In the field of military training, for example, the work of R. B. Miller is well recognized as having provided a basis for greatly improved rigor in the design of training curricula — one that is appropriate for the acquisition of the human competencies required for performance in man-machine systems.

In general vocational and academic training, E. J. Morrison's work in the development of vocational curricula for the vocational-technical school at New Quincy, Massachusetts, and that of Donald Maley in the development of vocational programs based upon the "cluster concept" at the University of Maryland stand as excellent examples of improved rigor and forecasting power.

On a more general level, the application of a number of theoretical principles has had a beneficial effect — notwithstanding the fact that they have often been badly overworked by some of their disciplines. Among these principles are those of operationalism, generally associated with the work of Ralph Tyler and the "curriculum evaluation movement," and applied to the defining of aims and objectives. Included also are the principles of stimulus-response contingency management associated with the work of B. F. Skinner, T. F. Gilbert and the "Neo-behaviorist movement" in curriculum design. Similarly, the work of systems theorists, such as Leonard Silvern, and the work of those whose concern has been with the principles of logical and/or psychological subject matter structures, as exemplified by the work of Robert Gagné and David Ausubel, have also had a beneficial impact on the field.

Yet the products of the educational technologist remain, as a whole, unusually crude in terms of their lack of forecasting power when compared with the output of other technologies — even within the social sciences. While crude implementations and lack of forecasting power appear to be necessary developmental stages in the history of any technology, it would seem that these stages have been prolonged beyond all reason in the field of curriculum design. New emphasis on rigorous theory building — both rational and empirical — surely is required. It will aid, first of all, in sorting and relating the rationales and techniques currently extant in the field, and, second, in providing a basis for significant and on-going educational research.

However, the problem of deriving a more powerful theoretical basis for curriculum design is a difficult one. As a number of authors have pointed out, curriculum decision making has always been suspect, at first because it was not based on theory, and then because it was. The early efforts at social science theory building in education and training have been notably unsuccessful. Those who advocate theoretically based design have been hard pressed to generate the required theoretical formulations. Their formulations have drawn criticism for three reasons: they are not scientific but normative and prescriptive — based upon common wisdom rather than on empirical science; they are not appropriate for the control of value-directed human behavior; and, most important, they fail to produce the sort of pragmatic payoff associated with such technologies as medicine and engineering.

Against this background, it can be argued that the historical lack of payoff in curriculum theorizing has been due, not to an inherent lack of appropriateness of the theoretical as opposed to the artful approach to instruction, as suggested by some, but to the *type of theorizing* that has been carried on. More specifically, the writer should like to take the position that, as a technology, the instructional enterprise ought to be primarily concerned with *technological* rather than with *scientific* theorizing. Some of the implications of this rather simple yet seemingly powerful notion will be examined in this essay.

The Prerequisite Nature of Curriculum Theorizing

A review of current literature in curriculum and instruction leaves the reader with little doubt as to its ultimate goal, namely to develop a scientific theory for curriculum and instruction. The literature is abundant with speculation as to the nature of such a theory and its relationship to theories of teaching, learning and/or curriculum (Johnson, 1967; MacDonald and Leeper,

1965; MacDonald, 1967; and Travers, 1967a, 1967b.) The development of scientific theories, such as those described by Beauchamp (1968) and Gordon (1968), for use in explaining and/or understanding curricular and instructional phenomena, appears to be a crucial step in improving the rigor of the curriculum design process. Yet the question must be asked as to whether such theories are of a prerequisite nature, either in terms of the obligations of the educational and training enterprises to society or in terms of the theoretical process by which theories for curriculum and instruction are likely to evolve.

It seems evident that the primary goal and obligation of education and training is to effect and control specific changes in educational and training environments. To this extent, it would appear that the prerequisite functions to be performed by these enterprises ought to be directed toward developing powerful design specifications and related techniques, and not to the ultimate understanding of the phenomena with which they work. Therefore, a *technological theory of curriculum and instruction,* rather than a scientific one, ought to be the first responsibility of the educational and training enterprises.

This position does not deny the crucial importance of sophisticated scientific understanding to technological innovation. Instead, it emphasizes the following: *Technological theorizing is methodologically different from scientific theorizing.* Scientific understanding belongs to relatively sophisticated fields of inquiry, and the "science of education or training" is surely not one. Relative technological sophistication in a given field is not dependent upon equivalent levels of scientific sophistication in related subject matter areas. Substantively related sciences and technologies develop in a parallel rather than in a sequential manner, the two being mutually supporting and interacting in their conceptual contributions to each other. And the sciences provide a climate for thought as well as many of the valuable conceptual tools employed by the technologist, but the technologist's methodology is not that of the scientist. The technologist is not limited to the inductive and deductive processes of theoretical science, but bases his methodology instead on "soundly cultivated judgments" (Wigglesworth, 1955). As Wigglesworth

(1955, p. 41) has pointed out: "To advise him to think scientifically would risk paralyzing his judgment rather than activating it." In short, technology is intrinsically a "black box" probabilistic activity, dependent only upon knowledge of inputs and required output topographies. Although the technologist welcomes scientific information concerning intervening phenomena and processes, his methodology is by no means dependent upon such data.

This defense of the prerequisite technological nature of curriculum and instruction implies a good deal more than the use of technology in instruction. During the last half of this century, much criticism has been directed against the use of technological concepts by the educational and training enterprises. Although much of this criticism appears to be well founded, it often fails to make clear the important distinctions between the use of technology as a principle of methodological decision and its use as a basis for: first, aims statements for instruction; second, criteria for instruction; third, possible decision strategies for instruction; fourth, instruments in the instructional system. In the first instance, the focus is on an "instruction for life syndrome;" in the second, an "efficiency and effectiveness syndrome;" in the third a "feedback," as opposed to an aesthetic or intuitive syndrome; and in the fourth case, the focus is the use of "engineering technology" or a hardware syndrome in instruction.

Sound bases for the criticism of such syndromes seem to exist, as described by Callahan (1962), Jackson (1968, pp. 159-171), MacDonald (1967), McLuhan (1963) and many others. However, this criticism appears to be based on a recognition of only the more obvious procedural attributes of technology, rather than on its more basic modes of functioning. It seems unlikely that those who have been so outspoken concerning the use of technology in this context would suggest that instruction is not praxeological in its goals and thus should not give attention to the investigation of appropriate technological modes of functioning.

Curriculum Design as Technology and Science: Some Functional Distinctions

There is, of course, certainly nothing new about the notion that the fields of curriculum and instruction, being praxeological in their outlook, are concerned with identifying what ought to be done, with describing and implementing the necessary strategy for doing it, and with evaluating the results. In spite of this, however, the literature in these areas continues to be primarily concerned with the scientific studies of the psychologist or sociologist. When technological issues are dealt with in the literature they are generally on a technologically unsophisticated, anecdotal and prescriptive basis. Given the technological nature of instructional goals, it seems that more attention should be given to developing more sophisticated technological descriptions of curricular and instructional design processes.

In order to demonstrate the crucial differences in the theoretical focus provided by these two decision systems, let us briefly review the essential differences in their content, goals, functions and evaluative criteria:

• While science focuses on investigating the behavior of components in abstract and surrogate environments in order to minimize variability and confoundedness, technology investigates the behavior of components in real world septic environments in order to maximize these factors.

• The goals of science include the control, explanation and understanding of phenomena, whereas those of technology are focused on optimizing the control of environments. As Fogel (1963, p. 4) points out, the scientist "does to know" while the technologist "knows to do."

• The scientist processes data in a manner calculated to lead him from a set of causal conditions to a related set of effects, and the technologist reverses this order. Starting with a desired effect, the technologist attempts to identify the required set of independent causal conditions. The scientific process by which this former activity is carried on is referred to as "discovery" and the latter is generally referred to as "invention." In the former case, the processes of induction, deduction and hypothetico-deduction are commonly employed. In the latter case, such logic and rationality give way to stochastic decision structures for relating means and ends. These structures are developed by analogical and metaphorical extension and by criterion trade-offs based on intuition and common wisdom, as well as on empirical science.

• The power of scientific theorizing depends primarily upon empirical sensory data inputs, whereas technological theorizing depends primarily upon the "hunches" of the technologist.

• While the outputs of the scientist are inductive and deductive explanatory statements, those of the technologist are forecasts that attempt to indicate in advance the extent to which a state of affairs can be anticipated by means of some set of independently selected variables (Finan, 1963, p. 530).

• Finally, scientific theories are evaluated in terms of their relative power for relating facts within a theoretical network, but technological theories are evaluated in terms of the probability of their forecasts. In the first instance, the criteria for evaluation include reliability and validity in explanation and prediction. In the second instance, reliability and fidelity in interpretation and forecasting are the criteria for evaluation.

Some Implications of Technological Methodology for the Fields of Curriculum and Instruction

If the instructional enterprise were to give prerequisite attention to the development of a more sophisticated technological methodology rather than to scientific theorizing, the following innovations might logically be expected: there would be renewed emphasis on the study of task, learner and instrumental variables associated with the acquisition of meaningful human capabilities as opposed to emphasis on the learning of capabilities of surrogate subhuman species. The study of the "how" of instruction might be emphasized more than the "why" of human behavior. A primary concern could be the invention of powerful instructional strategies, not the discovery of logical inductive or deductive systems of explanation. More emphasis might be placed on the compilation of handbooks containing artful, heuristic and highly operational, as well as scientific, theories of curriculum and instruction. The development of techniques for testing the forecasting and interpretive power of specific curricular and instructional design methods might take priority over testing the reliability and validity of principles and theories of instruction.

The Romans built fine bridges and roads, not because of their scientific sophistication in explanation and prediction, but because of their technological sophistication in interpretation and forecasting. Their inductive and deductive explanatory theories, judged by our present level of scientific knowhow, were primitive indeed. Yet, on the other hand, their technological output in bridge and road building was equivalent in many ways to our own. The difference is probably due to the prerequisite attention given by the Romans to technological theorizing.

It would be naive, of course, to suggest that man could ever descriptively control human behavior in the same manner as he can now control the behavior of many inanimate systems. These situations, however, appear to vary in degree rather than in kind. Both activities are intrinsically technological in nature, requiring the application of similar methodologies. They differ mainly in their levels of technological sophistication; that is, in the ratio of hard scientific data to that of their heuristic and artful design inputs.

Now let us examine the range of dependent and independent events that must be brought under the control of the curriculum designer, if his education and training specifications are to become increasingly more effective in their forecasting power.

Identifying the Critical Events in Curriculum Design

A review of aims, objectives and procedural statements that provide the substantive content of curricula leaves the reviewer with the uneasy feeling that all is not well. Not only do such descriptions and analyses of what ought to be done, and how to go about doing it, appear to be plagued with problems of terminology, but they appear to be over-simplistic and fragmented in the range of critical events that must logically come under the control of the curriculum planner and designer.

Clearly, the application of the principles of operationalism to the defining of curricular aims and objectives has been immensely beneficial in the improvement of their semantic meaningfulness; epistemological and ontological issues related to these same statements have seldom been subject to rigorous theoretical investigations* It seems abundantly evident that if the general rigor and forecasting power of curriculum designs are to be improved, the theorist must start with a study of the necessary and sufficient events that must be controlled by the designer before he can proceed to develop techniques for assuring their semantic meaning. In short, the key question at this stage in the development of the curriculum field is *not* "How ought curricular events to be identified, described, analyzed and ordered?" *but* "What curricular events ought to be identified, described, analyzed and ordered?"

The assumption made here is that the answer to this latter question, when arrived at within the context of technological decision structure, provides the starting point for the rigorous design of curricula. As Finan (1963) has pointed out, the technologist must, of necessity, start with a rigorous description of the desired dependent set of events; that is, a description of his finished product or process. Then, applying his own intuition and inventiveness, he must work backwards through his analysis to the set of independent events most likely to produce the required set of dependent events.

This problem of identifying and ordering the necessary and sufficient set of dependent and independent events for curriculum design is the issue to be dealt with here.

---

*Westbury (1969, pp. 4-5); one of the few to deal with these theoretical issues and to suggest their methodological implications for the curriculum field, points out that only five out of 178 works cited in the *Review of Educational Research* (1966) on curriculum are directed at basic theoretical issues.

Some Categories of Critical Events in Curriculum Design

A review of the statements characteristic of education and training curricula suggests that what are being described, analyzed and ordered (at a number of hierarchical levels) are most basically educational or training demands, their required institutional, material and/or human capabilities, and their contingent conditions of learning and/or instruction.

First of all, the curriculum designer seeks to identify, in considerable detail, the *demands* of the social milieu, the subject matter and/or the learner himself. Such a description provides, in effect, a verbal outline of the tasks to be performed and of the functional context in which the learner is intended to perform them. Rigor and forecasting power in curriculum design, as in engineering technology, appear to be dependent on a clear, unambiguous and comprehensive description of the functional characteristics of the completed product or process. Having derived such a set of dependent statements, through progressive descriptive and analytical distillations, the designer hopes he has arrived at a point at which he can infer, with a high degree of probability, a set of independent events for instruction. This set of independent events he expresses in terms of the institutional, material and/or human capabilities that are required to meet the above demands. Finally, having satisfied himself that he has generated such a set of capabilities, contingent upon the demands to be met, the designer then proceeds to describe and to analyze these capability statements until, as before, he can predict with a high degree of probability a second set of independent events. This second set consists of the instrumental procedures that describe the means by which the institutional, material and/or human capabilities are to be implemented.

As examples of this three-level distinction between various types of functionally related curricular statements, consider the following items abstracted from typical curricula: (1) to develop an appreciation of good design and the principles involved; (2) to give training in the basic skills and technology associated with the type of work the pupil expects to enter upon graduation;

(3) to study magnetic circuits involving various materials and air gaps; (4) to study the application of electronics to industrial control; (5) to perceive a change in the sound of a motor; (6) to differentiate resistors from capacitors; (7) to provide stimulus objects; (8) to provide verbal directions requiring recall of previously learned principles.

While some would question the semantic power of such statements, most recent graduates of programs in instructor training would likely recognize immediately each of the above eight statements as being either objectives, aims, goals, or procedural statements—depending upon the number of distinctions made and the terminology in vogue.

The preponderance of experienced instructors would also likely be quick to point out that these eight statements are probably all functionally related to each other in some subject matter context, and that they vary mainly in the analytical levels of activity they imply — the first being highly abstract and inexplicit with respect to the eighth.

Many instructors would also likely point out that, in addition to their differences in analytical specificity, these statements also belong to different but hierarchically related functional categories—statements one to four describe various levels of demand, statements five and six describe certain contingent human capabilities, and statements seven and eight describe certain related instrumental procedures for learning and instruction.

Finally, a few instructors would likely point out, if asked to criticize such statements, that all such descriptive and analytical statements ought to be made in accordance with the most recently available range of techniques for scientific and heuristic description and analysis, and for analytical, conditional and operational definition. Such techniques, they would point out, are designed to ensure comprehensive, specific and rigorous statements, with a minimum of vagueness and ambiguity.

The Validity of the Categories

Westbury (1969, pp. 12-13) has drawn attention to the face validity of this view as one of the necessary systems of events with which the field of curriculum must deal. He points out that a curriculum design methodology premised on a demand capability notion leads directly to a set of technical decision-points that can be described in terms of the resolution of the contrary equilibrium relationship between rigorously defined demand and capability descriptions. He goes on to suggest that, while there are many theoretical and practical problems associated with this simplistic view: (1) it does appear to be consistent with our intuitions about the range of problems with which the field of curriculum ought to be concerned; (2) it does provide a useful paradigm for dealing with categories of commonplaces, suggested by the generally accepted "Tyler rationale;" and, perhaps most important, (3) it does aid in dealing with the learner-curriculum issue on a one-to-one level that militates against ". . . educationally trivial manifestations or, alternatively, stipulations about subjects . . . without regard for their utility or meaningfulness vis-a-vis the student" (p. 13).

While the paradigm suggested here appears to be intellectually appealing, one must question its external consistency; that is, with its fit with the field from which it was abstracted.

Certainly, this view of the various events with which the curriculum theorist and designer must deal is not new. Ample evidence exists in the theoretical literature of the field for a concern for these demand capability and instrumental notions. They are evident in the writings of Gagné (1965a, 1965b, 1965c), Herrick (1965), Tyler (1950) and Walker (1969), to name but a few. Herrick, for example, pointed out that:

> The teacher struggling with the problems of where one's definition of objectives leaves off and the teaching program begins is realizing — perhaps for the first time — that this is always a matter of judgment. Carried to the extreme, the teaching program is the final definition of the meaning of one's objectives. The task is to define the essential attributes to the point where the outlines of method, instruction and evaluation are clearly worked out (Herrick 1965, p. 103).

The widely recognized works of Bloom (1956) and

Gagné (1963a) also provide well known examples of attempts to identify and order the content of two of the three categories of events noted here. Both these taxonomies deal with hierarchical orderings of cognitive knowledge and skills: Bloom's in terms of category one (educational demands) and Gagné's in terms of category two (the contingent human conditions of learning and instruction). Unfortunately, no direct link has been forged between these two taxonomies. This point is clearly made by Gagné (1965b, p. 21), who points out that while there is no simple one-to-one correspondence between his category system and that developed by Bloom, definable relationships and similarities do exist. Work currently underway in the field of task analysis (Miller, 1963, 1965) and capabilities analysis (Altman, 1966; Gagné, 1963) appears to be directed toward filling this gap. Indeed, it appears to be generally recognized by writers in the field of general curriculum theory, as well as by those in the field of education and training analysis (Gagné, 1965b, pp. 13-14), that the "task" is the fundamental analytical unit for describing subject matter demands. Once task variables have been rigorously described and ordered, at an appropriate level of generality, the required capabilities — institutional, material and/or human (initial and terminal) — will more than likely be inferable. The suggestion is also that the subsequent analysis of these capabilities will yield the instrumental procedures required to produce the necessary conditions for their implementation (Annett and Duncan, 1967, pp. 7-9).

Similarly, ample evidence exists in recent curriculum literature to suggest that the rigorous planning and design of instruction does indeed call for great precision in dealing with the range of dependent and independent events suggested here.

On one level, studies by Hoehn, Kaufman, Miller, Nunnelly, Wallis, and others (see Hoehm and McClure, 1960, and subsequent reports, Kaufman, Corrigan and Nunnelly, 1966; Miller, 1963, 1965; Nunnelly, Klemmer, Corrigan and Kaufman, 1966; and Wallis, Ewart and Kaufman, 1966) in developing the knowledge and skill capabilities required by technicians interacting with machines, in any one of a number of modes, are examples of the implicit use of such a category system.

On other levels, studies by Maley (see Maley, 1966 and subsequent reports) in the field of vocational training, by Morrison (see Morrison, 1965 and subsequent reports) in the fields of vocational and academic training, and by Miller (1969) in the field of management training all provide recent examples of the use of this category system in the rigorous design of curricula.

Summary and Conclusion

A number of attributes historically associated with the field of curriculum planning and design have been pointed out. It has been stressed that, in spite of a number of significant innovations, this field maintains the status of a relatively crude technology in terms of the lack of forecasting power of its products. Some of this lack of power has been attributed to the preoccupation of the field with scientific rather than with technological theorizing. Finally, attention has been drawn to a number of functional distinctions between curriculum and instruction — as sciences and as technologies. The implications of each of these distinctions for improving the rigor of the curriculum design process have been noted.

From this brief examination of both the attributes of technology and the field of curriculum design, it can be concluded that since curriculum design is indeed technological in its goals, technological modes of functioning ought to be examined much more closely by the curriculum designer. The efficacy of technology as a principle of methodological decisions has been clearly demonstrated historically in the engineering design of machine systems and more recently in the design of man-machine systems. The potential power of such a methodology for the field of curriculum design therefore seems evident. The prerequisite task in improving the rigor of curriculum design is to develop a conceptual structure for identifying the critical dependent and independent events with which curriculum designers must deal. This conceptual structure would describe, in effect, what curriculum designers do, or ought to do.

The curriculum theorist ought to look to technology as a

principle of methodological decision for assistance in developing a viable conceptual structure.

It has also been suggested that the sorts of descriptive statements used by curriculum designers — which are generally referred to as statements of goals, aims, objectives, or procedures — are logically divisible into three rather different but functionally related categories: educational or training demands; contingent institutional, material and/or human capabilities; and the necessary instrumental conditions of learning and/or instruction. While this three-level distinction is certainly not entirely new, it nevertheless has not been used to any great extent in helping to explicate the domain of critical dependent and independent events for which the curriculum theorist and designer are responsible.

In support of this view, some evidence has been offered as to the face validity of the category system, as argued rationally, and as seen in terms of the fit of the category systems with the field of events from which it was abstracted.

From this argument it can be concluded, first, that the curriculum theorist ought to be increasingly concerned with developing powerful category systems for organizing the demands, capabilities and instrumental procedures with which the designer must deal, given Finan's position on the general requirements for improving the rigor and forecasting power of technological specifications.

Second, I would conclude, along with Westbury (1969, p. 13), that a category system—based on the notions of demand and capability, with the necessary research as to the various aspects and elements these notions entail — provides at least part of the technical subject matter of curriculum inquiry.

Finally, such a category system provides a valid basis for developing a conceptual structure that will identify the range of stochastically and dynamically related decision-points with which the curriculum designer must deal. Without such a conceptual structure, the field of curriculum design will continue to lack the terminology required for meaningful communication amongst its practitioners, as well as the rationales and techniques required to produce rigorous curriculum designs with improved forecasting power.

REFERENCES

Annett, J. & Duncan, K. D.   *Task Analysis and Training Design.* Hull, England: University of Hull, Department of Psychology, 1967.

Altman, J. W.   Research on General Capabilities (skills and knowledges). American Institute for Research, Final Report, March, 1966.

Beauchamp, G. A.   *Curriculum Theory.* (2nd ed.) Wilmette, Illinois: Kagg Press, 1968.

Bloom, B. S. (Ed.) *Taxonomy of Educational Objectives: Handbook I: Cognitive Domain.* New York: David McKay, 1956.

Callahan, R. E.   *Education and the Cult of Efficiency.* Chicago: University of Chicago Press, 1962.

Finan, J. L.   The System Concept as a Principle of Methodological Decision. In R. M. Gagné (Ed.) *Psychological Principles in System Development.* New York: Holt, Rinehart and Winston, 1963, pp. 517-546.

Fogel, L. J.   *Bio-technology: Concepts and Applications.* Englewood Cliffs, N. J.: Prentice Hall, 1963.

Gagné, R. M.   Human Functions in Systems. In R. M. Gagné (Ed.) *Psychological Principles in System Development.* New York: Holt, Rinehart and Winston, 1963, pp. 35-75.

.... *The Conditions of Learning.* New York: Holt, Rinehart and Winston, 1966(a).

.... Educational Objectives and Human Performance. In J. D. Krumboltz (Ed.) *Learning and the Educational Process.* Chicago: Rand McNally, 1965, pp. 1-24 (b).

.... The Analysis of Instructional Objectives for the Design of Instruction. In R. Glaser (Ed.) *Teaching Machines and Programmed Learning: Data and Directions.* Washington, National Education Association, 1965, pp. 21-65. (c).

Gordon, I. J. (Ed.)   *Criteria for Theories of Instruction.* Washington: Association for Supervision and Curriculum Development, 1968.

Herrick, V. E.   Establishing and Using Objectives. In J. B. MacDonald, D. W. Andersen & F. B. May (Eds.) *Strategies of Curriculum Development.* Columbus, Ohio: Charles E. Merrill 1965, pp. 89-106.

Hoehn, A. J. & McClure, A. H.   The Development of Training Programs for First Enlistment Repairmen: I. Human Resources Research Office, Research Memorandum, July, 1960.

Jackson, P. W.   *Life in Classrooms.* New York: Holt, Rinehart and Winston, 1968.

Johnson, M., Jr.   Definitions and Models in Curriculum Theory. *Educational Theory,* 1967, *17* (2), pp. 127-140.

Kaufman, R. A., Corrigan, R. E. & Nunnelly, C. L. The Instructional System Approach to Training. *Human Factors,* 1966, *8* (2), pp. 157-162.

MacDonald, J. B. & Leeper, R. R. (Eds.) *Theories of Instruction.* Washington: Association for Supervision and Curriculum Development, 1965.

MacDonald, J. B. An Example of Disciplined Curriculum Thinking. *Theory Into Practice.* 1967, *6* (4), pp. 166-171.

Maley, D. An Investigation and Development of the Cluster Concept as a Program in Vocational Education at the Secondary School Level. University of Maryland, Report No. ERD-115-A, August, 1966.

McLuhan, M. We Need a New Picture of Knowledge. In A. Frazier (Ed.) *New Insights and the Curriculum.* Yearbook 1963, ASCD. Washington, D. C.: Association for Supervision and Curriculum Development, National Education Association, 1963, pp. 37-70.

Miller, R. B. Task Description and Analysis. In R. M. Gagné, (Ed.) *Psychological Principles in System Development.* New York: Holt, Rinehart and Winston, 1963, pp. 187-230.

.... Analysis and Specifications of Behavior for Training. In R. Glaser (Ed.) *Training Research and Education.* New York: Wiley, Science Editions 1965, pp. 31-62.

.... A Systems Concept of Training. *Training and Development Journal,* 1969, *23* (4), pp. 4-15.

Morrison, E. J. Development and Evaluation of an Experimental Curriculum for the New Quincy (Mass.) Vocational Technical School. First Quarterly Technical Report. Project No. 50009, June 30, 1965

Nunnelly, C. L., Klemmer, A. G., Corrigan, R. E. & Kaufman, R. A. The Instructional System Approach to Maintenance Technical Training: Development and Implementation Model. *Human Factors,* 1966, *8* (2), pp. 163-172.

Travers, R. M. W. Towards Taking the Fun Out of Building a Theory of Instruction. In *Rational Planning in Curriculum and Instruction.* Washington: National Education Association, Center for the Study of Instruction, 1967, pp. 33-53 (a).

.... Some Further Reflections on the Nature of a Theory of Instruction. Toronto: The Ontario Institute for Studies in Education, 1967, unpublished paper. (b).

Tyler, R. W. *Basic Principles of Curriculum Development.* Chicago: University of Chicago Press, 1950.

Walker, D. F. A Study of Types of Goal Statements and Their Uses in Curriculum Development Projects. A paper presented at the annual meeting of the American Educational Research Association, February, 1969.

Wallis, K. B., Ewart, W. L. & Kaufman, R. A.   Instructional System Approach to Flight Crew Training. *Human Factors,* 1966, *8* (2), pp. 173-178.

Westbury, I.   Problems in Search of Disciplined Attention or a Discipline in Search of its Problems: A Discussion of Some Assumptions in a Curriculum Theory. In symposium presented at the annual meeting of the American Educational Research Association, February, 1969.

Wigglesworth, V. B.   The Contribution of Pure Science to Applied Biology. *Annals of Applied Biology,* 1955, *42,* pp. 34-44.

6

Premature Instruction

George L. Geis

A key motto of the Now Generation, "do your own thing," may seem like an invention to those under thirty, but it appears to be only a rediscovery to those who have been around a bit longer. Everyday observations as well as data from psychological laboratories lead to the conclusion that one repeats those actions that have been rewarded in the past. In this way we each acquire a unique set of habits. So, in a sense, people have always been doing their own thing. Furthermore, we know from human and infra-human studies that it is not necessary for the reward

A version of this paper was originally prepared for a conference at the Center for Learning and Development, McGill University, November 21, 1969. The author expresses his gratitude to Patricia O'Connor, K. Brethower & D. Brethower for helpful comments and criticism as the paper was developed.

GEORGE L. GEIS is assistant professor of psychology at the University of Michigan.

to regularly follow the activity. An irregular schedule of reward, far from weakening the behavior, tends to *strengthen* it even further. Extrapolating from the laboratory to the complex and chaotic everyday world this fact alone may help explain why we do our own thing so often, even when it is inappropriate to do so.

We all have heard stories (possibly apocryphal) of medical cases in which a person in poor health is referred first to one specialist and then to another, each one claiming that the cause of the illness lies in *his* area of expertise. If a patient with a chest pain is sent to a cardiac specialist, the chances of the "cause" being a heart condition are high. If he should take a wrong turn in the professional building and end up in an allergist's office, the chest pains may be traced to the high pollen count. If he should have the misfortune to bungle into a psychiatrist's office his discomfort may be explained in terms of an overabundance of, or a glaring deficiency in, mother love.

Often the specialist is a solution in search of a problem. The heavy investment in building up one's expertise in an area, and the history of reward for the exercise of those skills, may lead to the misapplication of them. (In the above example, the problem might not even have been a medical one, and *any* medical solution would be inappropriate. The poor patient may simply have been sleeping on a bad mattress.)

In instruction, as in medicine, the professional does his own thing. Teachers teach; programmed instruction specialists develop programs; and centers to improve instruction insist on making such improvements. The instructional specialist, whatever his area or particular set of skills are, may see all problems as susceptible to instructional solutions.

In this essay, teachers and instructional designers are seen as agents of behavior change. Their function is to guide, elicit, modify and create behaviors. There are a great number of people similarly oriented, who consciously or unconsciously, intentionally or inadvertently, spend their professional lives attempting to change others' behavior: for example, architects, advertisers, psychotherapists, writers of guide books or cook books, and financial advisors. Teachers represent one subset of the class: "behavior change agents."

The behavior change agent is, of course, only one factor in the modification of another's activities. In addition, a person's immediate social and non-social environment, his history, his current motivational states and the like, act to produce his behavior at any moment.

It is naive and arrogant for one professionally involved in changing behavior to assume that he (or he and his colleagues) can manage to produce all kinds of modification in another person's behavior. It is especially impertinent (as well as self-defeating) for a person in instruction to assume that *all* behavioral changes sought can be brought about through teaching.

This essay originally began as a prescription for more effective design and development of instruction. In the preparation of such a prescription, it became evident that the conditions under which the prescription was to be used should be defined. Even the most effective medical treatment is at least useless and sometimes harmful when applied to the wrong patient. Similarly, a description of more effective ways of designing instruction could be worse than no description at all, if the procedures are applied indiscriminately.

Therefore, an attempt will be made to delimit the kinds of problems to which an instructional solution might be applied, i.e., it presents an analysis of the conditions under which it is appropriate to begin an instructional solution to a problem.

The analysis involves two activities: Verifying the existence of a problem and determining whether an instructional solution is appropriate. In approaching the matter this abstractly, it is necessary to set aside for the moment the real chronology of events. Typically an instructor comes to the attention of instructional designers with a "problem;" the instructor assumes *that* he must teach and *what* he must teach. This paper will approach the subject differently.* It purposely does not take into account existing instructional institutions or personnel and the demands to support them.

---

*The paper represents what is called a systems approach. Various attempts have been made to apply the systems approach to educa-

Step I. *Establishing the Need for a Consequence*

In a world which had no tradition of education and educational institutions, an instructional designer might begin by examining the environment for needs or problems. Some of these might be alleviated through the development and use of instruction.

Presumably all teaching is aimed at providing people with the ability to do things so that they can affect their environment in certain ways. The output of instruction is not merely the skills and knowledge that people acquire but a supply of people who act upon the world to produce certain effects (including effects upon themselves). Therefore, the proper place to start the process of generating instruction is at the end or output.

Education is a system to produce changes in the environment by developing mediators of such changes. The design of systems to produce changes in the environment ought to begin with identification of what changes are desired. A proper analysis, it is suggested, proceeds from effect, or consequence, to cause. ("Consequence" is similar to what Thomas F. Gilbert has called *accomplishment.*)

The observer, then, would begin by noting that there were certain needs not being satisfied. Broadly stated: Some things are happening which people wish would not happen and some things are not happening which people wish would happen.

Several actual examples may be useful in illustrating the application of Step I to real situations. The nursing educator brings a request to an instructional designer: improve the effectiveness of nursing education, perhaps by the use of expen-

tional problems. See, for example: Csayni, Attilla, Determining Objectives: A Behavior Systems Approach, *National Society for Programmed Instruction Journal,* Feb., 1968. Carter, Launor F. The Systems Approach to Education — Mystique and Reality, *Educational Technology,* April, 1969. Task Group 6: Systems Approach to Education, *Proceedings of Project Aristotle Symposium.* National Security Industrial Assoc., Washington, D.C., 1968. Lehman, Henry, The Systems Approach to Education, *Audiovisual Instruction,* Feb., 1968. Banathy, Bela H. *Instructional Systems.* Palo Alto: Fearon Pub., 1968.

sive media, through teacher training, or through any of a variety of "solutions." Step I is invoked. The educator is persuaded to examine, in a joint effort with other medical educators, the desired consequences of the nurse's behavior. The consequences of nursing education (along with the education of doctors, hospital personnel, and the like) involve the production of comfortable and healthy patients. The final output of nursing education, therefore, should *not* be considered an educated nurse but a comfortable and healthy patient.

Another example involves a request to "improve language learning." In language training the emphasis is almost always on the teaching of certain behaviors to the speaker. Looking at the area of instruction from the proposed "consequences point of view," it is obvious that the end point is *not* the behavior of the speaker but the effect upon a listener. Were we training children to push a cart, it would be obvious that we would not concentrate upon formal properties of the child's pushing behavior as much as we would upon his effectiveness in moving the cart. The aim of language, in a sense, is to move the environment about, using small muscles. Appropriate questions formulated for consideration by the language teacher included: What are the desired consequences of speaking, reading and writing a language? What are the effects expected and desired, when a speaker talks to a listener?

An interesting third example involved the development of instruction for interviewers in social work agencies. A common starting point for such instruction has been either the analysis of the interview into its component parts or an analysis of the behavior of the interviewer (for example, "the interviewer should learn to be supportive"). But these are, respectively, once and twice removed from a statement of final consequences. Step I was used as a starting point. Teachers and designers started by examining the conditions (including changes in interviewee behaviors) which lead to better family relationships, to temporary support for needy clients, to referral to an appropriate social agency, and the like. Often the goal of an interview is to obtain and evaluate information from a client and then to persuade the client to take certain actions which the interviewer feels are appropriate. The consequence is presumably that the client is happier, healthier or less a threat to society than he was before the process started.*

It is easy to see how quickly one moves from the specific and narrow limits of a traditionally defined "job" to a broader focus of a system designed to produce a consequence. In the care of a patient, in the solving of a client's problems, and in the education of a human being it is likely that many elements (human and non-human) will be involved. Closer examination of these components is the next task, Step II.

Before going on, two notes should be added.

The language and examples used in the description of this step so far may have implied that the sole aim of education is the development of demonstrable and specific knowledge and skills.

There is often a confusion in education between two aims. On the one hand, skills and knowledge seem to be taught for their own sake, and on the other, they seem to be vehicles for the development of traits, strategies, viewpoints and attitudes which, it is hoped, extend far beyond the content area.

For example, a history course eventuates in an examination or term paper in which content specific behaviors are supposed to be demonstrated. Yet most educators, and certainly the teacher of the course, would claim that producing a way of thinking is a major purpose, perhaps the major purpose, of the course. Similarly, the scientific viewpoint as well as a knowledge of chemistry is supposed to emerge from a course in chemistry. There are changes attributable to specific content being taught on one hand, and other changes for which the content is viewed as a carrier or medium (thus, the scientific viewpoint might as well be taught in a course in physics as in chemistry.)

---

*For an interesting attempt at stating behavioral goals for counseling, see: Krumboltz, John D. Behavioral Goals for Counseling. *Journal of Counseling Psychology, 13,* 3, 1966, pp. 153-159 and Krumboltz, John D. *Stating the Goals of Counseling.* California Counseling and Guidance Association, Monograph Number One, 1966.

This is not the place to go into the murky area of transfer of training or generalization — an unhappy history which, in modern times, begins with the teaching of Latin in order to produce more rigorous thinking. The point to be made does not require a lengthy discussion or analysis. It is enough to recognize here that content is often used as a medium for teaching general patterns of behavior.

The model described here may be applied to the production of those general patterns. However, examples involving knowledge and skill are used because they seem to present the clearest instances, those that are most easily examined and clearly illustrative of the points being made.

A second comment concerns constraints on objectives. Unfortunately, as described above, the development of goal statements might suggest an elitist and conservative (in the true sense of the word) view of education. Thus, it might seem that the educator alone determines the objectives of the instructional system; also it might appear that the role of the educator (or any agent of behavior change) is to fit his students neatly into existing molds. This need not follow from what has been said.

First of all, it is feasible (and, in the author's view, necessary) to engage all members of society, students as well as teachers, in the entire process being described. All concerned members of society must have a voice in defining needs and determining which deserve attention.

The apparent conservative bias may be further reduced if one more point is added here. Changes in what exists, and the capacity to produce further changes, can be viewed as continuing major societal goals. Goals may be derived not only from examination of the present but also from extrapolation of current trends to the future. (For example, as computer hardware was designed, it could be predicted that a new group of people — computer programmers — would be needed as part of the system.) The generating of people who are themselves flexible and who in turn generate change might well be Education's most important output. It is one that can be justified both in terms of benefits to the individual and to society.

Step II.   Defining the Components Necessary to Produce the Consequences

Having made explicit the needs and desired consequences relevant to the particular inquiry, one might next do a component, or systems, design. The aim of this effort is to specify the necessary components to produce the desired consequences.

Even a rough component analysis will usually reveal a division into human and non-human components. We are becoming more aware of the enormous amount of environmental change that can result from the use of non-human components in a system.

To return to nursing education as an example, one can observe that much that has to be done to make a patient comfortable in a hospital can be taken care of by non-human components. Certain tasks that were until recently thought to be exclusively human have been reanalyzed and appropriate equipment developed. Prototypes of the automated hospital, in which human intervention is minimal, already exist.*

The term "non-human" may include not only machines but also infra-human organisms. Although only a start has been made on the use of other animals as components of systems, the examples are noteworthy. Pigeons have been used to guide ballistic missiles (Skinner, 1960) and to inspect items on production lines (Cummings 1956). In both cases, they have been shown to be very good workmen, from the point of view of management. (Needless to say, there are objections from fellow workers.) These examples seem strange and, at the moment, trivial. Yet they reveal important problems. Replacing a man with a machine or even the suggestion that part of his job might be replaced by a machine can lead to trouble. We have not yet had librarians and accountants destroy computers (in the way that textile workers destroyed the first power mills) although the suggestion has been made publicly. The relationship

---

*See, for example, Brown, J. H. V. & Dickson, James F. III. Instrumentation and the Delivery of Health Services. *Science, 166,* Oct. 17, 1969, pp. 334-338.

between worker and automation is still to be worked out. The replacement of a human by a pigeon seems even more outrageous to most of us. Innumerable articles have been written reassuring teachers that they will not be replaced by teaching machines. Imagine the public relations work that would have to be done if lower animals were brought on the faculty! Not only is the component analysis difficult in and of itself but also it stirs up resistance and hostility, And yet, it is necessary.

Component analysis may lead to a restructuring of the system which produces the consequences desired. That restructuring may be in terms of the development of new non-human components; at least it will involve a restructuring of human jobs. In this second step, the analyst is likely to exclude more human tasks than he includes. He is likely to strip away many activities that were thought to be essential and were traditionally included in the training (and even in the performance) of the human components in the system. In addition, an examination of the present environment, the skills needed to accomplish the goals, and the skills as they are presently being exhibited, may reveal a number of components that are functioning very well. These can be subtracted out of the list of components to be designed or selected. In short: It is not always necessary to teach or develop the elements of the design. Some amount of cutting and fitting to make optimal use of what is available seems most desirable.

The analyst emerges from Step II with a system or several alternate systems which describe the components and the activities of those components necessary to produce a desired consequence.

Step III. Defining the Human "Job"

The human activities that emerge from a component analysis can now be classified into what may be prosaically called "jobs." Indeed, this step has traditionally been called "job specification." Historically, the description of a job has not arisen from the sequence of activities just described but from an examination of the present performance of a job holder.

For example, the nurse in action in a hospital is studied, and what she does is written down. These activities, including all of the superstitious behaviors as well as all the efficient ones that she engages in during a day, constitute a job description which often becomes the basis for training the next generation of nurses. If Steps I and II are carried out, the usual grouping of tasks into a job will often be found to have only traditional justification—it has just grown up; it is what people do—rather than what needs to be done.

In most academic areas, not even traditional job analyses have been performed. It would not be impossible to determine what historians do; but such a specification of their activities does not exist. The role or job of a clinical psychologist is somewhat specified, but that of an experimental psychologist is ill-defined or undefined. The activities of a good citizen, or an informed, thoughtful person remain even more mysterious.

The inexorable press of specialization has forced the analysis of job descriptions in many areas; medical education is a case in point. There are *some* general practitioners, but they are a good deal rarer than they were twenty years ago. Some medical schools, nevertheless, still teach a job which simply does not exist with the frequency that the curriculum would suggest. The country doctor, with his black bag, riding through the night in a one-horse shay, able to set broken legs and cure the colic, is a romantic figure — but hardly an appropriate model for present medical curriculum developers to consider.

Here is one more academic example. An analysis of the use by professional people of the foreign languages that they learned for their doctoral examinations reveals that most of them never read a foreign journal, never speak a foreign language, never publish in a second language. Either they should be doing so and we are failing to teach them effectively, or the requirement is an irrelevant one, at least as far as practical use of a foreign language is concerned. On the other hand, even informal observation reveals that many professional people in the academic world are required to write grant proposals for research and development. Rarely are the skills necessary for such an activity formally taught in a graduate school curriculum.

The definition of the human job often turns into the definition of multiple jobs. For example, time motion studies of dentists at work have indicated that much of what they do could be done by a dental assistant. Invoking the exclusion principle once again, one group of designers involved in the study have concentrated upon preparing training materials for dental assistants and teaching materials for dentists intended to persuade them to use, and equip them to use, the dental assistant effectively.

The point of this discussion is to illustrate that a job can grow in an evolutionary way out of the needs of the environment; and that probably its resemblance to traditional job categories will be slight.

It should be noted that there is often a confusion between pedagogic means and professional ends. The final task that a doctor is involved in may not require him to perform blood tests and microscopic examinations of the blood; however, for pedagogic purposes it may be necessary to teach this in order to teach something else. If what is being taught has no relevance to a job, existing or newly structured, or more broadly, to a real world activity, it must be justified in terms of its demonstrable pedagogic usefulness.

At this point, it is worth summarizing what one would have in hand if he had carried out Steps I, II and III.

1. He would have an explication of present and predicted need or a series of needs. Presumably, he would be forced to contrast his statement with other statements of needs that other people are generating, and some sort of preference scale or hierarchy would be developed.

2. An analysis and design stage would have been completed, which would reveal a system, or several systems, made up of the components necessary to achieve the ends, that is to say, to alleviate the need just described. The component analysis would reveal tasks that are, for one reason or another, to be assigned to human beings and tasks to be assigned to non-human components.

3. Presumably, the non-human tasks are of less interest to us here. They could properly be assigned to engineers (or, as

suggested, to animal trainers). The human tasks would then be grouped, or factored, into jobs. The exclusion principle would be applied both in separating human from non-human jobs and in attempting to set up job hierarchies for the human components (i.e., when possible, activities that can be handled at a lower level will be excluded from a higher level).

Step IV. Specifying Performance Criteria

The degree of precision involved in each of the previous steps has not been specified. It is likely, in most cases, that it will not be high. The lack of constraints in the early stages is probably beneficial. But at some point, for a variety of reasons mentioned below, criteria for the performance of each component in the system must be spelled out in detail.

Teachers, with some justification, think of the business of test development and testing as narrowing and confining to the instructional effort, sometimes directing the attention of the student and the instructor toward trivia. They are often familiar only with paper and pencil tests and, at that, with poor examples of tests. One useful thing that may come out of the "new look" in education is greater realization of the spectrum of instruments that can be used to record, measure and objectify human behaviors. An example is simulation.

Simulation has become part of the technology of education. Although its application has been mainly to teaching, some recent examples suggest it may prove equally useful in testing. When student doctors diagnose patients and prescribe treatment, interacting exclusively with a computer, it is only a minor tragedy if the computer as a patient fails to survive the recommended treatment, or passes away while waiting for the doctor to arrive at the correct diagnosis. Such simulated patients can be used to test not only the final behavior of the student doctor with regard to diagnosis and treatment but the sequence, or method, of inquiry he uses in arriving at those two terminal points. Teachers are being taught (and can be tested as well) in simulated classroom situations using filmed groups of students. Law students attend mock courtrooms. And sometimes science students are tested in the laboratory on techniques and experimental methodology. Expanding the range of testing techniques can help reduce antagonism to measurement and thereby increase the probability that relevant and comprehensive performance criteria will be stated.

The development of performance criteria has several benefits. Having thus made explicit and operational the behaviors represented by the shorthand of component analysis, the designer has a tool which allows him to determine the validity of his analysis so far. He can try out his criteria on master performers. If they are not able to emit some of the behaviors in the performance criteria test and yet can produce the results desired the designer should reconsider those criteria.* (Of course, that a master can execute a required task is no absolute guarantee that it is a necessary behavior.) The first important consequence of the creation of a performance criteria test, then, is the validation of the criteria themselves. We would expect that as he developed the performance criteria and examined the results of tests of the performance criteria on master performers (i.e., validity checking) the designer would repeatedly re-examine and revise the analysis and design emerging from Steps I, II and III.

Having developed adequate test instruments, the designer may find an alternative to instruction by using those instruments as selection devices. Somewhere there may be people who can do the things he wants done. It is often much more economical, and sensible in other ways, to select than to teach. Intelligent selection presupposes appropriate test instruments. When objective measures of performance, and of behaviors correlated with that performance, have been devised, one form of a selection instrument is available.

A third use of the performance criteria is as baselines against which the effectiveness of any treatment, instructional

---

*A classic instance of mismatch between predicted necessary behaviors and actual behaviors of master performers (in this case, successful executives) can be found in Whyte, William H., Jr. *The Organization Man*, Doubleday and Company, 1956, especially pp. 201-222.

or non-instructional, may be measured. The simple research design of *measure-teach-measure again* is a potent one regardless of whether the treatment is instructional or not (e.g., performance tests may be given to the student population previous to instruction and then afterwards to discover the effectiveness of the particular instructional treatment).

The last use of performance criteria to be mentioned here is as end points for treatments.* The designer of instructional material can work more effectively and efficiently if, as he constructs the map of instruction, he has the major terminal points available. Often instruction almost "falls out" of such criterion tests since what must be taught becomes obvious when one examines the tests and the acceptable answers or performance criteria.** With test instruments in hand, the designer can go on to the next step of examining, selecting or developing, and trying out possible solutions.

There is a similarity between Step IV and what others, for example, Mager (1962), have said about the need to state instructional objectives. However, there is a shade of difference between the sequence of events described so far which led to the statements of performance criteria, and the more traditional sources of objectives. Generally, statements of objectives are derived in part from the unique intuition and history of, and immediate controlling circumstances surrounding, the instructional designer. Another important contributing source, of course, is *content,* a static form of knowledge usually represented by textual materials. Arising from such sources, statements of ob-

---

*Descriptions of other uses can be found elsewhere; for example, see Gagné, Robert M. The Analysis of Instructional Objectives for the Design of Instruction. In *Teaching Machines and Programmed Learning, II* (R. Glaser, Ed.). National Education Association, 1965 pp. 21-63. And, Popham, W. James. Objectives and Instruction. In *Instructional Objectives.* A.E.R.A. Monograph Series on Curriculum Evaluation No. 3 (Ed. R. E. Stake) Rand McNally and Co., Chicago, 1969. Especially, pp. 40-43.

**In some cases the "solution" is even simpler: Giving the student or employee the criteria and allowing him to instruct himself in whatever way he chooses until he meets the performance standards.

jectives are likely to be a reworking of the same implied or poorly stated objectives that the instructional system is already working toward, however inefficiently. This is not to gainsay the important advances that are being made by those pressing for statements of educational objectives in terms of learner behavior. However, in the long run a mere restatement in behavioral terms of irrelevant educational objectives will not produce a marked improvement in education.

What *is* needed is a restructuring of curricula in terms of useful, functional behaviors, not mere testable statements of irrelevant goals. Curriculum redesign too often consists of reshuffling the same old pack of cards; making the symbols on those cards clearer and brighter does not change the basic constraints of the pack. To generate new and useful curricula one must move outside, to a new source, to the terminal activities or performances themselves.

Step V. Re-Examining the Performance Environment

Following the dictum "don't do your own thing" or "don't teach unless you have to," one would next re-examine alternative ways of producing the consequences desired. (Some have already been suggested, e.g., non-human components whenever possible might be substituted for human components.)

Mention was made of using performance criteria for *selection*. Training or teaching can be avoided if selection can solve the problem. When adequate test material is available, different populations may be tested and, by careful selection, people who can already execute the required tasks of the redesigned system can be brought into it. In highly mobile societies such as ours the concept of moving the man to the job is, of course, feasible.

The interaction of attempts at selection and component analysis need only be pointed out. If it is possible to select people who have certain patterns of skills that are needed in the redesigned system, the "jobs" can be redefined in terms of the available population. This rearrangement or reallotment of specific tasks can reduce the residual training or teaching problem.

A second way to avoid the necessity of teaching is through close analysis of the performance environment itself. Appropriate behaviors may be available in members of that environment but for one reason or another they are not called out or supported, an observation made by many people concerned with systems for changing behavior. G. A. Rummler has suggested the terms *knowledge* (what people have) and *execution* (what people do). Gilbert (1967) has contrasted performance deficit with ignorance: can do and won't *versus* can't do. Psychologists are familiar with the distinction between acquisition and performance. Different variables may operate, or at least be differentially emphasized, during acquisition and during performance (Geis, 1966).

There are many causes of discrepancies between learning and performing. What is learned may not be rewarded in the performance environment; what is learned may be punished in the performance environment; incompatible and more rewarding behaviors may be available in the performance environment; the stimulus conditions in the performance environment may be markedly different from those that obtained during acquisition. A re-examination of several critical variables in the performance environment may lead not to a design for instruction but to a redesign of the performance environment which, when tested, may prove to be sufficient.

Changes in the physical environment always ought to be considered. Changing the signals on a control panel may dramatically change the observer's performance. Placing materials on a lower shelf may increase the chances of use. A new handle on a machine can encourage better grasping. At the other end of this continuum is the addition of checklists of instructions which guide the performance bit by bit. (It is surprising how often a checklist plus instructions in its use dissolves the original instructional problem.)

In summary, one examination of the present performance environment may lead to changes in it which will eliminate or reduce the need for instruction. The environment should be examined with a second purpose in mind: The *maintenance* of the activities of new components. The design of an instructional system without a parallel design for maintenance in the performance environment is likely to make the instruction appear ineffective. As suggested above, it has been a long time since learning psychologists believed that behavior could be stamped in, in a way analogous to branding cattle. Today there is recognition of, and concern with, the maintenance of behaviors once established. The learning environment may be used to establish behaviors but the performance environment determines whether or not those behaviors will be exhibited. When the performance environment minimally supports the learned behavior, a deterioration of that behavior is likely. Our handwriting is a good example of this. Since it is primarily directed toward us or toward a sympathetic (and, incidentally, paid) secretary, most of us can note a gradual deterioration of what was a rather good hand to a scrawl unreadable by anyone but ourselves and our translator. Support systems for both the human and non-human components must be considered along with the design of the instructional system.* (Such a support system, for example, is the type and means of feedback for the performer. Thus: What are the effects of the consequences of performance to the performer, to his peers, and to his supervisors?)

In summary, the performance environment should be examined with two questions in mind:

(1) Is it possible to change some aspects of the present environment to evoke and support desired behaviors already present in the performance population?

(2) How must the environment be changed so that the behaviors acquired through instruction will be supported once the learner leaves the instructional system?

---

*For a discussion of maintenance in the context of training, see Brethower, Karen S. Maintenance Systems: The Neglected Half of Behavior Change. In *Managing the Instructional Programming Effort.* G. A. Rummler, J. P. Yaney & A. W. Schrader (Eds.), The University of Michigan, Ann Arbor, 1967, pp. 60-72.

Step VI. Considering Resources and Constraints

The re-examination of the performance environment may confirm that the design of an instructional system or component is indicated. The resources and constraints involved in the production and maintenance of such a system will now be considered. The real determinants of the success or failure of an innovation, regardless of its intrinsic worth, are such practical matters as cost and availability of personnel.

Since any change involves expenditure and reallotment of resources, it would seem appropriate, before setting up an instructional system, to ask a number of questions concerning cost. For example: What is the cost to the receiving, or terminal, system if the behavior under scrutiny simply does not occur? And then, suppose that the behavior is not taught. Will the final cost, in terms of deficiency of the terminal system, be greater than the cost of producing the behavior via instruction?

"Cost" can be interpreted broadly, and the concept of cost can be applied to other areas. For example, what is the value of the behavior to the learner and to other people? If there is no demonstrable value to the learner, the job of instruction may prove to be most difficult. If there is no value to others, the innovation will not be adopted or supported elsewhere.

Another cost-relevant consideration is the life-span of the instructional innovation or of the behavior the innovation produces. The rate of change in knowledge and skills is, in our society, geometrically accelerating. How long will what is taught be useful to the learner and to others?

Needs or goals are competitive. In everyday affairs they eventually become ordered in a hierarchy. Annual congressional debate and log-rolling results in a federal budget and legislation which define the select group of goals for which resources will be allocated that year. Cost of an instructional system may be considered in the context of a similar hierarchy. Should support be denied to the design and implementation of other behavior change systems in order to support the one being proposed?

Repeatedly, in this paper, attention has been paid to the problems of maintenance; the consideration of maintenance is appropriate in this step. Physical maintenance of an innovative facility (e.g., of the language laboratory) may prove to be too expensive for the existing instructional system. The support costs of an innovation should be estimated before the innovation is actually developed. The cost to the instructional system of maintaining the human components is, of course, equally critical in determining whether or not the innovation will last.

The cost of maintenance by the receiving system (i.e., performance environment) of the behavior to be taught must be considered. It was pointed out in the previous step that changes in the receiving environment often reduce or eliminate the need for new instruction of the people going into that environment. If new behaviors must be trained, then it is likely that the receiving environment will have to support those behaviors and probably will have to shift support or reallocate its resources to do so. Some of the more successful training efforts involve parallel training of supervisors with the supervised. In such cases there is clear recognition that if the supervisor is not specifically trained to maintain the trainee's behavior it will soon die out; the entire training program will have been a costly failure. The cost of maintaining the learner's behavior includes, in this case, the cost of training supervisors. Another, dramatic example is milieu therapy. This approach to psychotherapy recognizes that changes in the patient must be supported by his environment outside the therapist's office. The therapy, therefore, includes planned changes in the maintenance environment as well as the patient himself. The educational innovator might take heed.

Implementation and maintenance involve the development of subsystems concurrent with the development of the major system (e.g., the instructional innovation). It is impossible to predict with complete accuracy the course of implementation, the pressures on the maintenance system once it is in effect, the changing environment in which the innovation is located, etc. If a system is not designed to be adjustive and if data on its performance are not collected and fed back into the system, it is likely to wither or be destroyed. Only passing attention can be paid here to an important principle suggested by these statements: It is crucial to the maintenance of any system that some part of its resources be devoted to obtaining feedback on the performance of the system and some part to supporting a mechanism which responds to the feedback by producing changes when so indicated. (Instruction offers a negative instance. It is often a system without adequate means of gathering data on its performance and of converting the data it does obtain into recommendations for change.)

So much for constraints. The positive side of this step is "resources." Resources in the training environment and in the terminal environment which are presently untapped can be uncovered and used. Some examples may suggest the range of the resources that the educational innovator has at hand when constructing innovations and when seeking to have innovative behaviors maintained. Housewives, enlisted to grade English compositions, have proven to be useful aides. The each-one-teach-one system is often used by skillful teachers to relieve their own time pressures (in addition, there is some evidence that the student "teacher" learns as much as, if not more than, his tutee).* If the actual design and production of teaching materials is beyond the traditional resources of the system, the students themselves can often be utilized as curriculum developers. Involving students in the development of teaching materials may serve double duty: the materials can be used with other students and the developers learn a great deal in the process of development. The "world outside" can and should be used as a resource in the development of educational systems. As presently used most work-study programs and field trips represent only minimal and primitive use of the resources of the world beyond the campus walls.

It is unlikely at the present state of development of educational technology that detailed and accurate information can be gathered about resources and constraints. Yet some indicators of cost are available and should be used more extensively. In the past 15 or 20 years, enormous amounts of money and effort

---

*A well-tested innovative system involving students as staff is described in Keller, F. S. Goodbye, Teacher. *Journal of Applied Behavior Analysis, 1,* No. 7, 1968, pp. 79-89.

have been poured into educational innovations. Unfortunately, the life of even the best innovation is dramatically short. Evidence is mounting which indicates that an important contributor to the demise of many otherwise worthwhile educational innovations is the lack of attention paid to resources and constraints. The instructional systems designer might bear in mind these words of Machievelli (a man skilled in examining constraints and resources): "Any plan that does not carry with it its own plan for implementation is worthless as a plan and should, therefore, be abandoned."

Summary

This paper has proposed that a decision to design and develop any instructional system (as small as a chapter in a textbook, as large as a college curriculum) be deferred until six steps are carried out. It suggests that the *how* to teach problem be approached only after one has examined the questions of *when* and *what* to teach. The first concern of the instructional designer ought to be the definition and demonstration of goals and needs at the societal level. Solutions to problems that the needs present may, but do not necessarily, involve changing human behaviors. Furthermore, only some of those elements of the solution which do involve behavioral change are likely to require instructional systems. Finally, no such system should be developed until an inventory of relevant constraints and available resources is constructed and a plan for maintaining learned behavior is devised.

The decision to design and develop new instruction (or "improve" the old) is to be arrived at cautiously, only after excluding all other alternatives. The instructional systems that finally do emerge from this decision process will be undeniably relevant and must, inescapably, become efficient.

To the objection that teachers are involved in *Education* and "not merely" in instruction, the paper implies an answer. Many of the behavioral changes the "educator" wishes to produce require environmental modifications far beyond the scope of classroom and teacher. It is wise for him to consider not only the ends he wishes to achieve but the limitations of the means he has available for achieving them.

REFERENCES

Cumming, W. C.   A Bird's Eye Glimpse of Men and Machines" (pp. 246-256) & Verhave, T. The Pigeon as a Quality Control Inspector (pp. 242-246). Both in *The Control of Human Behavior* (Eds. R. Ulrich, T. Stachnik & J. Mabry), Scott Foresman Co., 1956.

Geis, G. L.   Retention — A Pseudo-Problem. *NSPI Journal, 5,* 2, Feb., 1966, pp. 10-13.

Gilbert, Thomas F.   Praxeonomy: A Systematic Approach to Identifying Training Needs. *Management of Personnel Quarterly, 6,* 3, Fall, 1967, pp. 20-30.

Mager, R. F.   *Preparing Instructional Objectives.* Palo Alto: Fearon Publishers, 1962.

Skinner, B. F.   Pigeons in a Pelican. *American Psychologist, 15,* 1960, pp. 28-37.

7

The Issue of Readiness in the Design and Organization of the Curriculum: A Historical Perspective

Edmund V. Sullivan

In order to frame this paper in a proper educational perspective, it may be said that the concept of *readiness* in the curriculum has been historically and is now one of the more polemical and controversial molecular issues in education. The term *molecular* is purposely used so that the reader will know that more molar educational issues take precedence over this question before the problem of readiness is even entertained. The role of the school in contemporary society, its educational objectives and the question of the moral limits of its influence, are but a few examples

The author thanks Mrs. Diane Hansen for the typing of this manuscript and is indebted to Mrs. Mary Stager for her critical comments and editorial assistance.

EDMUND V. SULLIVAN is associate professor of applied educational psychology at the Ontario Institute for Studies in Education, Toronto, Canada.

of the molar considerations which take priority over the question of "readiness" in curriculum planning. Thus far, it has been implicitly assumed that the reader already understands the term "readiness;" this is somewhat unfair, since one of the purposes of this paper is to clarify some of the reasons why it is a controversial term. In a sense, the reader's common sense definition of "readiness" is relied on, which, probably, in whole or in part, can be found in Webster's dictionary.

The word "ready" is defined by Webster's generally as follows:

— prepare or supply with what is needed for some act or event;
— suited or arranged for immedate use;
— immediately liable; likely;
— willing; disposed;
— dextrous; expert; etc.

"Readiness" is a noun briefly defined as follows:

— quality of being ready; promptness; alacrity;
— state or fact of being ready.

When these terms are extrapolated into their educational context, they obviously need a certain degree of precison on the part of the user if confusion is to be circumvented. This attempt at precision has not been demonstrated, in general, in educational circles; and this is probably one of the reasons why the polemics and controversy still crop up in contemporary educational theorizing. When the concept of "readiness" is used in educational curriculum planning, it is entrenched in implicit philosophical and psychological assumptions concerning the concept of mind, the definition of knowledge, and the way that knowledge is acquired and maintained. It will be shown, for example, that when a scholar such as Piaget, coming from a Kantian tradition, faces a Neo-Behaviorist coming from a British Associationist tradition, on the issue of "readiness," their controversy concerning this term stems from a long philosophical and psychological battle about the definition of knowledge itself, among other things. In its simplest form, no one would argue with Tyler's (1964) definition that "readiness" deals generically with the issue "when to teach;" in other words, it is first of all a temporal problem in curriculum planning. The difficulty ensues when different philosophical and psychological theories prescribe different times and different modes of attainment of a body of knowledge. It is here that the concept of "readiness" takes on different definitions, in accordance with the implicit assumptions of the theory within which the educational planner is operating. The attempt here will be to make explicit some of the implicit theories involved, and to show how they lead to opposing conclusions concerning the "when of learning" in a curriculum. The treatment will not be exhaustive, and the reader is referred to Tyler's (1964) excellent article on the same topic to see some of the "uses" and "misuses" of the concept of readiness that have taken place historically in American education.

Readiness and the Concept of Mind

When the discussion of readiness to learn is introduced in the pacing of a curriculum, one frequently finds that expert advice is sought from the discipline of psychology. Specifically, the areas of developmental psychology, learning theory and psychometry have, at one time or another, addressed themselves to the concept of readiness in curriculum programming. In spite of the fact that all these experts are psychologists, it has become obvious that different types of theories of development, learning and measurement have issued different prescriptions concerning readiness to learn — because they have vastly different conceptions of mind and how the mind assimilates information. In fact, some theories of psychology (e.g., radical behaviorism) deny the very concept of mind; but there are historical reasons for such a development, and when these are elaborated, the present topic may be more fully understood.

In a sense, the use of the term *psychology* is a misnomer in much of what is now known as modern psychology. The study (logos) of the soul (psyche) from its Greek origins honored a distinction or dualism between body and mind, but this distinction has been obliterated in many contemporary psychological theories. To some extent, this distinction of mind and body depends on whether the theorist thinks that the human person can be studied as a natural phenomenon, following laws similar to those followed by phenomena in the other physical sciences (e.g., physics). This development was continued in the writing of René Déscartes, and specifically in his thoughts concerning the mind-body dualism. Déscartes contended that reality involved two exclusive dimensions, that of extension and thought. Man partially participated in both these dimensions, in Déscartes' view, for he was a creature composed of both spiritual (mind) and corporeal (body) properties. The *mental* dimension of man was exemplified in such human activities as thinking, imagining, willing, being conscious, feeling, and so forth. The *corporeal* dimension was exemplified in such activities as breathing, digestion and other non-cognitive aspects of human existence. Déscartes attempted to unify this dualism by postulating their interaction in the pineal gland. This unification was unsuccessful, because his theory of mind-body interaction was never taken seriously. More important here, however, are Déscartes' views on how both mind and body were to be understood and explained. It was his conviction that man's corporeal existence could be explained by natural mechanical explanations, such as those given in the natural sciences of his day. This meant that bodily existence was determined by mechanistic laws that govern all bodies occupying space. Because of Déscartes' religious convictions, the mind of man was considered free and not subject, as the body was, to the laws of natural phenomena. The exclusion of the *mind* from the mechanistic world in a sense renamed psychology as a contender in the natural sciences. In the history of psychology up to contemporary times, three is a desperate attempt to consider this discipline a natural science; much of modern psychology has veered toward the explanation of all man's activities in naturalistic, mechanistic terms. The advent of behaviorism saw the total rejection of mind as a construct worthy of consideration, and, with Watson, the proper study of psychology became man's observed behavior, which was explainable by totally naturalistic means. Mind keeps creeping back, however, in the guise of *intervening variables* and *hypothetical constructs* and the probable reason for this is that, as fuzzy as the concept may be, it nevertheless emerges when theorists are honestly trying to understand many aspects of man's existence.

The 1960's saw a resurgence of old philosophical questions initiated by Déscartes, and the view that psychology is a natural science consisting of mechanistic explanations has been the subject of attack in many sophisticated theoretical circles. Sigmund Koch (1964) has challenged the primacy and importance of psychology's being a *natural science,* and has severely criticized the contribution of Behaviorism in its explanation and conception of man. Chomsky (1968) has launched a similar attack in his consideration of language development, and has rejected mechanical explanations of language acquisition. He reintroduces the concept of *mind,* and traces his theoretical concerns back to Déscartes. He maintains that the study of mind presents us with a problem of quality of complexity, and not merely one of degree of complexity. The phenomena of language cannot be explained by physical science strategies any more than can man's thought processes. Without further elaboration on these issues, it is hoped that the sense of controversy has been conveyed.

But why present this controversy? What does it have to do with educational readiness? This seems a long and circuitous route to travel, but if it is kept in mind that much of contemporary learning theory develops out of behavioristic psychology, it may be said that when the concept of "readiness" is tied to this tradition, it is implicitly operating from a distinct philosophical tradition with strong adherents and strong detractors in contemporary psychology.

To give a more complete picture of psychological influences on education, it is important to note that Behaviorism has not reigned supreme. Although Thorndike (1932) wielded a heavy influence on educational planning, Dewey provided many educational theorists and practitioners with an alternative view of the mind which was sympathetic to the Gestalt tradition in psychology (McDonald, 1964). Whereas Behaviorism drew from the British Associationists' philosophical tradition, as illustrated in the work of Locke, Berkeley and Hume, the Gestaltists' philosophical source was the "Continental European" tradition, exemplified by Kant. The Kantian tradition emphasized the *mind* side of the Cartesian dualism, whereas the British Associationists ventured out on its opposite counterpart. The two traditions have vastly different conceptions of the development and learning process as well as opposing conceptions of knowledge. Although it will be rough at the edges, an attempt will be made to show how different educational metaphors and their historical antecedents have led to different conceptions of learning and development in contemporary educational psychology. These conceptions are partially traceable to the different conceptions of man as previously discussed. It will be seen that the concept of *readiness* takes on different parameters depending on the educational metaphor and psychological theory that is being applied. Two conceptions of human development are initially pertinent here: (1) preformationistic and predeterministic conceptions of development, and (2) Tabula Rasa conceptions of development (Ausubel & Sullivan, 1970).

Preformationistic and Predeterministic Concepts of Development

Preformationist Approaches. The fundamental thesis of preformationism is a denial of the essential occurrence and importance of development in human ontogeny (Ausubel & Sullivan, 1970). The basic properties and behavioral capacities of man — his personality, values and motives, his perceptual, cognitive, emotional and social reaction tendencies — are not considered to be undergoing qualitative differentiation and transformation over the life span, but are presumed to exist preformed at birth. Nothing need develop as a result of the interaction between a largely undifferentiated organism with certain stipulated predispositions and his particular environment. Instead, everything is already prestructured, and either undergoes quantitative modification with increasing age or merely unfolds sequentially on a prearranged schedule. The concept of *readiness* is vitiated under preformationistic conceptions because there is no postulation of organism-environment interaction since development is denied in the growth process.

Historical antecedents. The origins of preformationistic thinking stem from theological conceptions of man and certain innate givens in his nature (e.g., Original Sin). An early embryological theory is found in the homuncular theory of human reproduction and prenatal gestation. The homuncular theory rested on the belief that a miniature but well-formed little man (i.e., homunculus) was embodied in the sperm, and when emplanted in the uterus simply grew to bulk, without any disorientation of tissue or organs, until full-term fetal size was attained at the end of nine months. Educationally, the disposition to perceive the infant or child as a miniature adult is largely an outgrowth of the ubiquitous tendency toward extrapolation or anthropomorphism in interpreting phenomena remote from one's own experience or familiar explanatory models. The theological variety of preformationism, allied as it was to a conception of man as innately sinful, inspired a rigid, authoritarian and pessimistic approach to education (Ausubel & Sullivan, 1970). Since ultimate form was assumed to be prestructured and complete in all of its essential aspects, one could at best only improve slightly on what the individual already was or was fated to become. Hence, it was not necessary to consider the child's developmental needs and status, the conditions propitious for development at a given stage of maturity, or readiness for particular experience. Readiness was considered irrelevant as a concept, because the child was not perceived as qualitatively different from the adult or as making any significant contribution to his own development. The arbitrary imposition of adult standards was regarded as self-evidently defensible. Fortunately, there are no contemporary counterparts of the approach in modern education.

Predeterministic Approaches. In contradiction to preformationism, predeterministic conceptions of growth satisfy the minimal criteria for a developmental approach. Successive stages of the organism are not merely regarded as reflective of a sequential unfolding of preformed structures or functions forever fixed at conception or birth, but as the outcome of a process of qualitative differentiation or evolution of form. Nevertheless, because the regulation of development is considered as so prepotently determined by internal factors, the net effect is much the same as if preformationism were assumed. Interaction with the environment and the latter's influence on the course of development is not completely ruled out, but its directional role is so sharply curtailed that it never crucially affects eventual outcome, accounting at the very most for certain minor limiting or patterning effects.

Historical antecedents. The first definitive predeterministic theory of child development was articulated by the French philosopher Rousseau (1712-1778). Rousseau postulated that all development consists of a series of internally regulated sequential stages, which are transformed one into the other in conformity with a prearranged order and design (Rousseau, 1895). According to this conception of development, the only proper role of the environment is avoidance of serious interference with the processes of self-regulation and maturation. It facilitates development best, not by imposing restrictions or setting coercive goals and standards, but by providing a maximally permissive field in which, unhampered by the limiting and distortive influences of external constraints, the predetermined outcomes of growth are optimally realized. Consistent with this orientation was Rousseau's belief that the child is innately good, that society constitutes the source of all evil, and that a return to a less inhibited and less socially restrictive method of child rearing would necessarily result in the unfolding of the individual's inherently wholesome and virtuous development proclivities. Implicit in the above is the educational growth metaphor of the plant (Scheffler, 1960). The metaphor is expressed in the parallels between the growing child and the *growing plant* and between the gardener and the teacher. As Scheffler points out, in both cases, the developing organism goes through stages of development that are relatively independent of the efforts of the gardener as teacher. In both gardening and teaching the objective is to help the organism flourish and care for its welfare by providing optimum conditions for the operations of laws of nature (Scheffler, 1960). Readiness from the teacher's standpoint is irrelevant here, since the timing is an endogenous organismic factor governed by the organism and not dependent on the environment. The educational implications of these doctrines may also be found in the educational writings of such men as Pestalozzi and Froebel; and, in more recent times, the writings of Neill on his Summerhill experiment.

The philosophical antecedents of predeterministic theories have psychological counterparts in the writings of Mall (1904) and of Gesell and his followers (Gesell, 1933; Gesell & Ilg, 1943). Since Gesell's position has more obvious implications for the educational concept of readiness, it seems appropriate to discuss parts of his theoretical position on the concept of development. In a sense, Gesell's theory of maturation reiterates Rousseau's emphasis upon the internal control of development (Ausubel & Sullivan, 1970). Gesell's theory capitalized on its general resemblance to the empirically demonstrable concept of maturation, which had gained considerable acceptance among behavior scientists, educators and the lay public. Actually, the latter concept dealt with non-learning (as distinguished from the learning) contributions to enhancement in capacity, rather than with the more general issue of the relative importance of internal and external regulation in development irrespective of the role of learning. Operationally it merely referred to increments in functional capacity attributable to structural growth, physiological change or the cumulative impact of incidental experience (i.e., learning). Gesell, however, used the term *maturation* in a very special and more global sense to represent the endogenous regulatory mechanisms responsible for determining the essential direction of all development, including that conditioned in part by learning and enculturation. Gesell (1933) theorized that developmental sequences are relatively invariable in all areas of growth, evolve more or less spontaneously and inevitably, and show basic uniformities even in strikingly different cultural settings. The role of the environment is relegated to a subsidiary function, merely supporting, inflecting and modifying but not generating the progressions of development. Since development follows an endogenous organismic timetable, the concept of readiness is relegated to a status similar to that found in Rousseau's philosophical position (see Gesell & Ilg, 1943). In other words, the organism itself takes care of readiness.

Contemporary counterparts. The most important contemporary theory with a posture toward predeterminism is the Piagetian stage model of cognitive development. Piaget's use of the term "stage of development" implicitly adheres to the notion that, as age is changing, the organism has at its disposal different intrinsic structures which enable it to process information in different ways. In theory, the concrete-abstract dimension that Piaget describes is attributed to these changing intrinsic structures. In order to assess the presence of a "stage," Piaget has deliberately questioned children on concepts that are *spontaneously* learned rather than directly taught in the school. If there are developmental differences in the way children view the world, it is wise to tap these structural differences by using concepts in which they cannot mimic adult responses. Thus, the use of questions which probe the child's spontaneous (versus learned) concepts guards against the child's giving information learned by rote, and, in this sense, enables one to see if there are differences between child and adult reasoning. Even a cursory reading of Piaget will establish the fact that this strategy has been a profitable endeavor.

The use of Piaget's stages as "readiness" indicators was first suggested by Hunt (1961) in his discussion of "matching" the environmental circumstances to the child's conceptual abilities. As Hunt points out, Piaget has frequently alluded to the importance of basing educational practice on the natural phases of the child's interaction with the environment, but he has only hinted at the principle that environmental circumstances force accommodative modifications in the child's cognitive structure. Some writers feel that Piaget's work has educational merit because it is important that there be an appropriate "match" between the circumstances that a child encounters and his present state of conceptual development.

> The description of the stages of intellectual development provided by Piaget are extremely helpful in the matching process as it is seen in a grosser sense. The periods between the various behavioral landmarks that

mark Piaget's transitions or stages are, in a sense, "critical periods" for various types of environmental encounters (Hunt, 1961, p. 273).

In the past several years, educational extrapolators of Piaget have attempted to deal with the "matching" hypothesis in practical curriculum prescriptions. For instance, Adler (1963) has suggested that if one follows Piagetian stages in planning curriculum, the world initially must be defined in terms of action-linked concepts, with the child encountering knowledge through his own actions (i.e., sensory-motor). During the stage of concrete operations, the teacher must deal with materials in terms of concrete samples; and, finally, the stage of formal operations allows the presentation of less concrete and more theoretical material.

This interpretation of Piaget's stages puts his normative sequences in a prescriptive context; that is, the stages of cognitive development in some way prescribe how the learning should take place at different levels of cognitive maturity. In a sense, it is hinting at the readiness of learning experiences in a particular subject matter area. Before expanding on the notion of readiness for subject matter, it is necessary to consider Piaget's definition of readiness. Piaget identifies the concept of readiness as synonymous with maturation (i.e., genic unfolding). His dichotomy between learning and development (Piaget, 1964) places his notion of "readiness" clearly on the side of some type of maturational unfolding. Piaget also states that learning cannot explain development but that stage of development can, in part, explain learning. Thus in Almy, Chittenden and Miller (1966), he states in the preface that:

> Development follows its own laws, as all of the contemporary biology leads us to believe, and although each stage in the development is accompanied by all sorts of new learning based on experience, this learning is always relative to the developmental period during which it takes place, and the intellectual structures, whether completely or partially formed, which the subject has at his disposal during this period. In the last analysis, therefore, development accounts for

learning much more than the other way around (1966, p. 5).

Piaget's educational position is quite similar to Dewey's, in the sense that the curriculum is to be geared to the child's cognitive level and not the converse. If learning should be geared to the child's present developmental level as Piaget insists, then the problem of "matching" the subject matter to the growing conceptual abilities of the child (i.e., his present cognitive structure) is a relevant consideration. Hunt (1961) maintains that when cognitive structure and subject matter are "mismatched" the learning experience is impeded and slowed down. It is, therefore, important that the changes in teaching strategy be based on changes that take place at critical points in the Piagetian scheme of development. The educational stress has thus far focused on the changes that take place between Piaget's stages of pre-operational, concrete operational and formal operational thought. It is interesting to note that they take place roughly at the periods of transition from nursery to elementary and from elementary to secondary schools (Sullivan, 1968). Several educators and psychologists have specifically applied Piagetian stages as indicators of "readiness" to learn in such areas as physics, mathematics and the social sciences and their attempts are critically evaluated elsewhere (Sullivan, 1967, 1969). For the moment, let us focus on the predeterministic elements in Piagetian theory, because of its obvious implications for the concept of readiness and its practical educational import within this theoretical orientation.

Piaget shares with other "stage formulations" of development the problem of attributing the on-going stage changes to some kind of genic unfolding. If taken seriously, a predeterministic position underlays the value of educational intervention and in many instances relegates it to a minor role in the development process. As discussed previously, Gesell (1954), in American psychology, exemplified predeterminism by attributing the development of his stages of motor and social development to genic unfolding of biological structures. Gesell theorized that developmental sequences are relatively invariable in all areas of growth, evolve more or less spontaneously and inevitably, and show basic uniformities even in strikingly different cultural settings (Ausubel & Sullivan, 1970). The effects of environment are only indirectly felt and its role is to support, inflect and specify, but not to engender, the basic forms and sequences of ontogenesis (Gesell, 1954).

It is clear that Piaget's consistent reiteration of the functional invariants of assimilation and accommodation (Hunt, 1969), as well as his emphasis on the effects of social experience (Piaget, 1964; Sigel, 1968), distinguishes his theory from Gesell's, at least in emphasis. Relative to Gesell, he is less a predeterminist along a predeterminist-interaction continuum, but is it valid to say that he is a full blown interactionist (see Hunt, 1969)? It is contended here that, in some ways, Piaget has invited being labelled as at least a modified predeterminist. It can be said without exaggeration that:

> Piaget . . . tends to ignore the effects of antecedent conditions and the environmental variables in development, relegating them to a place of definitely subsidiary importance to the unfolding of internal structures. This does not mean that he advocates a strict nativist position, for he has frequently emphasized the continual interaction between external and internal forces. Nevertheless, biological orientation and interest in structure leads him to take external factors for granted and to regard the form which this interaction takes as largely predetermined from the start. The only problem, then, is that of specifying the successive stages through which the organism passes; little leeway is left for differential manifestations of external conditions (Wohlwill, 1962).

This "little leeway" is seen in his complete lack of emphasis on direct educational intervention. In fact, it is in the statements that Piaget has made to educators that he is found most vulnerable to the accusation of predeterminism. This drawback is seen in his insistence on the dichotomy between development and learning. In considering the development of knowledge, Piaget (1964) has said the following:

The development of knowledge is a spontaneous process, tied to the whole process of embryogenesis. Embryogenesis concerns the development of the body, but it concerns as well the development of the nervous system, and the development of mental functions. In the case of the development of knowledge in children, embryogenesis ends only in adulthood. It is a total developmental process which we must resituate in its general biological and psychological context. In other words, development is a process which concerns the totality of the structures of knowledge (p. 8).

Piaget (1964) points out further a distinction between learning and development. For Piaget, learning should be considered as distinct from development:

Learning presents the opposite case. In general, learning is provoked by situations — provoked by a psychological experimenter or by a teacher, with respect to some didactic point, or by an external situation. It is provoked, in general, as opposed to spontaneous. In addition, it is a limited process—limited to a single problem or to a single structure (p. 8).

The reader will note that his concept of development is a spontaneous process tied to embryogenesis, while *learning* is provoked by external situations. Like Gesell, he notes that *embryogenesis* concerns bodily development, but also the nervous system and mental functions; thus *development* is a process which concerns the totality of the structures of knowledge. In Piaget's framework, *learning* is a more restricted process which is provoked by situations (e.g., teaching) and is limited to single problems or single structures. The classification of Piaget as predominantly a predeterminist (Ausubel & Sullivan, 1970), which seems rather shocking when one considers the factors he outlines for stage transition, can be justified because of the prime importance and prominence which he attributes to the equilibration factor. Piaget and his followers (e.g., Smedslund, 1961) deny that specific learning experience or training (practice), particularly of a verbal nature, or for that matter, education generally, has any significant influence on the emergence of stages of intellectual development. Vygotsky (1965) appears to have driven to the very heart of this rigid dichotomy when he discusses Piaget's notions of *spontaneous* concepts (i.e., concepts that develop through equilibration) and *non-spontaneous* concepts (i.e., concepts that are learned from external sources):

> There are errors in Piaget's reasoning that detract from the value of his views. Although he holds that the child in forming a concept stamps it with the characteristic of his own mentality, Piaget tends to apply this thesis only to spontaneous concepts and assumes that they alone can truly enlighten us on the special qualities of child thought; he fails to see the interaction between the two kinds of concepts and the bonds that unite them into a total system of concepts in the course of the child's intellectual development (Vygotsky, 1965, p. 84).

The educational problem with a stage theory such as Piaget's involves relating the notion of "intrinsic structure" to the on-going teaching-learning situation. This linking of the educational strategy to stage of development is complicated by the fact that Piaget in his research has attempted to keep them separate. One of the difficult educational dilemmas with Piaget's work is due to the tremendous stress that he places on spontaneous concept formation, while paying relatively minor attention to the formal concepts that are learned in school (Vygotsky, 1965). In this sense, the theory ignores the interaction between school-learned concepts and intrinsic structure (stage). With Piaget, "stage of development" affects the learning of school concepts but the reverse does not obtain. Aebil (in Kohnstamm, 1966) notes this stumbling block to making Piaget's developmental psychology fruitful for education:

> If Piaget in his developmental experiments demonstrates that at a certain age a certain operation exists, it does not have to be taught anymore. However, if the child does not yet have the operation at his disposal it cannot be taught (p. 3).

Kohnstamm (1966) views this as the basic problem with Piaget's theory for a number of reasons. The first is Piaget's belief that experiences in daily life are necessary for development, and that the child learns gradually from his own spontaneous experiences. There is no place in the theory for the systematic teaching of thought structures. The second reason is bound up with the fact that, for Piaget, the child's activity, not his language, is the main factor in cognitive development:

> In Piaget's view the social transmission of spoken language is not essential for the formation of operational structures. Therefore, all the words a teacher might use in trying to explain a certain Piagetian problem to the child are considered useless. If the child has had the necessary experience he will discover the insight into the problem all in due time; if he has not, the only thing a teacher can do is to teach the child to recite the rules parrot-wise without real understanding (Kohnstamm, 1966, pp. 3-4).

As will be pointed out later, a more generic conception of "cognitive readiness" can be considered without violating the assumptions of stage theories. This conception simultaneously considers maturation (genic) and prior learnings without treating them as discrete parts. The emphasis on learning as one of the necessary conditions for particular "stage of development" gives the educator greater latitude in experimenting with new subject matter if it is related to the previously learned subject matter. The formulation of Piaget's stage theory is of such a restrictive nature that in regard to the notion of "readiness" the temporal prescription is to simply *wait* for self-regulation to take place.

Tabula Rasa Conceptions of Development

In marked contrast to the preformationist and predeterministic doctrines of development which have been discussed is the Tabula Rasa position, which is derived from historical antecedents in British Associationism and has as its modern-day educational derivative approaches such as Behaviorism and Neo-Behaviorism. If the former (i.e., preformationist and predeterministic) approaches are considered as constituting one extreme of a continuum embracing various theories concerned with the regulation of human development, the latter ideological movements would have to be placed at the other extreme of the same continuum. They are referred to as Tabula Rasa (literally, "blank slate") approaches because they minimize the contributions of genic endowment and of directional factors coming from within the individual, and concomitantly emphasize the preeminent role of the environment in determining the outcome of development. The analogy which likens the neonate to a Tabula Rasa is aptly representative of their general thesis that no fundamental predispositions are inherent in the raw material from which behavior and personality develop, that human beings are infinitely malleable. All of the patterning, differentiation, integration and elaboration of specific and general behavioral content that emerges during the course of development is accounted for in terms of the unique stimulus conditions to which the individual is or has been subjected (Ausubel & Sullivan, 1970).

It should be noted, however, that the term "tabula rasa" is being used here in a very general sense, to denote extreme environmentalist positions such as those described above. In the more specific sense of the term, as employed by John Locke, the "blank slate" only referred to the ideational state of affairs at birth and not to the complete absence of developmental predispositions; as a matter of fact, in his discourses on education he placed much emphasis on the need for restraining the natural impulses of children. Furthermore, in the light of modern conceptions of cognitive and behavioral development, Locke's Tabula Rasa proposition cannot be regarded as indicative of an extreme position with respect to the nature-nurture controversy.

Historical antecedents. Consistent with and building upon the British Associationist philosophical tradition, Behaviorism as a movement in American psychology extended the Tabula Rasa position by emphasizing the behavioral plasticity of the organism and by denying subjective experience (except as a form of subliminal behavior). It rejected all developmental predispositions (except for reflexes and certain emotional responses) and conceptualized the human organism as a noncognitive response mechanism subservient to the control of conditioned stimuli (Watson, 1919). Similarly, in the area of child care and education, its advocacy of impersonal handling, strictness, regularity, and the importance of habit training was strikingly reminiscent of preformationist practices (Watson, 1928). Implicit in the above position is the educational growth metaphor of shaping (Scheffler, 1960). The metaphor is expressed in the parallels between the growing child as *clay* and the teacher as the molder or shaper of the clay from amorphous to specific forms. When this metaphor is being employed, the teacher's initiative, power and responsibility are brought into sharp focus (Scheffler, 1969). In line with Tabula Rasa conceptions of behavioral plasticity, the final shape of the clay is wholly a product of the teacher's choice of a given mold. Readiness, in this tradition, is a function of the teacher's initiative, with the child's inherent growth processes being generally ignored or skirted.

The earliest American proponent of the "Associationist" tradition in educational psychology was Edward Thorndike (1932). Thorndike viewed the learning situation as an *association* between sense impressions (stimuli) and dispositions to action (responses). These *bands* or *associations* or *connections* between stimuli and responses are strengthened by reinforcement or satisfaction and practice. Knowledge, for Thorndike, was the accumulation of these stimulus-response connections. Thorndike propounded a peculiar *law of readiness* which was grounded in physiological terms. Readiness had a physiological base in his postulation of a "conduction unit" which had to be *ready* to conduct if a connection or association was to be made. The law was quite vague and circular, and it sheds no light on the topic of readiness that is being dealt with in this paper. Nevertheless, the general thrust of Thorndike's educational theorizing indicates that readiness for learning is a matter of making the correct connections in the appropriate order with the accompaniment of a satisfying state of affairs (reward). There are few restrictions placed on the capacity of the organism and the teacher's role is to reward correct connections when they occur. Thorndike's position is quite in line with the Behavioristic thesis that knowledge and its acquisition is a matter of building up and rewarding stimulus-response connections. Skinner's (1968) conception of the learning process is one of the more current extrapolations of this viewpoint. Along with Thorndike, Skinner is quite optimistic about the plasticity of the organism for learning, as long as reinforcement takes place.

Contemporary counterparts. More pertinent to the present topic is the concept of "readiness" as propounded by the educational technologist Gagné (Gagné, 1968). It would be unfair to say that he is a Behaviorist (although he adopts some forms of their learning), yet his position is very closely aligned to the British Associationist view of knowledge acquisition. He is discussed here because he attempts to define "readiness" in quite different terms from Piaget, and this provides an interesting contrast in viewpoint. Gagné (1968) starts out to explicate his conception of "readiness" by distinguishing between two general processes, *learning* and *development*. *Learning* involves changes in behavior capabilities with respect to relatively specific forms of behavior, usually over relatively limited periods of time, i.e., hours, days, weeks (Gagné, 1968, p. 177). Gagné defines development as another major class of capabilities observed over longer periods of time (i.e., months, years). Gagné (1968) is justifiably disturbed by Piaget's underplaying of the role of learning in developmental change, and offers the following alternative to the Piagetian conception of cognitive development:

> The point of view I wish to describe here states that learning contributes to intellectual development of the human being because it is *cumulative* in its effects. The child progresses from one point to the next in his development, not because he acquires one or a dozen new associations, but because he learns an ordered set of capabilities which build upon each other in progressive fashion through the processes of differentiation, recall and transition of learning (Gagné, 1968, p. 181).

It is clear that Gagné places a marked emphasis on *learning* in the course of the organism's development. Although he postulates an interaction between genetically determined growth (i.e., maturation) and learning in the developmental progression, it is apparent that learning is paramount in his system, while maturation is simply assumed to be operating. His position attempts to explain the growth processes attributed to "equilibration" in Piagetian theory in cumulative learning terms. He postulates that all learning is hierarchically organized from simple to more complex forms of learning sequences. Readiness in this system is not attributed to maturation or equilibration but to the presence of prerequisite subordinate capabilities which form the foundation for the learning of more complex superordinate capabilities. *Readiness* appears to be totally independent of maturational construct, such as is seen in Gesell's work. For Gagné, the organism is *ready* if it has the necessary subordinate capabilities. The reason that development takes *time* is not that it is primarily maturationally governed, but simply that subordinate capabilities presented in the correct logical order take time to be learned (Gagné, 1968). Gagné further observes that when growth (development) is the dominant theme, educational events are designed to wait until the child is ready for learning. When learning is the dominant theme, the years are to be systematically filled with planned events of learning, and there is virtually no waiting — except for the time required to bring about those changes.

Gagné's criticism of Piaget's position represents a Tabula Rasa approach to the learning experience which virtually rejects the concept of development held by Piaget by making it solely "cumulative experience." It is unfortunate that when the polarities are dramatized, the proponents of both positions distort one another's concepts. Under these conditions the writer is sympathetic to Piaget when reading Gagné, and that the exact opposite obtains when concentrating on Piaget's prescriptions. As Cronbach (1964) points out:

> Somewhere between the dual approaches — enrich the environment and let development occur — there would seem logically to be some optimal curriculum of experiences arranged in some predetermined sequence with intervention by the teacher systematically regulated. But we do not know nearly enough about such questions (p. 77).

Gagné assumes that the answers to such questions lie in the logical *task analysis* of the learning situation that is of interest. Although he rejects a simple associationistic conception of learning, it may be safely said that the general position he espouses is a Tabula Rasa approach to development. Dewey's (1956) characterization of the early Associationists can be applied with equal force to Gagné's "cumulative learning" position.

> Subdivide each topic into studies; each study into lessons; each lesson into specific facts and formulae. Let the child proceed step by step to master each one of these separate parts, and at last he will have covered the entire ground. The road which looks so long when viewed in its entirety is easily travelled, considered as a series of particular steps. Thus emphasis is put upon the logical subdivisions and consecutions of the subject-matter. Problems of instruction are problems of procuring texts giving logical parts and sequences, and of presenting these portions in class in a similar definite and graded way. Subject-matter furnishes the end, and it determines method. The child is simply the immature being who is to be matured; he is the superficial being who is to be deepened; his is narrow experience which is to be widened. It is his to receive, to accept. His part is fulfulled when he is ductile and docile (Dewey, 1956, p. 8).

An Interactionist Approach

To recapitulate, the concept of readiness to learn takes on different prescriptions for curriculum programming, depending on the conception of mind and the theory of development within which the theorist operates. The concept of mind and knowledge acquisition are closely linked to the theorist's concept of development, and there are usually historical precedents for this linkage. Mechanistic explanations of development have generally fallen within the Tabula Rasa conceptions of development wherein content of the mind is very dependent on environmental input.

The mind within this context is a *mechanical mirror* (Langer, 1969) in which the child is born empty of psychological content and into a world of coherently organized content. In a sense, the child's mind is like a mirror in which the child comes to reflect his environment. Consistent with our own interpretation is Langer's (1969) historical perspective on the mind as a *mechanical mirror:*

> In the history of philosophical thought this thesis has been based upon two central assumptions. The first is that the content of the mind can be analyzed into constituent elements. Historically, this meant speculating about the building blocks or atoms, such as impressions and images, of which the mind is presumed to be composed . . .
>
> The second assumption is that external forces impinge upon the child's sensorium and leave elementary impressions. Thus Locke maintained that the mind is an empty slate before sensory impressions mark it. Ideas, as Hume put it, are merely the faint images of these impressions. These images are the elements or simple ideas that make up the mind, and complex ideas are the associations of elementary or simple ideas. We may therefore characterize the growth of the mind from this point of view, as the quantitative accumulation and association of elements supplied by the environment (pp. 4-5).

These two assumptions are present in both Thorndike's and Gagné's concepts of intellectual growth.

Non-mechanistic explanations of development have normally fallen within the tradition of "predeterminism," but this is not absolutely necessary, and predeterministic theories have generally given the organism considerable credit for its own growth. Like Kant, Piaget stresses the importance of "structures" which have to be present if knowledge is to be assimilated. Piaget's contribution to this tradition is the postulation of the *development* of intrinsic structures, whereas within the Kantian tradition there was no development implied. Piaget's model of the mind is quite different from the mechanistic conceptions of knowledge acquisition. Langer (1969) has characterized Piaget's conception of mind and knowledge acquisition as that of an *organic lamp*. Within this perspective, man is conceived as an *active* agent in the developmental process.

Hopefully it is clear by now that the concept of readiness takes on different parameters depending on the tradition within which the theorist operates. The traditions discussed thus far have emphasized two extreme conceptions of development which make rather different prescriptions about the *readiness* of the learner for knowledge acquisition. The Tabula Rasa conceptions see the child's mind as essentially a passive sponge, and place considerable emphasis on the teaching input that the environment provides. The "predeterministic" theories have given the organism an *active* and *dominant* part in its own development of knowledge, and the teaching input is undervalued. The Tabula Rasa conceptions put the problem of *readiness* in the teacher's hand, whereas readiness in the predeterministic tradition depends on only the learner. A third position is introduced here which is labeled *interactionist* because it attempts to conceptualize the organism-environment interaction in less extreme polarities than the views previously discussed. Because of its different theoretical stance from predeterministic and Tabula Rasa approaches, the prescriptions on *readiness* to learn will be somewhat different, and a different conception of knowledge acquisition will be advanced.

Vygotsky's Interactionist Approach. The presentation of Vygotsky's (1965) theory of conceptual development here serves to illustrate an interactionist position in contrast to the predeterministic and Tabula Rasa approaches. Vygotsky's (1965) approach toward the understanding of concept formation involves the distinction between *spontaneous* and *nonspontaneous* concepts. Spontaneous concepts refer to those concepts of reality that are developed mainly through the child's own mental efforts (i.e., incidental experience). In operating with spontaneous concepts (e.g., house, dog, red, etc.), the child is not conscious of the concepts, because attention is centered on the object to which the concept refers but never on the act of thought itself. Spontaneous concepts are characteristic of the preoperational stage of development. Nonspontaneous concepts (or scientific concepts) are those which are acquired in school and are characterized by consciousness and deliberate control over the act of thought itself. Nonspontaneous concepts are characteristic of the operational stages of development. Vygotsky (1965) developed his *interactionist* position by asking two main questions concerning the development and interrelationship between the above mentioned concepts:

> What happens in the mind of the child to the scientific concepts he is taught in school? What is the relationship between the assimilating of information and the internal development of a scientific concept in the child's consciousness? (Vygotsky, 1965, p. 82.)

Vygotsky commences by criticizing two prevailing schools of thought, because of the way they treat the above mentioned concepts. The Tabula Rasa position which is exemplified by Associationist theorists (e.g., Thorndike) holds that scientific concepts have no inward history and are absorbed ready-made through a process of understanding and assimilation. Vygotsky maintains that this viewpoint fails to stand up under scrutiny, either theoretically or practically, since investigations of the process of concept formation reveal that a concept is more than the sum of its associative bonds formed by memory and mental habit, and is, rather, a complex act of thought that cannot be taught by drilling. Learning scientific concepts is accomplished only when the child's mental development has reached the requisite level.

> The development of concepts, or word meanings, presupposes the development of many intellectual functions: deliberate attention, logical memory, abstraction, the ability to compare and differentiate, These complex psychological processes cannot be mastered through initial learning alone (Vygotsky, 1965, p. 83).

> Because instruction and development are treated as identical, there is no question of the relationship between scientific and spontaneous concepts.

> Predeterministic approaches to concept formation, although recognizing the distinction between scientific and spontaneous

concepts, are criticized because they fail to see the interaction between the two kinds of concepts in the course of the child's intellectual development. Spontaneous concepts, acquired through incidental experience (i.e., self-regulation), assume primary importance in Piaget's theorizing and are considered as the primary indicators of intellectual development. Vygotsky (1965) in commenting on this viewpoint, notes that the theory considers instruction and development to be independent.

> Development is seen as a process of maturation subject to natural laws, and instruction as the utilization of the opportunities created by development. Typical of this school of thought are its attempts to separate with great care the products of development from those of instruction, supposedly to find them in their pure form (Vygotsky, 1965, p. 93).

Vygotsky believes that the two processes (i.e., development of spontaneous and scientific concepts) are related and constantly influence each other. Because spontaneous concepts develop through the incidental experience of the child, while scientific concepts result from school instruction, it is felt that they must differ in their development as well as in their functioning. However, these two variants of the process of concept formation must influence each other's evolution. The interrelation of scientific and spontaneous concepts is a special case within a much broader subject: the relation of school instruction to the mental development of the child. Vygotsky contends that the rudiments of systematization first enter the child's mind by way of his contacts with scientific concepts and are then transferred to spontaneous concepts, changing their psychological structure from the top down. In Vygotsky's view, instruction precedes development and is partially influential in the development of more advanced spontaneous concepts. Vygotsky (1965) however, carefully distinguishes his position from the Tabula Rasa approaches already propounded.

> We found that intellectual development, far from following Thorndike's atomistic mode, is not compartmentalized according to topics of instruction. Its course is much more unitary, and the different school

subjects interact in contributing to it. While the processes of instruction follow their own logical order, they awaken and direct a system of processes in the child's mind which is hidden from direct observation and subject to its own developmental laws (p. 192).

Vygotsky obviously avoids the Tabula Rasa conception of the organism by postulating certain systems of thought that the child has which are somewhat independent of instruction yet are influenced by tuition. It seems that Piaget has uncovered many of the thought processes that Vygotsky claims are hidden from direct observation. From an interactionist's perspective it would be interesting to see how instruction affects these spontaneous processes. As Vygotsky (1965) points out:

> Since instruction given in one area can transform and reorganize other areas of child thought, it may not only follow maturing or keep in step with but also precede it and further its progress (p. 96).

Here I would like to cite one example, a study by Ojemann and Pritchett (1963), where Piagetian "stages" of development are used within Vygotsky's framework of development and instruction. Within this context, Piagetian-based concepts have not been used as prescriptions of readiness to learn or profit from instruction, but rather as assessment procedures indicating the success of school instruction. Two factors differentiate this type of approach from the majority of studies quoted thus far in discussing the relevance for education of Piaget's work. First of all, the study does not use Piaget's theory to determine the structure and sequence of the curriculum. Second, these authors do not share Piaget's assumption that spontaneous concepts (intrinsic structure) can only be altered by the indirect internalized activities of the child. In other words, they share Vygotsky's (1965) assumption that non-spontaneous school-learned (scientific) concepts can alter the child's spontaneous concept formation. The study concerns the concept of "specific gravity" in kindergarten and first grade children. The assessment of children in the pre-test studiously avoided using Piagetian materials on "specific gravity" and this approach was maintained in the "guided teaching" phase. Piaget's assessment of specific gravity was only given in the post-test; this guarded against the criticism that the children would be rotely parroting answers supplied by the teacher. After a pre-test, the children were randomly assigned to either an experimental or a control group. The experimental group had a three-session learning program designed to guide the child's perceptions to relevant aspects of the specific gravity concept. The "guided experiences" consisted of calling the child's attention to those aspects represented by "weight of object" and "weight of an equivalent amount of water" while ignoring other aspects of the objects, such as shape, color, form, etc. The control group did not receive these experiences. The results indicated that the experimental group made a significant gain over the control group on the post-test series and this gain was also evidenced in Piagetian assessments of specific gravity. One would like to have known the comparability of the Piaget tests with the other tests of specific gravity because Piagetian items were not utilized in the pre-test. Nevertheless, the study does give tentative evidence that Piaget's spontaneous concepts can be significantly altered by the non-spontaneous (scientific) concepts that are learned in school. This result, although contradictory to Piaget's assumption, is completely compatible with Vygotsky's interactionist position. The use of Piaget's assessment in the post-test indicates some generalization of the learning experience beyond the strict confines of the learning context.

Readiness for a learning sequence is far less dogmatically presented in the Vygotskian framework. The organization of the material and the way it will be presented is partially dependent on the intuitions of the teacher. Vygotsky admits that different temporal sequences are possible in a learning task but he demands that the learning take into consideration the conceptual orientation of the child where possible. This ambiguity makes any rigid concept of readiness impossible and forces the educator to ask relevant questions, aside from strictly the readiness issues, in deciding whether instruction is to be given now or at some later point in time. The crucial issues, in other words, are whether accelerated learning is reasonably economical in terms of the time and effort involved, and whether it helps children *develop-*

mentally in terms of their total educational careers. The answer to these issues cannot be found within the confines of a psychological theory of growth and development, for:

> Even if it be demonstrated that young children *can* learn this or that "advanced" process, we should still need to decide whether it is desirable and appropriate for them to do so. Sociologically, we may ask whether this is the best way for children to spend their time and energy. Intellectually, we may ask whether this is the most suitable preparation for future intellectual activities. Emotionally, we may ask whether "early" systematic instruction in reading, mathematics, or what have you, will have a harmful effect upon motivation, or upon personal and social behavior . . . The point we are trying to make here is simply this: Just the fact that children *can* learn this or that does not *by itself* mean that we, therefore, must require them to do so at some young age or in some early grade (Tyler, 1964, pp. 223-224).

Postscript

The treatment of "readiness" in this paper makes no pretense of being exhaustive. The historical focus was an attempt to give the reader a kind of perspective in which to view psychological theories and make understandable their frequent conflicting prescriptions on readiness to learn in the curriculum. The focus of the paper ignored the possible treatment of readiness that is possible within the psychometric treatment of contemporaneous individual differences. A brief and simple minded example will seem to illustrate the possibilities of this approach in the consideration of readiness. Let us assume that children are grouped on the basis of some personality measure (e.g., anxiety). If high-anxious and low-anxious children are separated, the question can be raised about the readiness of children to learn a subject under different kinds of instructional strategies. If it is found that high-anxious children appear to learn mathematics when the instructional strategy is highly structural but not when a "discovery" tactic is used, the concept of readiness can then be tied to differential instructional strategies which interact with individual differences found in children. This approach, while complex, is rather promising.

REFERENCES

Adler, M. *Some Implications of the Theories of Jean Piaget and J. S. Bruner for Education.* Toronto: Board of Education for the City of Toronto, Research Service, 1963.

Almy, M., Chittenden, E. & Miller, P. *Young Children's Thinking.* New York: Teachers College Press, Teachers College, Columbia University, 1966.

Ausubel, D. P. & Sullivan, E. V. *Problems and Methods in Child Development.* New York: Grune & Stratton, 1970 (in press).

Chomsky, N. N. *Language and Mind.* New York: Harcourt, Brace Inc., 1968.

Cronbach, L. Learning Research and Curriculum Development. In R. E. Ripple & V. N. Rockcastle (Eds.) *Piaget Rediscovered: A Report of the Conference on Cognitive Studies and Curriculum Development.* Ithaca, N. Y.: School of Education, Cornell University, 1964, pp. 73-77.

Dewey, J. *The Child and the Curriculum.* Chicago: University of Chicago Press, Phoenix Books, 1956.

Gagné, R. M. Contributions of Learning to Human Development. *Psychological Review,* 1968, *75*(3), pp. 177-191.

Gesell, A. Maturation and the Patterning of Behavior. In C. Murchison (Ed.) *A Handbook of Child Psychology.* Worcester, Mass.: Clarke University Press, 1933, pp. 209-235.

.... The Ontogenesis of Infant Behavior. In L. Carmichael (Ed.) *Manual of Child Psychology.* New York: John Wiley, 1954, pp. 335-373.

Gesell, A. & Ilg, F. L. *Infant and Child in the Culture of Today.* New York: Harper, 1943.

Hunt, J. McV. *Intelligence and Experience.* New York: Ronald Press, 1961.

.... The Impact and Limitations of the Giant of Developmental Psychology. In D. Elkind & J. Flavell (Eds.) *Studies in Cognitive Development: Essays in Honour of Jean Piaget,* Oxford University Press, 1969, pp. 3-66.

Koch, S. Psychology and the Emerging Conception of Knowledge as Unitary. In T. W. Wann (Ed.) *Behaviorism and Phenomenology: Contrasting Bases for Modern Psychology.* Chicago: University of Chicago Press, 1964.

Kohnstamm, G. A. Experiments on Teaching Piagetian Thought Operations. Paper presented at the Conference on Guided Learning of the Educational Research Council of Greater Cleveland, 1966.

Langer, J. *Theories of Development.* New York: Holt, Rinehart &

Winston, 1969.

McDonald, F. J. The Influence of Learning Theories on Education (1900-1950). In E. R. Hilgard (Ed.) *Theories of Learning and Instruction.* Sixty-third Yearbook of the National Society for the Study of Education. Part I. Chicago: National Society for the Study of Education, 1964.

Ojemann, R. H. & Pritchett, K. Piaget and the Role of Guided Experiences in Human Development. *Perceptual and Motor Skills, 1963, 17,* pp. 927-940.

Piaget, J. Cognitive Development in Children: The Piaget Papers. In R. E. Ripple & D. N. Rockcastle (Eds.) *Piaget Rediscovered: A Report of the Conference on Cognitive Studies and Curriculum Development.* Ithaca, New York: School of Education, Cornell University, 1964, pp. 6-48.

Rousseau, J. J. *Emile.* New York: Appleton-Century-Crofts, 1895.

Scheffler, I. The Language of Education. *American Lecture Series.* Springfield, Illinois: Charles C. Thomas, 1969.

Sigel, I. E. The Piagetian System and the World of Education. Unpublished manuscript, Merrill-Palmer Institute, 1968.

Skinner, B. F. *The Technology of Teaching.* New York: Appleton-Century-Crofts, 1968.

Smedslund, J. The Acquisition of Conservation of Substance and Weight in Children. *Scandinavian Journal of Psychology, 1961, 2,* pp. 11-20; 71-87; 153-160; 203-210.

Sullivan, E. V. Piaget and the School Curriculum: A Critical Appraisal. *Bulletin No. 2,* The Ontario Institute for Studies in Education, 1967.

.... Piagetian Theory in the Educational Milieu: A Critical Appraisal. *Canadian Journal of Behavioral Science, 1969, 1*(3), pp. 129-155.

.... *The Role of Inter- and Intra-Age Individual Differences in Planning Teacher Training Programs.* An invited chapter for Teachers College, Columbia University, 1968.

Thorndike, E. L. *The Fundamentals of Learning.* New York: Teachers College, Columbia University, 1932.

Tyler, F. T. Issues Related to Readiness to Learn. *Theories of Learning.* Sixty-third Yearbook of the National Society for the Study of Education. Chapter 9. Chicago: National Society for the Study of Education, 1964, pp. 210-239.

Vygotsky, L. F. *Thought and Language.* New York: MIT Press, 1965.

Watson, J. B. *Psychological Care of the Infant and Child.* New York: Norton, 1928.

Wohlwill, J. S. From Perception of Inference: A Dimension of Cognitive Development. In W. Kessen & C. Kuhlman (Eds.) Thought in the Young Child. *Monographs of the Society for Research in Child Development,* 1962, *27*(2 Whole No. 83), pp. 87-106.

8

A Curriculum Is a Set of Specifications of Which of the Following: A. Stimuli, B. Responses, C. Both A and B, D. Neither A nor B

William A. Deterline

Suppose we encounter a society in which many people have for many years worked diligently and skillfully to develop curricula. Suppose also that in this society each curriculum is a set of specifications of stimuli, information, or presentations, to which large groups of students are to be subjected; that is, there are no specifications that state with precision what capabilities and competencies the students are to develop as a result of the information — just details of what the information is to consist. And suppose that there are no "real world" paths, specifying any relevance of a curriculum or components of a curriculum to

WILLIAM A. DETERLINE is president of Deterline Associates.

anything in the real world; nothing to inform the student in detail just what the components are to be used OUT THERE. Suppose also that students are kept completely in the dark about the relevance of the curriculum to the real world, and about what is expected of them as they proceed through the curriculum. Suppose — well, the reader gets the idea.

Webster is quite accurate, of course, in defining *curriculum* as "a course or set of courses." There is no reference to relevance, performance, effectiveness, or learning — just a set of courses. That's what we call "telling it like it is."

Consider the two extreme ends of a continuum — a continuum, not a dichotomy — along which are varying degrees of emphasis on stimuli and responses. At the stimulus end of the continuum there is no concern whatever for response considerations; no one cares what the students are to do in response to the information presented or what they can do upon the completion of the instruction; attention is directed exclusively to the questions of what to tell the student, and what to show him. At this extreme we might concentrate on the development of textbooks, films, slides, demonstration kits for teachers, teachers' manuals and other presentation materials. The results of such an effort can be quite elegant, and can make significant inroads on the many problems facing schools and teachers. The emphasis is on technically accurate, interesting, clear, well-organized subject matter, on the presentation of content, on the stimulus side of teaching and learning. Obviously, all of this is important along the entire continuum, so the *stimulus* emphasis should remain the same from one end of the continuum to the other. What does vary is the attention given to the *response* aspects of learning. Consider the extreme right hand end of the continuum shown in FIGURE 1. Although we are dealing with a continuum, we have shown the importance of stimuli and response considerations at only seven points on the continuum. At the extreme right, equal emphasis is given stimuli and responses. At this extreme, the desired responses would be identified *first,* and those response specifications would facilitate the identification and selection of the content — stimuli — that are to produce the responses. In more familiar terms, the specification of the instructional objectives, in terms of the terminal performance capability of the students, provides the maximum guidance and direction for the selection and design of content presentations. At the other end of the continuum, the content is selected because it appears logically to be a relevant part of the subject matter, and the form, media, methods, examples, problems and clarification are all selected on an artistic and intuitive basis, without very much attention to the desired *change* in the students that the presentations are to produce. Traditionally, curriculum design and development has been stimulus-oriented, on the left half of the continuum shown in FIGURE 1. Some attention has, of course, been given to the response considerations, in the form of workbooks and tests. But as we move to the right we begin to see instructional materials and events being designed more in relation to outcomes, and the specifications of the desired outcomes provide more detailed direction for the artistic and intuitive development of content. This is what is meant by instruction that is *response-oriented*.

Where do curricula come from? Traditionally, they have been stimulus-oriented, because they have been, in effect, a body of content that has through the years come to be identified as a course, or set of courses. By their nature, curricula are stimulus-oriented. Textbooks in most cases define curricula — not vice versa. Considerable effort has been expended in many subject areas to develop well-written textbooks around which teachers can work. But specifications no more clearly drawn than textbooks and related materials are really no specifications at all.

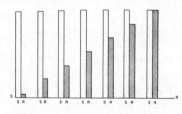

FIGURE 1

A "package" of stimulus material does not indicate what the students should be able to do after being subjected to the content and related experiences. It might be a pleasant little exercise in academic freedom to provide a textbook and related materials and say only that each teacher can develop his own course from the content. But shouldn't the curriculum specialists have more responsibility and expertise than that? Certainly no one would claim that curriculum design and development is in any way a science, or a professional activity, or an objective methodology. It is, to date, primarily an artistic endeavor, content oriented, with little or no concern for what the students should be able to do after being subjected to a specific curriculum (although "specific" is not a characteristic except in the eyes of those who feel that content arrangement and clarification is all that there is to it!)

The myths of training and educating are readily visible in curriculum design activities and their consequences. In spite of masses of data to the contrary, many curriculum projects seem to be based on the assumption that any technically accurate presentation, if interesting and attention-getting, will teach — *something or other.* Certainly a presentation must be technically accurate and interesting, but *that is not enough.* Certainly a curriculum should consist of more than technically accurate information, and more specifications than simply "Here, present this!" Curriculum design, development and implementation, like teaching, and like teacher education, must eventually come to grips effectively with the problems: *what is to be taught,* and *how it is to be taught.* These problems will not be resolved, and school will not improve appreciably until *curricula become student-behavior centered* and *teaching becomes student-behavior-change oriented.*

Perhaps the most promising developments — those that might bring about some of these changes — are those underway at many of the Regional Educational Laboratories. Because a major part of their mission is to develop instructional materials and products that produce specified and measurable outcomes, the Labs have had to learn from the experience, successes and failures of programmed instruction. And what this invariably leads to is instructional objectives, interactive instruction (with continuous student activity and feedback), and thorough testing and revision of the materials and procedures until they do in fact achieve their objectives. And many colleges and universities have — through experimentation with the computer, or with multimedia learning centers, or with some approach to individualized instruction—developed complete courses, or modular segments of courses, based on an applied response emphasis. And wherever this has been done, existing curricula have been found to tell only part of the story, and to provide only part of the necessary information. The response specifications should dictate the stimulus specifications, not vice versa. We should decide what the students are to learn, and how that learning is to be manifested and measured, and then the necessary stimulus events and components can be selected or developed. This appears to be more reasonable than blindly putting together stimulus components, with no clear picture of what they are to accomplish. The curriculum specialist should, if his curricula are to be complete, become involved in *both* the stimulus specifications and the response specifications. If he does not, then each school, Lab, or other development or production center will have to do the most critical tasks itself, probably without adequate coordination, and without the help of the curriculum specialists who should have done it in the first place!

The curriculum specialists, committees and study groups of the educational world are influential, powerful and entrenched. They typically represent *the* Word in their subject matter areas, and are generally considered prestigious and highly competent — individually and collectively — in their fields. If innovation is to come to their curriculum activities, they, not the instructional technologists, will have to bring it about, because they own all of the marbles. And many of them have so far rejected the behavior-oriented approach to curriculum design. That is to be expected. The work of a lifetime, and the methods and procedures that have proven to be at least partially effective, are not likely to be discarded simply because people, from other fields, say that there is now a better way. But isn't the whole idea to try to improve education? Isn't it worth trying *anything* that even faintly looks promising? Can we turn our backs on *any* approach that has data to support it, and then repeat the errors of the past and point to them with pride as something innovative and something better than the previous model of the same thing?

Every subject matter has its own educational mystique, its educational myths and its educational superstitions. Instructional decisions are made intuitively, and are almost always stimulus-centered. The empirical sciences are no more empirical in their curriculum projects than any other subject matters. Does a new curriculum result in more learning, more learning of those outcomes that are thought to be important? How can we tell, if no one bothered to specify in detail just what the outcomes are to be, or why they are thought to be important? Although it starts at the curriculum design level, many teachers, professors and training directors join in the chorus: "That approach might be fine for subjects A, B, or C, or in settings, X, Y, or Z, but my students and my requirements are different!" Certainly they are, but learning is not, and the outcomes-orientation can be used as a curriculum development procedure for any subject, in any setting. The real kicker is that it is more difficult, and it must be done right, because any deficiencies are quickly identified. That isn't true of the stimulus-design approach, which has no accountability whatsoever! Is it surprising that much of curriculum design, like much of teacher training, has been only a perpetuation of the past, resisting empiricism, the outcomes-orientation and the notion of accountability?

One objection to this behavior-oriented approach is that it might "dehumanize" the schools. But has the reader visited a school recently? Has he observed the conditions under which teachers and students take part in the "educational process"? Aren't schools now, under present conditions, rapidly losing the battle and becoming more "dehumanized" each year? There is nothing inherent in the behavior-oriented approach, unless foolishly applied, that "dehumanizes" instruction. And there are increasing numbers of us who feel that this approach is the most promising direction we have for "rehumanizing" education, making teaching a dignified and true profession, and offering students the quality education that they deserve.

9

Student Unrest
and the Curriculum

E. G. Williamson

A very intriguing article appeared in the April, 1969 issue of
Educational Technology with regard to the experience at Montclair, New Jersey High School in which students began to use
an experimental computer as an aid in their educational and
career exploration. The students, under the direction of Super,
have access, by means of this new technological improvement, to
a comprehensive library of occupational and educational facts
stored in data processors. The student loads reels of film into
the device after using the typewriter to identify himself to the
system. He explores further printed instructions; and then
images related to his interests are projected onto the unit's
screen. The illustrated information includes actual work situations that give the student a feeling for the job in which he is

---

E. G. WILLIAMSON is dean of students and professor of psychology
(retired) at the University of Minnesota.

interested. This is, indeed, a wonderful advance over the laborious methods of the past in which the counselor tried to compress into his own memory process all the information about which he had read or observed and then translated it into words so that the student would understand these data in relationship to his own choice of career.

This magnificent technological improvement of information giving may not be perceived by some students as particularly relevant to their choices and decisions. In fact, such a system, for some individuals, not all by any means, might very well convince them or reconvince them that they are being negated or alienated by impersonal machinery and bureaucratic rigidity, and that their worth as persons or individuals is being computerized. One remembers with horror the third revolution at Berkeley in the fall of 1964 in which a huge reproduction of an IBM card was held up as a symbol of this supposed depersonalization of the relationship between the schools and the individual. It is not, indeed, being argued that all technological innovations present this risk, but, rather, that unless some kind of a protective process is built into the use of technological innovations of this sort, their use could augment and accelerate the so-called alienation of students. A large part of today's unrest, although by no means all of it, can be attributed to the supposition that some students feel that they are the "low man on the totem pole."

Learning of a philosophic or moral (value) nature takes place best in the mutually respectful context of human relationships. Certainly those, including Super, who innovate efficient apparatus to facilitate learning subscribe to that point of view about education at all levels. Indeed, the development of each student to his full potential *is* the central issue, and everything about education is a means to that end. This we all accept, but the crucial problem is: how does each student perceive what we adults do with youth? Perhaps some misperceive us and our work. How can we communicate to students so that they *believe* and accept our "good" intentions? That is *the problem* central to radical and revolutionary youth. They do not believe that we are being honest with them. They assert that adults are hypocritical. We mouth moral platitudes and then do evil. What can be done about this basic problem of how we are perceived by students?

We do not wish to return to the good old days when everything was done by hand or not at all. But, rather, the rioting, denegation, unrest and violence of the last decade, and of this decade, has sensitized us to this depersonalization as a great risk which we must do something about, even as we attempt to take advantage of the twentieth century technological advances. Special emphasis must be placed on the student and the curriculum as well as the extracurriculum in which much of the current unrest is manifested.

Some of the restless and revolting students today do not, at any level of education, want to learn what parents, teachers and administrators say is appropriate, and are prepared to teach them. Why? That is the starting point of our query. Does the student sometimes revolt with violence against what is done to help him because he considers that we are trying to force him to conform to the prevailing elite capitalistic system? Does the student feel resentful because what we give him is conducive to well-behaved middle class expectations and conformity?

Fortunately, the unrest has not yet fully and widely descended below the high schools, but no doubt it will soon take various lower forms. There may be some hope for surcease there, because of the greater susceptibility of younger aged children to conform to what is expected of them in the schools. Indeed this induced conformity of younger age children is singled out by those students who advocate unrest or destruction of society because it is believed to be one of the great sources of alienation and unrest in later years.

For example, the radical organization known as Students for a Democratic Society contends that schools teach conformity to the prevailing bureaucratic system, which is capitalistic from the Marxian point of view. This molding, they contend, occurs at all levels of education. As a psychologist would put it, this is indeed "conditioning" through which the individual, as the result of training and experience, accepts as his way of life the style of living of the well-behaved, white middle class. That is, the individual will become well-behaved according to the Calvinistic point of view, with respect to speech, dress, vocation, politics, war service and ideology. The latter is held as a hypocritically superficial doctrine from the point of view of the SDS advocates because so many adults live according to other, conflicting value commitments. One must reply rationally to the SDS contention about teaching conformity through raising children and adolescents to be well-behaved according to middle class standards. What else would society do but teach according to some chosen set of standards and expectations? Indeed, if one studies the cultural and anthropological literature about primitive tribes, one concludes that all tribes molded, manipulated, nudged and rewarded children and youth according to the wisdom of the elders. That is, the elite or ruling class, as the SDS would say, set the standards of expectation of the youthful members of the tribe. This fact does not justify the practice, according to youth today, because they insist that they have a right to participate in setting their own standards of behavior!

Man's history is replete with the undesirable results of excluding the young from participating in the establishment of standards of behavior. In the historical record it is quite clear that the Russian 19th century revolutions destroyed the Czar elitism over the peasants. But in the 1917 revolution a new political elite of "elders" installed their own standards of expected behavior which were as rigid in terms of conformity as was the Russian system before the earlier revolution. The same observation might be made about the Nazi destruction of the Weimar republic. This was Germany's first attempt to get rid of the old system of rigid Prussian elitism, reinforced by heredity, tradition, bureaucracy of the civil service, and by the military. The Nazi elite immediately installed their own rigid system of conformity. This kind of substitution of one form of conditioning for another does not free the individual, as the SDS implies by insisting on participatory democracy. Indeed, one concludes that there must be in every organized society some prevailing hierarchy of social structure and values. Even in ancient Greece, which was the first so-called republic, there was a ruling elite class above a slave economy in which women had no rights equivalent to those of the ruling men. Thus, we are now importuned by SDS to change the course of history.

In the pluralism of our organized society, there is more than one dominant, competing hierarchy or mode leading to value conflicts. And one is puzzled, as an educator, as to how students are effectively taught to choose "the truth" about "the proper style" of living from among the many available alternatives. This is the same as saying: how do we teach the resolution of conflicts among competing modes or methods of conditioning or manipulating? Moreover, how do we teach students to "live with" and strive to resolve conflicts among competing beliefs and philosophies?

Nevertheless, we see that there is a lack of explicitly perceived (to the student) alternatives, a seriously neglected aspect of the curriculum in many schools at all levels. Perhaps, even the technological improvements of the kind mentioned previously at Montclair, New Jersey don't really get at the problem of teaching students. How does the student evolve his own choice of what kind of a life style he wishes to follow while at the same time being molded by the surrounding societal, family and school ecology? This, indeed, is a neglected aspect of technological improvements in the modern curriculum. It is small wonder that many of the restless students today say that adults are not addressing themselves honestly to the real source of their complaint and conflict. And one wonders if there would not be a new molding according to a new hierarchy of values if the SDS, or the violent students, or the unrestful students, were in authoritative positions of leadership.

The essential aspect of this crucial problem is that the absolutism of the individual reformer is proposed as a substitute for the then absolutism of the ruling hierarchical class. But, beyond this point of view, many of the students indicate that they are revolting against all external authority over the individual. Some go on to contend that freedom is indeed the freedom of the individual to do as he pleases. But we admonish them in vain that even freedom of speech has its limits when it interferes seriously with the freedom of others. And so it is with any freedom. The restless youth forget that even Thoreau, Ghandi and King were cognizant of this restriction on individual freedom. Youth fail to see, and we fail to teach them, in spite of the technological improvements in teaching methods and materials, that the exercise of autonomous freedom exacts a price or consequence when it infringes upon the freedom of other individuals. One needs to perceive the unknowns in understanding "rights" every teacher, and administrator, faces in dealing with students.

Western civilization has oscillated between attempted or desired absolutism of the tribe and some individual or group against its opponents. This has led to anarchy and revolt among visible adults (war, union strikes, etc.). Under these conditions, it is small wonder that youth resort to restlessness and revolt.

Shocking as it is to some, young and old, a degree or form of "imposed" or required restraint faces every individual in the exercise of his own individual freedom. For example, the controversy over restraints with regard to sex, drugs, political beliefs, political action and the like have continued over the ages.

Even in self-chosen communes, with supposedly common belief, *by common consent or imposition* of a few aggressive leaders, rules of behavior, speech, thought, or conscience arise to restrict absolute freedom of individualism.

This is the price that must be paid for retaining membership in any organized society or any organized part of society. This is a paradox, one we have not been able to teach to many children and adolescents. Do we adults understand "truth" phrased in such paradoxes? But such is the history of successive changes in Western civilization. In no organized society, even in the land of Marxism, can there be absolute freedom for the peasants.

In every democracy there are loose-fitting restraints imposed on some individuals, or self-imposed (internalized is the psychologist's term). Each person is free to pay the price of conformity about some behavior in return for freedom to exhibit other desired or valued forms of behavior. Some individuals seek to destroy society and modify or otherwise change the restrictions on their freedom by rational persuasion or by violence. Or they may renounce membership in a given group and withdraw and organize a new tribe, commune, or some form of community of those who are like-minded in the freedom which they desire above all restraints. How do we aid students to learn this lesson of man's history and thus to forge their own hierarchy of restraints and freedom to attain a style of maturity?

In this decade, we are experiencing a major wave of rejection and revolt against the hierarchical elitism of some members of the capitalistic ruling class. This is a revolt against the tribal elders who seem to have concluded that the restraints and values of the Victorian, Calvinistic, Western culture are fixed and immutable and not to be changed through societal or personal innovations. Such is reported to be the perception of Western civilization.

Despite the economic and technological revolutionary changes which have produced many improvements in creature comforts through communications, education and welfare, we still face conflict with youth over what they perceive as the rigid rules of the Victorian period. One longingly turns to John Gardner's concept of The Self Renewing Society as the hope of the future. To be sure, the least of societal change is often achieved only after violent behavior on the part of those who want to impose the "new culture" on others. Indeed, one hunts for instances of orderly, planned societal change.

This contemporary revolt against the "old" (the "Establishment") order of tribal mores and folkways has today centered in the younger generation, especially in high school and college youth. Everything newly discovered or innovated by the young is thought by them to be a significant improvement. They also feel that there is a conspiracy of the elders to condition the young (through child rearing and education) to conform, that is to accept the old way of life. It is true that one can pick out instances in history — Russian history, European history and Oriental history — in which the bourgeois revolted against the entrenched economic rulers and set up a new dictatorship that exhibited some forms of benevolence. One has to question whether or not the new is any better than the old, although some great improvements have been made in freedom of thought, conscience, speech, choice of vocation, creature comforts, communications, etc.

Currently, non-whites (beginning with the repressed and

regulated Negro, young and old) are revolting with violence against the culture in which for three hundred years they were at the bottom of the hierarchy of status and privilege. One is tempted to apply to this revolt the formula: repression-frustration-revolt, which of course is a variation of Freudian psychology. Perhaps this sequence makes some orderly sense out of disorder, violence, rejection, intransigence and otherwise rejection behavior of contemporary youth, even though we know that our motives are designed to help them achieve some degree of satisfaction and success in our culture. But they are not willing to accept the contention that we are "telling it as it is." Perhaps this cultural disorder is world-wide because of increased communication across national barriers. The members of the younger generation learned from each other both the concept of regulation and enforced conformity and also their low status in the hierarchy of determining what kind of a life is the "good life." That is, they have no voice in determining standards of behavior apart from revolt. Marcuse and other Marxists currently insist on their formula as the proper explanation of the present-day chaos, at least as dramatized and over-reported by the news media, as the drama of conflict that is irrational and violent as contrasted with the social planning of rational change from the old to new forms of culture through encouraged and stimulated innovation of both young and old.

Some adults advocate and practice the increased use of their authority to "crack down" on the young radicals who demand change and replacement of the old ways of living. It is very tempting, of course, to apply this kind of repressive discipline in anger, but by acting in this way we merely reinforce the contention of the younger members of society that adults are rigid, bureaucratic, arbitrary and unilateral in their decision-making as to the nature of the "good life." There are many leading educators, however, who do not advocate cracking down but rather continuous restructuring of generational relationships, especially in the schools, through the use of rational confrontation, and by mutually seeking to identify desirable changes in the old style of living. Included among these moderate liberals are Harold Taylor, Sidney Hook, Buell Gallagher, and many others. Such a moderate reaction in the face of violence calls for the innovation of radically new roles for the young and the enhancement of their dignity as persons worthy of full participation in decision-making. That is, what is needed are radical changes in students' perceived, or misperceived, roles within home and school. This revolution of rational confrontation might be called a new form of joint partnership with mutual respect. Of course, if one waits until there is violence and armed conflict, it becomes very difficult, if not impossible, to bring about rational dialogue and peaceable confrontation.

Recently, events at the Carnegie-Mellon Institute (Pittsburgh) provided an impressive example of rational innovation. For about a year the Dean of Students, student leaders and faculty have been engaged in a continuous, thoughtful, rational reflection, review and evaluation of all of the regulations inherited from the past that governed students. Although the outcome is uncertain, it is an impressive demonstration that there can be rational discussion as opposed to irrational violence. This is the kind of participatory democracy which many SDS advocates talk about but few really propose. Instead they propose that they and they alone should dictate the requirements to be imposed upon the young. This is merely substituting the dictatorship of a splinter group of the young for the dictates of adults.

What will happen to the many individuals who do not exhibit overt behavior and are therefore ignored by SDS and other radical groups? Indeed, no one seems to care about the "silent ones," including the commuters who do not participate but merely sit on the sidelines, go to class faithfully, and in other ways conform to the accepted behavioral standards. The "Silent Majority" also receives little attention from the news media as compared with the "Vocal Minority." Members of the education profession should take a hard look at this neglected group of students.

Having stated a point of view with regard to the innovation of technological apparatus and an interpretation of the basic causes of unrest, revolt and violence, let us turn to a more positive statement of what can be done through the efforts of teachers and administration in the schools. How do we aid students, indeed all youth, to learn the linkage of freedom and responsibility without perceived denegation to second-class citizenship? Does this mean that every decision in the school must be preceded by a plebescite in which there is assured equality of all participants — students, faculty, administrators, parents, citizens, and the like — that is, one man one vote?

How do we teach respect for the racial and societal history of experiences without choking off innovation of the new by old or young? How do we satisfy the adolescents' urge to denegrate the adult leaders even if society must first be destroyed? How do we teach internalized restraints on freedom without curbing the individual's innovative capacity and subordinating his sense of worth? How do we teach students to deal with conflict and controversy among competing value hierarchies and commitments? In a pluralistic society as contrasted with the simple minded societies in which there was, presumably, a unitary orthodoxy, or official doctrine, expectation, or value commitment, how do we teach the individual that the traditional wisdom is only one of many alternatives in man's effort to find livable answers to his philosophic queries and hypotheses? How can adults learn these truths?

These are basic questions which educators must strive to answer through participatory discussions and dialogues with each new student generation. Educators must make a concerted effort to avoid rigidity of outlook, belief and action even though they may be reinforced by societal laws and customs.

Is violence and revolt the only possible way of bringing about desirable change in the societal requirements expected of the young and the old? There are many other ways that can be utilized if adults will but enter into a kind of rational discussion or interchange of ideas with the young. Societal issues and their desirable reconstructions and the consideration of alternative methods of living the good life are open-ended hypotheses (not carved-stone truths) which call for continuous re-evaluation, rather than bureaucratic rigidity.

Seven suggestions are offered for exploration. They are not complete, simple answers to the questions that have been raised, but rather they indicate areas of discussion that may bring about an easing of the tension and, thereby, lead us to use our rational powers to find solutions that we can live with, at least until someone innovates better answers.

1. All individuals, regardless of age, should learn to appreciate and become well informed about the long, tragic history of man's struggle to achieve freedom — that is, the history of war, politics, great leaders, and the various methods of resolving man's problems. Most revolting students, however, do not want to do their homework and study history, which they consider to be merely one more way that adults have invented to condition youth to conform to the established order. How can we teach them to respect man's history and to learn from it *and to go beyond it* to new methods of trying to solve man's age-old problems?

2. Every student, active or inactive, commuter or resident, should be encouraged, pursuaded, manipulated and nudged to learn firsthand about the contemporary unsolved problems of man. Field work in the ghetto or inner city with the culturally deprived, with racially different groups, and with different religious groups, especially those organized in close knit communities, would be extremely helpful in achieving this goal. To learn that mankind has evolved alternate and sometimes competing and conflicting answers to the great philosophic queries is a sobering experience. One can understand the desire of many individuals to cling in ignorance to a particular formula as though it were the only one; but, surely, an educated person must be prepared to deal with rationally innovating societal changes now or in the future.

3. Every student should acquire some direct, immediate experience with the political apparatus of his city and state through field work, through visits, through personal contacts and through conferences with political leaders, because all of them are trying to find legal and political solutions to man's great unsolved societal problems. This is particularly true at the present time with regard to racism and poverty, and also with regard to nationalism, which a few decades ago took the provincial form of "America first."

4. In line with John Dewey's concept of educating youth to prepare for the rational, continuous reconstruction of society, every individual student should learn to commit himself to doing some "social good." This he may do in any number of forms, but this he must do if he is ever to acquire any deepseated appreciation and empathy for those whose lot in life is degrading of their feeling of self-worth.

5. How do teachers, parents and counselors learn how to hold effective seminars, discussion groups, conversations and dialogues — especially involving speakers and advocates of current and therefore controversial issues of the community and society? It is a relatively easy matter to secure discussions and seminars among those who are like-minded and who advocate relatively similar solutions to society's unsolved problems. But how to deal with those who advocate radically different solutions is another question which pedagogues and counselors for the most part have not yet faced as technique, even with our technological innovations. Students must be taught to listen respectfully, even though they do not agree with alternative proposals or solutions to society's ills. There surely is more than one road leading to Rome, and many different methods of solving society's problems. An educated person should not dismiss that with which he disagrees in a summarily arbitrary and dictatorial manner. He must do his homework in depth and understand something about the nature of the alternative with which he initially, at least, does not agree. It is a very difficult problem to teach students and adults (taxpayers and parents!) how to face and deal with controversial issues; that is, with those who advocate different points of view and different solutions to society's ills. This is especially difficult in public institutions because of the proximity of the citizens, the taxpayers and the parents who wish their young to be indoctrinated with "the" truth established in carved-stone from Mount Sinai. Without being *wishy-washy* and giving equal credence to all proposed alternative solutions to society's problems, how does one critically examine thoughtfully and respectfully the various advocacies, particularly when the dialogue takes place in the midst of violence and controversial emotions and vituperation? This is

by no means an easy task for the school teacher and for the counselor, and it is small wonder that they stick to the "safe" topics and leave to the outside radicals in the political arena, who have the dramatic hold on the news media, the controversial topics and sure-fire solutions to these great unsolved problems. How can the young be taught to deal with controversy in a rational, intelligent way rather than in the emotional manner which is so characteristic of our "adult" political campaigns?

6. The pedagogical method should go even further. Students should be taught, encouraged and aided to read and think in depth and to put their thoughts systematically into writing defending a particular alternative solution to a specific problem, such as racism or poverty, and giving thought to the many historical proposals that are found in the books and pamphlets of the past. This kind of in-depth reading, thinking and writing holds for whatever topic of controversy interests each student. What we are trying to do, or what we should try to do, is to help students learn to read conflicting sources rather than restricting themselves to the literature of indoctrination which merely reinforces their own initial conclusions or beliefs. Teachers and counselors should be very careful to make sure that they are accepted as open-minded without being empty-minded, and should make it clear that they may have a tentative hypothesis with regard to the questions under consideration, but that they are still open to the influence of new data. Surely all educators, including counselors, can earn respect, even though they do not secure agreement, if they buttress their own particular hypothesis with some kind of rational in-depth argument. By advocating the open-ended discussions, the counselor and teacher can serve as a model of the type of person who can deal with problems of contemporary life and future planned change which is thoughtful rather than violent.

7. In many instances the counselor can help the student to do such thinking, reading and writing in depth using as his subject matter, or thesis, his own relevant occupational interest, or the several alternative possible choices which interest him. There is always a great deal of controversy in the literature with regard to all occupations and their historical development. For

instance, the founding father of the counseling profession, Frank Parsons, was himself a social radical — an innovator proposing radical changes, many of which today seem rather commonplace and to be taken for granted. But in his day he advocated this kind of thinking and reading in depth as a part of the preparation of the well occupied and employed individual who derives great satisfaction, not only in terms of his paycheck but also in terms of his insightful understanding of his contribution to the betterment of organized society.

10

The Student-Centered Curriculum

Bruce W. Tuckman

The purpose of this essay is to describe a concept known as the student-centered curriculum. The student-centered curriculum concept will be described in terms of a series of postulates which provide a basic definition of what the student-centered curriculum is to be. From these postulates, propositions are then derived which describe the way the student-centered curriculum would be constructed and how it would operate.

Postulates

Postulate 1. A curriculum must be defined in terms of its goals as they apply to students.

A curriculum must have a purpose. Its purpose ostensibly

BRUCE W. TUCKMAN is associate professor of education at Rutgers University.

is to provide students with experiences that will lead them to attain certain desired end states. Pre-specification of these end states provides a guide for the direction of the instructional process as well as a basis for determining if the instructional process has been a success. Thus, a curriculum must be defined in terms of the educational goals of students.

It is considered reasonable to further assume that educational goals may be broken down into three broad areas, i.e., (a) occupational, (b) civic/citizenship, and (c) personal/social.

Of maximum importance is the point that desired goals or end states are here posited as part of the basis for defining the curriculum.

Postulate 2. Occupational goals are, for a large majority of students, those requiring less than a bachelor's degree.

Today, approximately 20 percent of the young people in the United States obtain a bachelor's degree. The remaining 80 percent fall into one of the following categories: high school dropout, terminal high school graduate, two-year college dropout, two-year college terminal graduate, or four-year college dropout.

Postulate 3. A curriculum must be defined in terms of the psychological structure (learning style) and educational experiences (what has already been learned) of students.

It is necessary that the curriculum be defined and developed in such a way as to be meaningful in terms of the way people learn.

Second, learners do not come to any learning situation without having had prior experiences. In defining a curriculum which centers on students, it is necessary to consider the relevant prior learning experiences that students have had as they relate to the curriculum at every point. To this end, one must be sensitive to the issue of transfer of learning.

Postulate 4. In terms of learning style, learning of the concrete must precede learning of the abstract.

Jean Piaget, the eminent European developmental psychologist, has in the course of a 40-year career shown that children learn concrete operations before they learn abstract operations and that, moreover, abstract operations cannot be learned unless concrete operations are learned first.[1] Thus concrete learning style and materials must precede the abstract.

Postulate 5. Learning can be maximized by controlling the sequence towards some goal and locating the student in that sequence.

This postulate contends that learning is an experience which requires that the conditions under which it is likely to occur be controlled. The contention is that learning is not a haphazard occurrence.

To the extent that one can associate the conditions of learning with those that are relevant for a specific person, one should be able to produce learning. This position has been well documented by Robert M. Gagné, in his book *The Conditions of Learning.*[2]

Postulate 6. Learning is most meaningful when a person learns through interaction with his environment.

In the interdependent learning model, the individual learns through interaction with his environment. This is in contrast with a unilateral model where some agent establishes external criteria and affects the behavior of individuals in terms of these criteria through the use of rewards and punishments.

Propositions

Proposition 1. The curriculum must be vocationalized in order to: (a) meet a student's future employment needs, and (b) provide a concrete context for learning.

Since as many as 80 percent of today's young people will enter the work force with educational experiences at less than the bachelor's level, it is necessary that instructional activity be provided to help students master the skills and competencies that they will need for entry into the occupational world.

A second reason for vocationalizing the curriculum is to take advantage of the postulate that concrete learning must precede abstract learning. The vocational context is a highly concrete one, within which previously considered abstract concepts may be more easily mastered by students, particularly those students whose experiences heretofore have not provided a great opportunity for the mastery of concrete concepts.

Proposition 2. Behavioral objective identification must precede curriculum development in order to identify goals and facilitate evaluation.

If the curriculum is to proceed from a delineation of goals, then the identification of goals must be the first step in the curriculum development process. Moreover, these goals must be identified and specified in behavioral terms in order to provide meaning to all who must follow in the process and contribute to the development of the curriculum. The place to begin is with goals, and behavioral objectives are a form of goal statement with enough specificity to make them usable by curriculum developers and evaluators alike.

Proposition 3. Behavioral objectives must be analyzed to provide sequences of learning experiences.

The behavioral objective is a good place to begin the process of identifying sequences of experience that will ultimately constitute the curriculum. Such sequences of experience are meaningful only in terms of what they add up to, that is, where they end up. In order to guarantee that such sequences end where you want them to end, one begins at the end point and works backwards.

Proposition 4. A model for combining sequences and thus students in sequences must be developed which is consistent with the psychology of human function and the three classes of goals.

A curriculum cannot consist of an infinite or near infinite series of disconnected sequences. Each sequence can take on additional meaning by being grouped and connected to other sequences which relate to it not only in terms of the goal object, but in terms of the nature of skill or competency or knowledge which the sequence is an attempt to facilitate. The practical requirements of a learning situation necessitate some form of packaging of the sequences. The form the packaging has taken thus far in our educational history has been by subject matter. However, subject matter is not inherent to the learning experiences nor to the learner. Perhaps it would be more meaningful to use some characteristics which are inherent in both the subject matter and the students who are to learn them as a basis of clustering learning experiences. Characteristics which are descriptive of human function and equally consistent with the three classes of goals — occupational, civic/citizenship, personal/ social — should be maximally effective, since the curriculum is to be defined in terms of both of these kinds of characteristics.

Proposition 5. "Individualized" instruction can be approximated in groups, but these groups will be shifting rapidly in membership over time.

Individuals will be simultaneously instructed when they are at the same point in the same sequence. This proposition argues against individualized instruction in the sense which we have come to think of it, namely, students working by themselves with relatively impersonal presentation devices or books, often linked to a computer to provide them with equally impersonal feedback. Many have argued against individualized instruction and opted for a major role for the teacher who can provide the "human element." If a curriculum were to be built around learning sequences, there is no necessary reason why each student should go through a sequence in isolation from all other students.

However, these students will not constitute a group in the rigid manner in which that term is presently used within the educational establishment. While students may exist as a group for a particular learning experience or sequence of experiences, for the *following* learning experience they may each find themselves as parts of other groups.

Proposition 6. Learning must be propagated through learning experiences, i.e., "hands on" experiences, rather than lecturing by the teacher.

Materials must be prepared to allow students to learn through their environment. The environment must be structured to maximize the probability that the desired learning will take place. To this end, one concentrates not on writing lesson plans, but on writing experimental units, i.e., participation exercises, which provide a vehicle for learning experiences.

Conclusions

The student-centered curriculum ultimately will be built on the basis of the postulates and propositions described above. It will be a goal-oriented curriculum in that it will begin by a specification of goals broken down into the three goal areas identified. It will reflect the progression from concrete to abstract, using the vocationalizing experience as a context for concrete learning as well as a way of providing young people with occupationally-relevant experiences. It will be made up of a series of sequences which are analyzed from specified goals.

Once the goals and the sequences are identified and combined, the next step undertaken will be to develop specific learning materials to achieve the goals that have been set forth.

At the same time that the curriculum is being constructed, it will be valuable for individuals to examine the physical and administrative structure of the educational system as we now know it. Any curriculum which is built based on the propositions and postulates described in this paper—that is, any truly student-centered curriculum — will require an administrative structure and perhaps a physical one which differs in many respects from that presently in existence in the majority of school districts in the United States. The student-centered curriculum would require a non-graded school. It would do away with the traditional concept of ability grouping and tracking as it is presently practiced in most American secondary schools. It would require modular scheduling and a computer system for record keeping and sequence coordination.

Additional demands different from those presently in existence will be placed upon the guidance systems of the schools, whose activities will have to be closely coordinated with the student-centered curriculum.

In conclusion, the advent of a student-centered curriculum, should it ever come to pass, would require some *basic changes* in the instructional system.

REFERENCES

1. For a synthesis see J. H. Flavell. *The Developmental Psychology of John Piaget*. Princeton, N. J.: Van Nostrand, 1963.
2. R. M. Gagné. *The Conditions of Learning*. New York: Holt, Rinehart & Winston, 1965.

11

The New Curriculum Design in Special Education

Norris G. Haring

A curriculum is a plan for the arrangement of information and experiences which educators consider necessary for children to cope successfully with life. This general view of curriculum involves the teacher in arranging the variables of instruction to produce the behavior sought — an approach that encompasses what to teach, how to teach, and how to improve teaching (Bellack, 1969). The child and his own development, as well as the final goals of instruction, are influences on the final design of the curriculum. Consequently, a curriculum designed effectively starts with the child at his level of entering behaviors and guides him efficiently and effectively toward terminal objectives. The overview that follows identifies the influences from which the newly

Norris G. Haring is director of the Experimental Education Unit at the Child Development and Mental Retardation Center, University of Washington.

emerging curriculum design in special education has arisen and, in addition, discusses the developments resulting from these influences, as well as examples of their application to exceptional children.

Influences on the New Curriculum Design

A clear picture reflecting the exact influences on curriculum design is not available, for researchers have not yet begun to analyze experimentally these forces outside the curriculum (McNeil, 1969). However, it seems apparent that three types of influences have had impact on the new design in the curriculum of special education. The increased awareness of educators of the need to specify instructional objectives in ways that can be measured has had significant results. Influences upon curriculum have taken the form of (a) programs which individualize instruction; and (b) programs which require active responses from children. Behavioral research and technological developments have provided additional impact. Behavioral research has helped educators to identify behaviors that can be measured during performance. Technology has provided the tools both for instruction and measurement (Blackhurst, 1965).

The interaction of these influences eliminates the possibility of identifying one which might have functioned as the dominant factor. Even the specific contributions of each are difficult to pinpoint, for upon close inspection one seems to have arisen from the other and yet parallel developments are also at times apparent. It has become obvious through the review, however, that the influences of behavior principles and the tools of technology have, throughout their mutual development, interacted quite significantly upon advances in special education curriculum.

Behavioral Research as an Influence

Behavioral objectives. The most important influence on special education has been a recognition of the importance of specifying the terminal objectives of instruction around which to design the curriculum. The need to specify terminal objectives as *observable behavior* (Mager, 1962) became obvious as research in the behavioral sciences (Honig, 1966) began to have impact on education (Ferster & Perrot, 1968; Haring, 1969, 1970). This need has placed the educator in the position where he can be specific about behavioral requirements of specific curricula, which, in turn, has made it possible for him to arrange an instructional program in a sequence that involves successive approximations (Lumsdaine, 1965), i.e., progressive steps, that lead toward terminal objectives.

Behavioral approach to handicapped children. The influence of behavioral research has, in addition to this contribution, been much more pervasive, for it has provided a behavioral approach to the identification and management of exceptional children. While, as categories, the medical and psychological classifications have offered some function in classifying children, they have proven to be nonfunctional as the teacher deals with learning and behavior in the classroom. Consequently, special educators have begun to view the handicapped child in terms of his educational deficits (Stolurow & Davis, 1965). The child may be seen to have deficits in pre-academic or academic skills, or, where indicated, he may lack vocational skills useful to him. The child may lack language skills that are essentially verbal behavior. He may lack the social skills (Patterson & Reid, 1969) necessary for behavioral interactions involved in cooperation, competition and exchange (Lindsley, 1966; Mithaug, 1970a; Mithaug, 1970b). Or the child may be deficient in behaviors considered sensory-motor skills. Identification of exceptionalities in terms of observable behavioral deficits provides information specific to making decisions for modifications that can be accomplished in an educational setting.

This behavioral view of the exceptional child has had two major effects on special education. One has been the realization that the effects of environmental modifications can change some deviancies in development. This has brought educators to focus on very early identification and treatment of handicapping patterns of development (Public Law 90-538) almost at the prevention stage. The growing awareness that learning results from the *process* of instruction (Mowrer, 1969) is a second major effect of this view. Kopstein's (Hickey, 1968) definition of teaching is an apt representation: ". . . a rigorous definition of teaching must be the complement of an accepted definition of learning. Any generally acceptable, operational definition of learning shows teaching to be simply a beneficial control and regulation of a learner's stimulus environment" (p. 45).

Adaptation of procedures of experimental analysis. Research in the behavioral sciences has also provided a set of procedures — experimental analysis (Skinner, 1965; Sidman, 1960) — which, in varying adaptations, has become the newest curriculum design in special education. Application of procedures of experimental analysis in the classroom has provided the teacher with a functional way to plan, implement and evaluate a curriculum designed to satisfy specific terminal objectives.

Educational Technology as an Influence

Development of programmed materials. The long recognized need for an effective means of individualizing instruction (De Cecco, 1964) has produced the demand; the technology of education (Skinner, 1968) has responded with self-instructional programs in which children can perform at their own rates. This demand has proved to be the second greatest influence on special education (Carson, 1969), an influence which credits this field as giving birth to the movement to individualize instruction (Ofiesh, 1969).

The precision made possible by a programmed arrangement of materials to be learned has greatly assisted educators in teaching children with learning deficits. This to some degree explains the rapidly spreading application of programmed instruction in special education. Programmed materials, as a form of instruction, meet the requirements for individualization to the degree that the specific program develops the specific skills for which it was designed (Lange, 1967). Too many programs fall short of instructional objectives, a fault of the programmer, whose responsibility it is to make his program instructional through a series of behavioral evaluations prior to marketing the product (Markle, 1967). Programmed instruction in special education, as in regular education, is gaining a new breadth of meaning to include the total programming (Haring & Lovitt, 1967) of a learning environment for a specific portion of the total classroom session.

Development of instrumentation. Programmed instruction has been instrumental in the development and use of the teaching machine, which, in turn, has served as a catalyst for the introduction of the computer (Bushnell & Allen, 1967). The computer (Jerman & Suppes, 1969; Robertson, 1968), when introduced into education, made possible a more refined application of these earlier influences. One refinement has been that terminal objectives can be stated more precisely in behavioral terms, enabling software (the curricula, per se) to be programmed, evaluated and revised. In addition, the computer offers refinements in curriculum developments because of its potential for sorting bits of information into sequencing and branching arrangements. Through the use of the computer (a) more precise behavioral objectives can be implemented; (b) bits of information can be arranged in linear and branching sequences; and (c) feedback can be obtained that is essential to program revisions. The availability of computerized instrumentation for display of instructional stimuli and for measurement of performance to obtain a continuous evaluation of performance has accelerated the scientific progress of education.

Development of systems analysis. Probably the final influence, whose impact is just beginning to be felt, is a systems approach (Saettler, 1969; Carson, 1969; Ofiesh, 1968) to curriculum design. Systems analysis (Stolurow, 1967), as applied to education, has developed along with programmed instruction and computer programming because of the nature of the requirements for the design and evaluation of both. It is a dimension of technology, not necessarily automated, which provides a framework within which a curriculum (a) can be designed to meet specifically defined objectives; (b) can be implemented as planned; and (c) can be evaluated, then modified on the basis of the evaluation in order to approximate more closely the terminal objectives. At the present time, however, as far as the teacher in the special classroom is concerned, a systems analysis is more a model for administrative strategy in decision making than a tool for instruction. Systems analysis will prove to be especially useful for designing and evaluating comprehensive curricula which may include one or more of a large number of different media, including computer assisted instruction. Without a method of evaluating the use of these media, and their timing, it is impossible to make on-going decisions about a more effective curriculum design.

Developments in the Technology of Special Education

In order to meet the educational objectives for the individual handicapped child, the special education curriculum is increasingly designed to focus on (a) the total classroom environment; (b) the effective use of a variety of media; (c) the process for implementing and evaluating the plans; and (d) the behavior of the child. These four features of curriculum design together are important to educational technology, the growth of which can be attributed in large measure to the influences just described and to the development of the instrumentation and procedures which have made its application possible.

Based on the urgent rationale that effective teaching on a large scale requires that educators either model the master teacher or master the teaching model (Stolurow, 1965), educational technology has followed two lines of development. Educational technology refers both to hardware (automated and non-automated instrumentation) and to a systematic process of instruction, regardless of the media used for presenting the information of the curriculum (Gagné, 1968). Either dimension of educational technology is actually a process, whether the presentation of instructional stimuli is planned, implemented and evaluated through instrumentation or accomplished systematically by the educator himself (Heinrich, 1968). Instrumentation and automation are seen as the product of technology. But the total gains from technology are not achieved without the full use of systematic instructional procedures. In the early stages of the application of technology, the special educator borrowed bits and pieces to apply to his instructional design. With increasing refinements in behavior modification and intervention, however, the educator is beginning to specify his requirements of technology. Such interrelationship can only result in benefits for technology as well as education.

Any process of instruction that includes the identification of behavioral objectives and a process by which they will be carried out and evaluated is an example of the application of technology. Thus educational technology can be applied at any level to the solution of instructional problems.

In the natural setting, educational technology is being applied in two ways: 1) through automated and non-automated media for display and measurement as part of the task of in-instruction, and 2) as a set of procedures which systematize instruction (Silverman, 1968).

Educational Technology as Automated and Non-Automated Media

Over the past two decades, automated and non-automated media have shown an accelerated growth in the types available as well as in their frequency of use. Programmed and non-programmed materials, very simple teaching machines like the Bell and Howell Langauge Master (Crouch, 1967), the World Book Cyclo-teacher and the overhead projector (Wyman, 1969), and the very complex instrumentation of computer assisted instruction well represent the range of media available. Each type of medium, regardless of its simplicity or complexity, has one or two functions: either it displays instructional stimuli or it provides both a display of stimuli and some measurement of performance.

Display media. Media which display information (Silberberg & Silberberg, 1969) are extensive and abundant. For example, educational television, films, filmstrips and slides have been available to the special class for a long time. Programmed instruction is a much newer development, offering much greater opportunitiy for individualized instruction. The feasibility of programmed instruction has been demonstrated on children with all types of exceptionalities — mental retardation, slow learner, speech deficiency, aphasia, school dropout, deafness and cultural deprivation (Pfau, 1969). It has been especially used where their learning deficits have involved the lack of skills in initial reading, math, spelling, written language and handwriting (Haring, 1970). Programmed materials designed around other content areas have had limited applicability to handicapped children because the reading requirements are too difficult.

Display and measurement media. Teaching machines — in any degree of complexity—provide capabilities of both display and performance measurement to facilitate educational objectives for the child. One of the simplest and most functional to date has been the Language Master, manufactured by Bell and Howell, which can present and record auditory stimuli to develop both visual and auditory discrimination and which can be easily managed by the young child. It is an excellent illustration of a medium that can facilitate individualized instruction inexpensively.

Some machines feature specific types of display to suit a handicapping condition, such as those used in Project LIFE (Pfau, 1969) for hearing impaired children. These machines feature a master-response control unit for teaching reading skills to deaf children as early as five years of age.

Another form of instrumentation — the conjugate reinforcement servo* — has been developed and used to measure the preferences for various types, rates and degrees of intensity in the auditory presentation of information to mentally retarded individuals (Lovitt, 1968). Through conjugate reinforcement, two variations in auditory stimuli are simultaneously available for presentation to the child, who indicates by his response pattern on a handswitch which variation he prefers. The potential offered by such precision in response measurement for assessment of skills and for evaluation of instructional conditions, as they affect performance, has barely been tapped.

The Talking Typewriter (Moore, 1963) has, in the recent past, offered a semi-computerized program in elementary reading for autistic, mentally retarded and maladjusted children

---

*Behavior Research Co., Kansas City, Kansas.

(Pines, 1965), and is currently being evaluated with disabled readers (Zaslav & Frazier, 1969). Although research results have not been obtained to substantiate the success of this instrument, many users have been highly pleased with, at least, short-term effects.

The most complex teaching machine is the computer, now at a stage of development where software programs are becoming available in very elementary form to assist the on-going program of classroom instruction in one of several subjects.

Following the development of programmed instruction and teaching machines as the two major educational developments of the late 1950's and early 1960's, the computer, as it assists instruction, promises to be the major educational development of the late 1960's and early 1970's (Feldhusen & Szabo, 1969). Most computer programs to date have involved computer assisted instruction (CAI) rather than developmental programs; and, although by 1968 five hundred public and private schools had had some degree of CAI programming as part of the curriculum (University of Washington Summer Computer Assisted Instruction Project, 1969) and 25,000 children below college level to date have had some degree of exposure, only about 1,000 children in special education classrooms have had this opportunity.

Currently, only five programs for handicapped children have included the computer as part of the curriculum design. The Experimental Education Unit of the Child Development and Mental Retardation Center at the University of Washington presented a summer CAI program to children exhibiting a wide variety of handicapped conditions as well as to a group of deaf children (University of Washington Summer Computer Assisted Instruction Project, 1969). The program of drill-and-practice in arithmetic, emanating from Stanford University, was utilized in an initial attempt to evaluate the efficacy of CAI for teaching handicapped children. Stemming from this groundwork, there is currently underway, within five selected school districts in King and Pierce Counties, and at the Experimental Education Unit, a more extensive CAI project. A total of 22 terminals, provided with input from a local computer facility, will be placed in different settings for children having a wide range of ages and handicapping conditions. The concern of the project, as children are instructed in elementary math and language, centers primarily (a) on the efficacy of CAI for handicapped children; (b) on the conditions which might increase its effectiveness; and (c) on the training necessary to prepare teachers and administrators to utilize the features of CAI in ways that facilitate instructional objectives. Probably the most unique feature of the project is the test to be given the expensive presentation of stimuli the computer provides when comparisons are made with student performance in a parallel program presented in workbook format. In addition to comparing learning rates to stimuli with and without the computer, the project is directed at determining (a) optimal conditions for evaluating the project; (b) optimal length of terminal use by the child; and (c) the influence of different settings and different reinforcement conditions on the adequacy of CAI programming.

Gallaudet College (Finch, 1968) is conducting a pilot project using an arithmetic drill-and-practice program for deaf children with computer input from Stanford University. It is also developing a model secondary school for the deaf which will include capabilities for the use of computer in meeting instructional objectives.

Four educational settings in Oregon participate in a mobile CAI program which teaches problem solving and "understanding computers." Students at the Oregon School for the Blind, the Oregon School for the Deaf, the State Penitentiary School, and McLaren School for Boys (Pembroke, 1968) respond to these programs on a periodic basis.

A third computerized program (Lang, 1969) is in the experimental stages for automating Wolpe's (1958) behavioral therapeutic technique for desensitizing phobias. Early results show that this on-line computerized presentation of stimuli associated with the phobia and adjusted according to the patient's pattern of response is just as effective as using a live therapist. This new development promises to be an effective approach to the treatment of other psychopathological processes.

One other computer program relevant to the needs of

handicapped children involves a mobile instruction unit (CAI Study Designed to Help Student with Minor Handicap, 1969) being developed to present inservice training to classroom teachers to give them skills to identify minor handicapping conditions, such as vision and hearing deficits. When a program such as this can be extended to include training in the identification of behavior and learning deficits, using identification procedures which lead directly to improve teaching conditions, computer programming will be extremely functional for professional training. in special education.

Other machines, mostly in the design or early development stage, feature prosthetic devices which can assist the child to make the necessary responses, such as a computer terminal that would have response keys embossed with braille (Blackhurst, 1965).

A view of computer programming currently available to children in regular classrooms provides a panorama of its applicability to the needs of exceptional children. Regular class elementary and secondary students (not to mention college students) in California, Kentucky, Mississippi, Tennessee, Pennsylvania, New York, Michigan and Washington respond to computer programs for elementary reading, math, spelling, mathematical logic, social studies, grammar, vocational and technical skills, problem solving and "computer understanding" (Jerman, 1969). To any one student only one or two of these programs are available, however. Most of these programs are supplementary curriculum programs of drill-and-practice. An increasing number are beginning to be tutorial, thus more developmental. Tutorial programs, including those involving simulation, are geared to the answers and questions the child presents to the computer, a further advancement in individual instruction.

Although the results of CAI programs, with various groups of mostly normal children, do not definitely identify whether or not the skills developed have been accomplished more effectively than when the teacher presents the same information, results do show that instruction is equalized from child to child when using CAI. Undisputedly, CAI has had its greatest effects in geographical areas where educational opportunities are lacking and socioeconomic standards are low (Suppes & Morningstar, 1969).

Computers offer tremendous promise to education when used with good software and when their use is evaluated within a larger curriculum design. Suppes (1968) predicts that within the next five years the drill-and-practice programs in math and reading alone will reach between 200,000 and 800,000 children. Furthermore, he predicts that in ten years this application may reach between one and ten million. In addition to their contributions to skill development for both the handicapped child and the teacher, computers will facilitate educational research designed to explore the variables of the teaching-learning process.

These media, in addition to their value in display and measurement, have also proven to have reinforcing value and can be used to motivate performance.

Any medium, however, is only as effective in achieving educational objectives as the effectiveness of its specific application. If this form of technology is to benefit special education, it must not simply be appended to current instructional approaches, but instead must be incorporated into the operational program in such a way that instructional objectives are facilitated. Systematic plans must be designed for the use and evaluation of media in line with instructional objectives for the individual child. The use of electronic, mechanical and electromechanical devices to speed up the process of learning will reshape our previous concept of the teacher as a key professional who supports the learning process, for his role will be both managerial and supportive (Joyce, 1969).

The importance of these media to special education is registered in the increasing demand for curriculum or instructional materials or media specialists (Kraft & Latta, 1969; Watson, 1968; Kelley, 1969) to assist the teacher in planning for instruction. It is also seen as important in the development of two types of media centers, one within the school building (Herman, 1969; Owen & Compton, 1968; Wood, 1969; Singer, 1968) for use by the child, and the other often within its own structure (King, 1969) to provide for the teacher the dissemination, evaluation and further development of all forms of media.

Media specialists. The great variety of available instructional material and media has spawned a need for a new specialist — the instructional material or media specialist (Glaser, 1968). This specialist will be concerned with the effective use of all instructional resources to promote the most learning with the least time and expense. His primary responsibility is to assist the teacher in the use of available resources to meet his stated objectives. His focus is and will be to design curriculum plans that include the teacher's activities, the use of materials and other media, as well as the interaction of both. With the increased expectations of instructional and media specialists, however, it probably would be too much to expect one person to assume responsibilities for equipment as well as for materials. The earlier expectations that librarians should assume the roles of audiovisual specialist and materials specialist might serve as a lesson here. Because of the total needs of both areas and the diverse service requests, their attempts were not entirely satisfactory. Quite probably the "audiovisual specialist" of the schools of yesterday will be the instructional materials specialist of the schools of tomorrow.

A hierarchy of educational planners is actually developing. The prototype for any specialist in this hierarchy may well be the resource teacher (Haring, 1969), whose role has most recently been refined through training in the use of classroom measurement and evaluation procedures that focus on the process of instruction. Resource teachers have been trained to help the special class teacher directly with instructional plans designed to meet specific problems in classroom management and instruction.

Educational planners within the next ten years will also function at the school district level, where the task of curriculum design increases in complexity with an increase in the number of variables to consider.

Where curriculum specialists operate from Instructional Materials Centers, they may be directly responsible for instruction to children who come to the Center periodically for individualized programming. These specialists increasingly will have at their disposal a variety of information retrieval systems. Even computer assisted instruction and the "talking typewriters" are coming under the direction of the instructional materials specialist (King, 1969).

Media centers: Local and national. Media centers at the school level are being designed for easy access and independent use by the student, whether within the classroom (Weisberger & Rahmlow, 1968) or another room. Both settings are increasingly useful in providing the student with a large amount of information through a variety of media as he is guided toward terminal objectives. These centers, when well equipped to provide information, may include individual carrels having "dial access" to a computer storing a wide variety of information for problem solving, individual use of filmstrips, movies, discs, tapes and programmed instruction integrated with multi-media formats. They are staffed by specialized personnel.

Use of these facilities varies widely, currently. Some are used simply to provide the child the opportunity to browse for information. Others are used when the child is to make a specific report or to bring to the attention of the child specific areas of interest. These facilities will be used most effectively, however, when they are programmed as part of the child's total curriculum activity, where it is planned that at a certain time the use of the center will facilitate specific skills (Gerletti, 1969).

On the national level, several types of media centers have been organized for the dissemination, evaluation and development of media to implement the design of curriculum for exceptional children. Directly and indirectly they are also involved in teacher training. Since the development of four centers for the deaf (McIntyre, 1969), the Special Education Instructional Materials Center (SEIMC) Network for Handicapped Children and Youth (Erickson, 1969) has been developed and is becoming an effective program for the dissemination and demonstration of a wide variety of instructional resources. The seventeen special education centers comprising the network (a) contain libraries of instructional materials to be used by personnel in the area; (b) publish regular newsletters and provide library services by mail; (c) sometimes provide field specialists; (d) sometimes have mobile units for reaching the teachers; and (e) coordinate a system to centralize information in conjunction with the CEC Information Center. Overall, the centers provide consultation, inservice training meetings, and information on educational methods and media. The CEC Information Center (Soeffing, 1969) is one of the ERIC Clearinghouses which prints abstracts of publications in the literature of special education and abstracts of available instructional materials. The National Media Center for the Handicapped (Ofiesh, 1969) is the most recently developed national program. This center will provide the additional feature of a demonstration school.

Systematic Instruction in Special Education: The Second Form of Educational Technology

Educational technology as systematic instruction or as a systems approach to achieving educational objectives was not initially singled out as a technology in its own right, although it was a necessary parallel to the development of non-automated and automated technology. Today, however, it is recognized as a technology whether functioning with or without instrumentation or programmed instruction. It is more comparable to the broad definition of programmed instruction, i.e., programmed environment.

This form of technology is characterized by three major features of instruction: (a) systematic arrangement of conditions for learning; (b) continuous measurement of child performance; and (c) evaluation of the overall effect of the instructional conditions. This form of technology has progressed to the point where, in the classroom, it primarily involves procedures of continuous measurement of child performance. In addition, because teachers using these procedures have identified behaviorally the skills they expect to see the child achieve and the intervening steps in the development of these skills, these teachers are able to assess where each child is in relation to the objectives and the stimuli that might be selected and sequenced to begin an individualized program. Precise identification and sequencing of specific conditions of instruction require attention to: 1) those stimuli that occur before the child responds to the task; 2) those that occur immediately after each unit of response to each "bit" of the task; and 3) those events or reinforcers that can be provided after the total task is completed. It has become essential to attend not only to the conditions which cue or prompt the desired response, but also to those which motivate performance, thus maintaining, attending and responding accurately to a task.

This is not a methods approach to instruction but an *instructional process*. Although a methods approach and a systems approach to instruction both involve a set of procedures, a systems approach includes a procedure for continuous measurement and systematic evaluation of results, which may in turn change the original input. The lack of built-in measurement procedures in a methods approach may result in perpetuation of that method without reliable evaluations. Requirements of this second dimension of technology parallel the requirements of instrumentation. That is, both require, as part of the process of instruction, the determination of precise behavioral and instructional procedures. Together they permit valid information to be obtained from the child's performance that reliably reflects the effects of the curriculum design. This means total programming of the instructional environment during intervals of each daily class session when the teacher's activities are directed toward specified objectives.

The application of this dimension of technology has reached such a degree of precision in some educational settings, mainly special classes, that a central data bank is in the developmental stages which will evaluate and disseminate information on conditions that cue and reinforce child performance. Specially designed computer forms have been prepared on which the teacher or researcher is to identify the instructional conditions used as well as the relevant behavioral data about the child's performance under these conditions. Data from projects conducted anywhere in the country using procedures adapted from those of experimental analysis can be pinpointed and summarized on these forms, which are then sent to the data collection center.

Although the use of these forms is in a very early stage of development, it is a direction that is bringing research procedures into the classroom as instructional procedures, producing results precise enough to be replicated by others and to be used as information to store for future access.

Within this area of educational technology, special education will be credited with providing an area for the application of a precise adaptation of procedures of experimental analysis (Lindsley, 1964; Haring & Phillips, in press), a major contribution to the beginnings of a behavioral science base to instruction (Glaser, 1965).

New Factors of Curriculum Design

New curriculum design in special education is characterized by the achievement of an ever increasing degree of individualization of instruction. Second, it is characterized by a systematic approach for designing, implementing and evaluating (using child performance data) the process of instructing the child so that he acquires specific information and specific behaviors. Third, there is a greater emphasis on academic content, with, in addition to a wide variety of printed media, the use of instrumented media wherever feasible for accomplishing terminal objectives efficiently in terms of time and cost. Fourth, as opposed to initial concentration on deviant behaviors or other special handicapping conditions, there is an evaluation of entering academic, social and verbal behaviors of the child that leads directly to educational programs that modify and build on these repertoires, thus emphasizing the rapid developmental potential of early childhood rather than the deviance. The new preschool programs for handicapped children, now subsidized by Public Law 90-538, underscore the fact that there is no need to wait, for example, for the development of eye-hand coordination and form and letter discrimination before beginning instruction. In early childhood, many skills are not as dependent on readiness as they are on training. This fact, alone, is having a powerful effect on curriculum design.

New Curriculum Design as Total Programming

New curriculum design in special education reflects the glimmerings of the science of teaching. The most comprehensive application of the new curriculum design in special education takes one of two forms. One type of application involves the addition of some form of CAI to classroom instruction in an additive way, although not as a coordinated part of the total curriculum design. The other type involves the use of systematic procedures applied to some portion of the total curriculum each day. As yet, no programs involve a design using both complex instrumentation and systematic instructional procedures, other than those built in to the software program.

Programs primarily involving instrumentation, which have already been identified, are self-contained. As these instrumented programs meet objectives for which they are designed and employed they represent total programming for the duration of stimulus presentation. However, the curriculum of special education is broader than the technology of instrumentation can supply, at least at present.

The special class teacher as he applies the new design, selects and arranges environmental conditions and events as they play a role in instruction. These conditions and events are not only those that prompt specific types of responses from the child, but also specific conditions which do and can function to reinforce classroom performance — reinforcement being the key factor in motivation (Ferster, 1961; Nolen, Kunzelmann, & Haring, 1968; Girardeau & Spradlin, 1964). The specific features of the new design also materialize as the teacher incorporates procedures of continuous measurement of performance into his daily instruction. When teachers plan and carry out instruction in line with the new design, they are engaged in a type of engineering as they construct an educational environment designed to shape student thinking and behavior.

Examples of the Application of New Curriculum Design

There are a number of examples of the new curriculum in classrooms across the country. Within any of these programs currently exemplifying new curriculum design, several new factors which advance instruction are prominent. All involve technology and measurement. The two major factors in these programs are the *selection* and *arrangement* of environmental conditions and events which influence learning. In many ways these programs represent either the application of a systems analysis or the application of a more precise set of procedures — experimental analysis. These programs are systems or processes of instruction, as they embrace: terminal objectives, a program of instruction, measurement, and evaluation of the achievement of objectives.

The new design, represented by various adaptions of the basic features, is visible under a number of different labels: experimental education (Haring, 1970), precision teaching (Lindsley, 1964), behavior modification (Haring & Hayden, 1969), engineered classroom (Hewettt, 1967), contingency management (Haring & Kunzelmann, 1966; Haring, in press), and contingency contracting (Homme, 1969). Regardless of the label, this new design is being applied widely to handicapped children (a) exhibiting all types of exceptionalities (Haring & Kunzelmann, 1966; Nolan, Kunzelmann, & Haring, 1968); (b) mentally retarded (Birnbrauer, Wolf, Kidder, & Tague, 1965; Girardeau & Spradlin, 1964); (c) severely disabled in reading (Haring & Hauck, 1969); and children with (d) conduct problems (Quay, Werry, McQueen, & Sprague, 1966; Becker, Madsen, Arnold & Thomas, 1967) and emotional disturbances (Hewett, 1968). This design is also being applied extensively to children disadvantaged (Wolf, Giles, & Hall, 1968) and delinquent (Tyler & Brown, 1967).

The technological significance of each of these exemplary programs is that each describes a direction, how to get there through the instructional program and other experiences, and a way to evaluate where the child is in relation to the design. In addition, each program focuses not on the deviancies but on the behavioral deficiencies of children, a focus on accelerating positive behaviors rather than on decreasing a pathology. In this way, curriculum is designed to build terminal objectives similar to the specific performance expectations required for normal children, as well as the additional objectives necessary for effective work with handicapped children.

A number of methods are also being used with exceptional children in addition to these exemplary programs. When these methods begin to incorporate terminal objectives, which the selected materials and experiences are arranged to achieve, and when evaluation procedures are also included as part of the process of instruction, they too will become systems of instruction.

The best curriculum design in special education will incorporate both dimensions of technology to the fullest. Within a systematic curriculum designed to meet specific objectives, several forms of non-automated as well as automated media, including the computer, where feasible, will be employed and evaluated. This approach permits continuous revision of the process in the original design to accomplish the desired product.

Summary

New curriculum design in special education shows a convergence of two strong influences: 1) the recognition of the importance of individualized instruction; and 2) the growing effect of the procedures of experimental analysis with an emphasis on the individual child and the conditions which, when applied to well-defined behaviors, produce specific results. In contrast to the design of the curriculum of the past, the new design in the curriculum of special education is broader, possibly more content oriented, certainly directed at the behavioral components of learning, totally defined in behavioral terms, and managed within a system.

What appears to have emerged as the overall curriculum design is the technology of teaching or teaching according to applied scientific principles of behavior. This means the use of systematic procedures and the inclusion of instrumentation where economically feasible and functionally appropriate for effective individualized instruction. In particular, the design builds on sequences of behaviors (or behavioral chains) and begins with a focus on early childhood for more effective prevention and amelioration.

The new curriculum design underscores three important features of instruction. First, academic skills can and should be developed through systematic arrangements of cues, placing the teacher in a managerial role for designing, implementing and evaluating curriculum. Second, materials and other media used to cue responses should be selected and arranged so as to prompt equal response units. In this way, a continuous measurement of performance can be obtained that reliably reflects the effects of the materials and instructional procedures. Third, decisions concerning instructional conditions are based on this continuous record of performance.

Great variation in the application of educational technology can be observed throughout special classes and programs for exceptional children. In some classes, the most advanced use of instrumentation, educational media and resources is being demonstrated. Still in other special classes the methods, materials and equipment being used have not advanced very far. Certainly rapid change in instructional procedures and materials is being effected, for which educational technology is responsible in large measure.

Observation of the current curriculum design in special education not only reveals remarkable variation in precision, but also (a) growth in the application of more scientific procedures and (b) increasing visibility of the new design in a number of programs. Teachers are changing from dramatic artists to managers of all resources available for instruction.

There is reason to believe that educators will look toward special education for the opportunity to use more precise procedures for instruction. This development in special education is the growth of a new discipline, which, as Silverman (1968) describes it, is "midway between the science of learning and the day-to-day practical problems of teaching. This new discipline would require people trained in behavioral science, exposed to the problems of teaching, and unafraid of devices" (p. 3) and of measurement procedures that permit evaluation of instruction.

REFERENCES

Atkinson, R. C.   Instruction in Initial Reading Under Computer Control: The Stanford Project. *Journal of Educational Data Processing,* 1967, *4,* 175-192.

Becker, W. C., Madsen, C. H., Jr., Arnold, R. & Thomas, D. R.   The Contingent Use of Teacher Attention and Praise in Reducing Classroom Behavior Problems. *Journal of Education,* 1967, *1,* 287-307.

Bellack, A. A.   History of Curriculum Thought and Practice. *Review of Educational Research,* 1969, *39,* 283-292.

Birnbrauer, J. S., Wolf, M. M., Kidder, J. D., & Tague, C. E.   Classroom Behavior of Retarded Pupils with Token Reinforcement. *Journal of Experimental Child Psychology,* 1965, *2,* 219-235.

Blackhurst, A. E.   Technology in Special Education. *Exceptional Children,* 1965, *31,* 449-456.

Bushnell, D. D. & Allen, D. W. (Eds.)   *The Computer in American Education.* New York: John Wiley & Sons, 1967.

CAI Study Designed to Help Student with Minor Handicap. *Educational Media,* 1969, *1,* 17-18.

Carson, L.   Computer Assisted Instruction — What It Can Do for Education. *Educational Media,* 1969, *1,* 14-17.

Carter, L. F.   The Systems Approach to Education: Mystique and Reality. *Educational Technology,* 1969, *9,* 22-31.

Crouch, E.   The Language Master in the Classroom. *Audio-Visual Media,* 1967, *1,* 31-34.

DeCecco, J. P. (Ed.)   *Educational Technology: Readings in Programmed Instruction.* New York: Holt, Rinehart & Winston, 1964.

Erickson, D.   The Instructional Materials Center Network for Handicapped Children and Youth. *Audiovisual Instruction,* 1969, *14,* 41.

Feldhusen, J. F. & Szabo, M.   A Review of Developments in Computer Assisted Instruction. *Educational Technology,* 1969, *9,* 32-39.

Ferster, C. B.   Positive Reinforcement and Behavioral Deficits of Autistic Children. *Child Development,* 1961, *32,* 437-456.

Ferster, C. B. & Perrott, M. C.   *Behavioral Principles.* New York: Appleton-Century-Crofts, 1968.

Finch, R. H.   *Selected Program Activities in the Education of the Deaf.* U. S. Department of Health, Education, and Welfare, Washington, D. C., 1968.

Gagné, R. M.   Educational Technology as Technique. *Educational Technology,* 1968, *8,* 5-14.

Gerletti, R. C.   What Is a Media Center? *Audiovisual Instruction,* 1969, *14,* 21-23.

Girardeau, F. L. & Spradlin, J. E. Token Rewards in a Cottage Program. *Mental Retardation Journal*, 1964, *2*, 345-351.

Glaser, R. Toward a Behavioral Science Base for Instructional Design. In R. Glaser (Ed.) *Teaching Machines and Programmed Learning, II: Data and Directions.* Department of Audio-Visual Instruction National Education Association of the United States, 1965.

Glaser, R. Educational Technology as Instructional Design. *Educational Technology*, 1968, *8*, 1, 5-6.

Haring, N. G. *Attending and Responding.* San Rafael, California: Dimensions, 1968.

Haring, N. G. The Application of Functional Analysis of Behavior by Teachers in a Natural School Setting. Final report, U. S. Department of Health, Education, and Welfare, Office of Education, Bureau of Research (Grant No. OEG-0-8-070376-1857-032), 1969.

Haring, N. G. Experimental Education: Application of Experimental Analysis and Principles of Behavior to Classroom Instruction. In C. Rickard (Ed.) *Unique Programs in Special Education.* London: Pergamon, 1970.

Haring, N. G. & Hauck, M. A. Improved Learning Conditions in the Establishment of Reading Skills with Disabled Readers. *Exceptional Children*, 1969, *35*, 341-352.

Haring, N. G. & Hayden, A. H. The Contributions of the Experimental Education Unit to the Expanding Role of Instruction. *College of Education Record*, 1968, *34*, 31-36.

Haring, N. G. & Kunzelmann, H. P. The Finer Focus of Therapeutic Behavioral Management. In J. Hellmuth (Ed.) *Educational Therapy* (1), Seattle: Special Child Publications, 1966.

Haring, N. G. & Lovitt, T. C. Operant Methodology and Educational Technology in Special Education. In N. G. Haring & R. Schiefelbusch (Eds.) *Methods in Special Education.* New York: McGraw-Hill, 1967, 10-48.

Haring, N. G. & Phillips, E. L. *The Analysis and Modification of Classroom Behavior.* New York: McGraw-Hill, in press.

Heinich, R. Educational Technology as Technology. *Educational Technology*, 1968, *8*, 1, 4.

Herman, D. Now It's Hard to Keep Them Away from the Terminals When It's Not Their Turn. *Educational Media*, 1969, *1*, 4-7.

Hewett, F. M. Educational Engineering with Emotionally Disturbed Children. *Exceptional Children*, 1967, *33*, 459-467.

Hewett, F. M. *The Emotionally Disturbed Child in the Classroom.* Boston: Allyn & Bacon, 1968.

Hickey, A. E. *Computer Assisted Instruction: A Survey of the Literature.* Newburyport, Massachusetts: Entelek, 1968.

Homme, L. E., Csanyi, A. P., Gonzales, M. A. & Rechs, J. R. *How to Use Contingency Contracting in the Classroom.* Champaign, Illinois: Research Press, 1969.

Honig, W. K. *Operant Behavior: Areas of Research and Application.* New York: Appleton-Century-Crofts, 1966.

Jerman, M. & Suppes P. Some Perspectives on Computer Assisted Instruction. *Educational Media,* 1969, *1,* 4-7.

Joyce, B. R. The Development of Teaching Strategies. *Audiovisual Instruction,* 1969, *13,* 820-827.

Kelley, G. B. Technological Advances Affecting School Instructional Materials Center. *Audiovisual Instruction,* 1969, *14,* 42-48.

King, W. H. The Emerging Role of the Instructional Materials Specialist. *Audiovisual Instruction,* 1969, *14,* 27-28.

Kraft, R. H. & Latta, R. F. Systems Engineering Techniques: Embarrassment or Opportunity for Today's Educators. *Educational Technology,* 1969, *9,* 9, 26-30.

Lang, P. J. The On-Line Computer in Behavior Therapy Research. *The American Psychologist,* 1969, *24,* 236-239.

Lange, P. C. *Programmed Instruction.* The Sixty-Sixth Yearbook of the National Society for the Study of Education. Chicago: University of Chicago Press, 1967.

Lindsley, O. R. Direct Measurement and Prosthesis of Retarded Behavior. *Journal of Education,* 1964, *147,* 62-81.

Lindsley, O. R. Experimental Analysis of Cooperation and Competition. In T. Verhave (Ed.) *The Experimental Analysis of Behavior.* New York: Appleton-Century-Crofts, 1966, 470-501.

Lovitt, T. C. Free-Operant Preference for One of Two Stories: A Methodological Note. *Journal of Educational Psychology,* 1967, *58,* 84-87.

Lumsdaine, A. A. Assessing the Effectiveness of Instructional Programs. In R. J. Glaser (Ed.) *Teaching Machines and Programmed Learning, II: Data and Directions.* Department of Audiovisual Instruction, National Education Association of the United States, 1965.

Mager, R. F. *Preparing Instructional Objectives.* Palo Alto: Fearon, 1962.

Markle, S. M. Empirical Testing of Programs. In P. C. Lange (Ed.) *Programmed Instruction.* The Sixty-Sixth Yearbook of the National Society for the Study of Education. Chicago: University of Chicago Press, 1967, 104-138.

McIntyre, K. Media Systems and the Handicapped Child. *Audiovisual Instruction,* 1969, *14,* 21-23.

McNeil, J. D. Forces Influencing Curriculum. *Review of Educational Research,* 1969, *39,* 293-318.

Mithaug, D. E. The Development of Cooperation in Alternative Task Situations. *Journal of Experimental Child Psychology* (In Press.) (a)

Mithaug. D. E. A Functional Analysis of Cooperation, Competition and Exchange: Some Suggestions for Theoretical Linkages Between Processes. *Journal of Experimental Child Psychology* (In Press). (b)

Moore, O. K. *Autotelic Responsive Environments and Exceptional*

Children. Hamden, Connecticut: Responsive Environments Foundation, Inc., 1963.

Mowrer, D. E. The Language of Behavioral Engineering. *Educational Technology,* 1969, *9,* 8, 34-36.

Nolen, P. A., Kunzelmann, H. P. & Haring, N. G. Behavioral Modification in a Junior High Learning Disabilities Classroom. *Exceptional Children,* 1967, *34,* 163-168.

Ofiesh, G. D. A National Center for Educational Media and Materials for the Handicapped. *Audiovisual Instruction,* 1969, *14,* 28-29.

Ofiesh, G. D. Tomorrow's Educational Engineers. *Educational Technology,* 1968, *8,* 13, 5-10.

Owen, F. W. & Compton, C. L. The Learning Centers in Palo Alto. *Journal of Learning Disabilities,* 1968, *1,* 36-43.

Patterson, G. R. & Reid, J. B. Reciprocity and Coercion: Two Facets of Social Systems. In C. Neuringer & J. Michael (Eds.) *Behavior Modification in Clinical Psychology.* New York: Appleton-Century-Crofts, 1969, in press.

Pembroke, B. R. Computers in the Classroom. *Scholastic Teacher,* May, 1968, 14-15.

Pfau, G. S. Programmed Instruction: An Exploration into Its Effectiveness with the Handicapped Child. *Audiovisual Instruction,* 1969, *14,* 24-27.

Pines, M. What the Talking Typewriter Says. *New York Times Magazine,* May 9, 1965.

Quay, H. C., Werry, J. S., McQueen, M. & Sprague, R. L. Remediation of the Conduct Problem Child in the Special Class Setting. *Exceptional Children,* 1966, *32,* 509-515.

Robertson, T. F. The New Impact: Technology in Education. In N. G. Haring & A. H. Hayden (Eds.) *Instructional Improvement: Behavior Modification.* Proceedings of Workshop at Western Washington State Hospital, 1969.

Saettler, P. Instructional Technology: Some Concerns and Desiderata. *AV Communication Review,* 1969, *17,* 357-367.

Sidman, M. *Tactics of Scientific Research.* New York: Basic Books, 1960.

Silberberg, N. E. & Silberberg, M. C. The Bookless Curriculum: An Educational Alternative. *Journal of Learning Disabilities,* 1969, *2,* 9-14.

Silverman, R. E. Two Kinds of Technology. *Educational Technology,* 1968, *8,* 1, 10.

Singer, I. J. Media and the Ghetto School. *Audiovisual Instruction,* 1968, *13,* 860-864.

Skinner, B. F. What Is the Experimental Analysis of Behavior? *Journal of the Experimental Analysis of Behavior,* 1965, *9,* 213-218.

Skinner, B. F. *The Technology of Teaching.* New York: Appleton-Century-Crofts, 1968.

Soeffing, M.   The CEC Information Center on Exceptional Children. *Audiovisual Instruction,* 1969, *14,* 42-43.

Stolurow, L. M.   Model the Master Teacher or Master the Teaching Model. In J. D. Krumboltz (Ed.) *Learning and the Educational Process.* Chicago: Rand McNally, 1965.

Stolurow, L. M.   Programmed Instruction and Teaching Machines. In P. H. Rossi & B. J. Biddle (Eds.) *The New Media and Education: Their Impact on Society.* Garden City, New York: Doubleday, 1967, 136-192.

Stolurow, L. M. & Davis, D.   Teaching Machines and Computer-Based Systems. In R. Glaser (Ed.) *Teaching Machines and Programmed Learning, II: Data and Directions.* Department of Audiovisual Instruction, National Education Asociation of the United States, 1965.

Suppes, P.   Computer Assisted Instruction. *Nation's Schools,* 1968, *82,* 52-53, 96.

Suppes, P. & Morningstar, M.   Computer Assisted Instruction. *Science,* 1969, *166,* 343- 350.

Tyler, V. O. & Brown, G. D.   The Use of Swift, Brief Isolation as a Group Control Device for Institutionalized Delinquents. *Behavior Research and Therapy,* 1967, *3,* 1-9.

Ullmann, L. P. & Krasner, L.   *Case Studies in Behavior Modification.* New York: Holt, Rinehart & Winston, 1965.

University of Washington Summer Computer Assisted Instruction Project. Report by the Experimental Education Unit of the Child Development and Mental Retardation Center, University of Washington (Title VI-A Project), 1969.

Watson, P. G.   Instructional Strategies and Learning Systems. *Audiovisual Instruction,* 1968, *13,* 841-846.

Weisberger, R. A. & Rahmlow, H. F.   Individually Managed Learning. *Audiovisual Instruction,* 1968, *13,* 835-839.

Wolf, M. M., Giles, D. & Hall, R. V.   Experiments with Token Reinforcement in a Remedial Classroom. *Behavior Research and Therapy,* 1968, *6,* 51-64.

Wolpe, J.   *Psychotherapy by Reciprocal Inhibition.* London: Oxford University Press, 1958.

Wood, E. K.   Potbellied Stoves, VTRs and Electronic Hardware. *Audiovisual Instruction,* 1969, *14,* 44-47.

Wyman, R.   A Visual Response System for Small-Group Interaction. *Audiovisual Media: International Review,* 1969, *3,* 21-25.

Zaslav, S. S., & Frazier, R. I.   The ERE and the Disabled Reader. *Journal of Learning Disabilities,* 1969, *2,* 48-49.

12

Innovations in the Elementary School Curriculum

Henry J. Otto

As the writer pondered the task of preparing this paper, several questions came to mind. What is an *innovation?* Are innovations something entirely new and different or merely noticeable modifications of some former practice? Are innovations to be identified by what one reads in the professional literature or by what one can observe in school and classroom practices? If innovation is mere change, in what ways, if any, have the objectives and content of children's classroom activities changed in the last 40 to 50 years? What has been the lasting impact of the major curriculum movements of the 20th century? What recent curriculum movements are affecting the elementary school? What *curriculum* changes are implied in *organizational* changes? What

---

HENRY J. OTTO is professor of educational administration at the University of Texas at Austin.

are the present cross currents which impinge upon the elementary school?

Not all of these questions can be answered to everyone's satisfaction in a short paper, but the writer has attempted to make some observations and statements without undue overlap with the other papers in this collection or the extensive literature on educational change.[1,2,3] Perhaps it is well to define innovation as a dichotomy to include major change in an existing practice as well as the addition of something new or the complete elimination of a pre-existing practice. The initial use of a motion picture or an overhead projection to bring broader content or a clearer understanding of a topic already being taught represents a major change in content and method. If a school already offered science on a regular schedule and then adopted one of the new elementary science programs it would represent a major change in an existing practice. The addition of a foreign language to the program or the elimination of school banking as a weekly activity would illustrate the second meaning of innovation. Our literature is generally very unclear when the word *innovation* is used. Presumably it is legitimate to identify innovations from two sources, the professional literature (including courses of study) and actual practices in the schools. Again, the professional literature has left us confused about the sources used when innovations are discussed. Both sources of information may be valuable, but each author should identify the source of his information.

Have Objectives and Content Changed?

Since textbooks remain as the heart of the instructional program, it is clear that content has changed to the degree at least that textbooks have been updated over the years. Updating of content does not necessarily mean a change in goals sought in the instructional program, nor does it result in a change in the subjects offered. Except for the addition of foreign language in some elementary schools, there has been no change in the subject offering in elementary schools since physical and health education were added in the 1920's.

As a matter of fact, if the criterion for judgment is what actually transpires in classrooms, there is precious little information to tell us whether objectives and content have changed during the past 50 years. No one has ever attempted to provide comprehensive data, even on a representative sample basis, of instruction in elementary schools as it actually takes place. No doubt an important reason for this absence of information is the lack of proper research tools for gathering such data. Some writers have given us glimpses of what actually happens in classrooms, but such accounts are usually limited to one school, such as the reports of Collings (1923),[4] Washburne (1932, 1963),[5] Clapp (1939),[6] and Cunningham (1946),[7] whereas others are limited to a few classrooms in one or several schools, as reported by Flanders (1964),[8] Bellack (1966),[9] and Jackson (1968).[10] To anyone who is familiar with what went on in elementary schools 40 years ago and with what goes on in such schools today, it seems clear that much change has taken place — but we cannot document the characteristics of those changes. To the writer it also seems evident that the undocumented changes are areas of school operation, pupil services, teacher-pupil relations, etc., and *not in the basic objectives and subject offerings of the schools.*

There have been two major pronouncements on objectives within the past 30 years. *The Purposes of Education in American Democracy* appeared in 1938[11] and *Elementary School Objectives* was published in 1953.[12] Both statements say about the same things; both are cast in general performance or behavioral language, and both had wide reproduction in professional books. There is no way of knowing to what extent either statement has influenced what actually happens in elementary school classrooms. Chances are that tradition and local community pressures have had more influence over school practices than these national pronouncements. Lee theorized, however, that the teacher's role and the teacher's behavior were being influenced by current changes in education.[13] He saw three crucial respects in which educational goals can be seen to be in transition: (1) the change from personal aims and needs of students toward meeting the broader national needs; (2) from the broad commitment to the psychosocial development of pupils to the cultivation of intellectual power and the understanding of the disciplines; and (3) from a conception of education as having a fixed beginning or end to education as continuous and endless and thus replacing the notion of "third grade arithmetic" or "freshman English." Based upon his goal changes, Lee projected three important changes in teacher behavior: (1) from the pluralistic to the singular — from the diversified to the specialized, with increasing stress on knowledge and mastery of subject matter; (2) away from the teacher being a source of data and a dispenser of knowledge to a growing stress upon "learning how to learn" and a catalyst in stimulating the urge to inquire and the oversight of student effort; and (3) from a didactic to a tutorial role.

The writer has grave doubts about the extent to which the changes Lee mentioned have actually modified classroom practices in the majority of elementary schools in 1970 from what they were in the 1950's. If the neglect of individual differences, pupil psychosocial needs, and the implied emphasis on academic performance had actually taken place, the percentage of non-promoted pupils should have increased (which it did not), the percent of the eligible age group entering high school should have decreased (the opposite happened), and the percentage of the eligible age group graduating from high school should have decreased (the opposite happened). Other forces have been at work to contravene the impact of theoretical considerations.

The Impact of Previous Curriculum Movements

One way of assessing the long term impact of current curriculum movements is to examine what happened to earlier ones. Several such efforts can be scrutinized. During the 1920's and 1930's, there was much ado about character education.[1] No one knows how extensively this movement permeated school programs, but the topic has been ignored in the literature since the 1930's. If schools had taken the idea seriously and stuck with an effective program, some of the current societal turmoil might have been avoided.

The activity movement had its heyday in the 1920's and 1930's.[15] This movement, indirectly sponsored by the Progressive Education Association, contained many excellent educational ideas which some groups are now trying to recapture. The idea of the pupil being actively engaged in purposeful enterprises, teacher-pupil planning, provision for individual differences, and diversified learning activities caught the imagination of teachers, particularly in the primary grades. Many misunderstood and misused the idea, but many of the inherent tenets of the activity concept can be found in elementary schools today. The movement, as a broad curriculum plan, fell into disrepute under the onslaught of post-World War II critics of public education.[16]

The mental health movement began in the 1930's.[17] It had some precedents in the activity movement and the earlier concern for adapting instruction to individual differences. The theme was sustained during the 1940's and 1950's by forces outside of the education field, such as the growing burden on public funds to support the number of adults who had to be institutionalized, the increasing number of adolescent suicides, and the expanding role of psychiatry as a branch of medicine. The concept of dealing with "the whole child" helped schools to maintain a continuing interest in children with problems; a disturbed child could not be expected to be a good student. The movement received a major boost in Title I of the Elementary and Secondary Education Act, with its provision for the employment by the schools of psychologists, counselors and home visitors or school social workers. The concern of schools for children's mental health as well as that of teachers is undoubtedly greater now than it was in the 1930's

In chronological sequences, the interest in intercultural education should be considered next. It began in the late 1930's, then lost a place of prominence in the professional literature during the 1950's, but again appeared with vigor after the Civil Rights Act of 1964.[18] Intercultural, intergroup and interracial education are all in the same vein, and their neglect by the public, the labor unions, and by the schools prior to 1960 may be an important cause behind present civil turmoil. Now, many groups are trying to lock the barn after the horse has disappeared. New approaches and greater vigor characterize the current methods of dealing with the problem. The importance as well as the neglect of broadly based social education in elementary schools brought two books into the market.[19] Both books were intended as texts for college courses and inservice teacher education programs. The fact that neither book sold enough copies to justify its publication attests to the low level of interest by professionals in this area. By 1957 the public and school people were striving for academic supermen who could match scientific progress being made in the Soviet Union.

During World War II there was a tremendous scramble for nutrition education in the schools, but not much has been heard about this since 1950; except in so far as adequate food for children of indigent parents became institutionalized in the school milk program and in the Elementary and Secondary Education Act. Conservation education had about the same fate. It was highlighted during the late 1940's and the early 1950's.[20] No one knows how much of the latter two movements ever penetrated into classroom programs, but both seem to have been forgotten in the professional literature, as leaders in the field struggle with the structure of the disciplines and discovery learning.

The community school concept, like nutrition and conservation education, emerged during the 1940's and remained alive in the literature into the early 1950's.[21] The idea was not a new curriculum for the schools, but a major departure in the way the school program would be related to community resources and problems and thereby bringing parents into close working relations with the efforts of the schools. Field trips, the use of resource persons, and joint involvement of pupils, teachers and parents in community improvement projects were stressed. The basic idea was to build many bridges between the school and the community to achieve a "community oneness" in the education of children and youth. There are no data to show how extensively individual schools or whole school systems adopted the full concept, but one result was the expanded use of field trips and, to a much lesser degree, the use of parents as resource persons in the instructional program.

Currently, parent participation in school affairs is again in the limelight, but the concept has new dimensions. Instead of the school staff seeking parent participation, the parents are demanding a decisive role in school affairs.[22] In the Ocean Hill-Brownsville decentralization experiment in New York City, the local school board in this disadvantaged area would have the power to determine educational policy, to allocate school funds, and to hire and dismiss teachers. The parent role now calls for jurisdiction over the curriculum, demanding that the latter be made relevant to the backgrounds and problems of disadvantaged students. The guidelines for Head Start classes require a parent advisory committee and that parents be employed as teacher aides.

The most important and the most lasting curriculum movement during the past 50 years has been the concern for more adequate provisions for individual differences among pupils. This movement has had a long history, starting with the St. Louis quarterly promotion plan (1862) designed to save time for repeaters, followed by the Pueblo Plan (1888), the Cambridge Plan (1893), the Batavia Plan for coaching laggards (1898), the Santa Barbara Concentric Plan (1898), Burk's Individualized Instruction (1913), the Dalton and Winnetka Plans in 1919, and then Detroit's X-Y-Z Grouping Scheme (1919). No major movements can be identified with the concept of adapting instruction to individual differences until the mid-50's epidemic to provide special schools and classes for academically talented pupils.[23]

During the interim between 1920 and the early 1950's, several other developments ensued which gave a continuing thrust to the importance of adapting instruction to individual differences.[24] Special classes for all types of exceptional children were expanding in the larger school systems; the activity and mental health movements made their contributions; and intraclass grouping became popular, at least in the primary grades.

Currently the movement to adapt instruction to individual differences is very much alive. It is emphasized in the literature dealing with education of disadvantaged students, in team teaching, in nongraded programs, and in programmed instruction.

There is an important difference in the emphasis on how and what to individualize in these several movements. The emphasis in most programs for the disadvantaged calls for major changes in content, method, and even some change in objectives. Some of the same emphases are found in the literature on nongradedness although nongraded ideas to date have concentrated largely on teaching the conventional program better. Team teaching and programmed instruction attempt to modify rate and amount learned in the conventional offering.

If professional literature is used as the basis for appraising the survival of the curriculum movements described in the preceding paragraphs, the result probably is as follows: There is no evidence of important changes over the past 30 years in objectives and content, except through updating the content of textbooks and whatever change may grow out of the new urge to provide special programs for the disadvantaged. Character, nutrition and conservation education have lost their appeal as special emphases or programs. Intercultural education was lost as foreign language in the elementary school became the dominant interest. A cycle has been completed from high interest to low or no interest to high interest in the activity movement, the community school concept, and adaptation of instruction to individual differences; each of these is now very much alive, with new dimensions.

If comprehensive data on what actually transpires or has transpired in the past in elementary school classrooms are used as the basis for describing trends, one is left without any answers. Such data simply are not available. Visits to schools then and now make it evident that schools are not like they were 40 years ago, but the differences are due to the way children are viewed, understood, treated and accommodated in the school organization. The differences do not lie in the goals sought in the instructional program. The 3 R's, science, social studies, physical education and the fine arts still constitute the scheduled offering. It is unlikely that these basic components of the elementary school curriculum will change in the foreseeable future. The specific objectives sought within each are now under consideration by various groups.

New Curriculum Revision Movements

Physical education underwent a major revision during the past 15 years. In 1955, for the first time in our national history, physical fitness became a national concern of top government officials in peacetime.[25] In 1956, the President's Council on Youth Fitness was appointed by President Eisenhower. The movement was encouraged by subsequent Presidents, was renamed the "President's Council on Physical Fitness and Sports" and in 1967 became an agency in the Department of Health, Education, and Welfare. In 1967, this Council published a revision of its 1961 edition of *Youth Physical Fitness*. This publication, since its first edition, has provided the basis for improved school programs in physical education. The American Association for Health, Physical Education, and Recreation published and standardized a physical performance test; California published its own Physical Performance Test for California. Only meager data are available regarding the introduction of a systematic program of physical fitness exercises into elementary school physical education programs. No doubt the introduction of this new emphasis in physical education has been widespread in school systems, with professionally alert supervisors and special teachers of physical education.

Systematic instruction in one or more foreign languages in public elementary schools began in the 1950's, the movement being spearheaded by the Modern Language Association. Some foreign language has been taught in some elementary schools, mostly private, for many years, but the current movement was aimed at all elementary schools, particularly the public schools. Whether offering instruction in a foreign language represents a clear-cut addition to the school program depends on the administrative arrangements. It cannot be considered an addition to the regular offering if classes are scheduled before or after school hours on a fee basis. Most school systems that have added instruction in a foreign language have placed it within the regular school day. Itinerant native speakers of the language being offered or instruction via television have been the prevalent methods. Some of the states with state adopted textbooks have added texts in the foreign language to the state adopted list. The conflicts associated with this offering will be discussed in a later section of this paper.

The movement to add sex education to the health education program in grades 5 or 6 or in the junior high school developed during the 1960's. Various approaches are being tried in different school systems, but as yet there is no general acceptance of the idea. There is much controversy among parents as to whether this is a function of the school or the home as well as over the what and the how of such instruction if the school is to do something about this problem. Here, apparently, the need for sex education has grown out of societal problems and at least some segments of society are turning to the schools to solve the problem through education.

The most dramatic, and perhaps the most controversial, curriculum movements reside in the efforts by many groups to restructure the content of existing subjects and to add content from heretofore neglected fields. These new remodeling programs affecting the elementary school include five in mathematics (including computer-based instruction at Stanford University), three in science, five in the social studies (including one in anthropology and two in economics), two in English, one in music, and one in health education. Each of these programs is described at some length by Goodlad and his associates and will not be elaborated upon here.[26] These several programs can best be described by quoting from *The Changing School Curriculum*. Goodlad and associates state, "If previous eras of curriculum development can be described as child centered or society centered, this one can be described as subject or discipline centered. The ends and means of schooling are derived from organized bodies of knowledge. Further, the curriculum is planned by physicists, mathematicians and historians, and students are encouraged to think like these scholars. The word 'structure' has replaced 'the whole child' in curriculum jargon . . . The current curriculum movement is marked by an updating of content, a reorganization of subject matter, and some fresh approaches to methodology in fields traditionally taught in the schools."

New hope appears to be on the horizon for success in school for non-English-speaking beginners, most of whom come from disadvantaged homes. Several Early Childhood Education Centers have been established to test various approaches to the education of children between the ages of two and five. At least two of the regional laboratories are developing and field-testing bilingual materials and teacher-guides so that non-English-speaking five- and six-year-olds can be taught in their native language as well as in English. The most extensive activity in this field is being carried forward by the Southwest Educational Development Laboratory, with headquarters in Austin, Texas.

Curriculum Changes Implied in Organizational Changes

From the early beginnings in St. Louis in 1862 to the present, the favorite method for achieving school improvement has been to make organizational changes. Witness the cyclic favor for multiple-track plans, special classes of all kinds, ability or achievement grouping, departmentalization, vestibule classes, and after school or Saturday programs. Now, we have a revival of some of these, in the form of team teaching, nongradedness, departmentalization, a longer school year, and a longer school day. Each of these is discussed briefly in terms of their implications for curriculum change.

The theorists who advocate team teaching do not mention curriculum change. Their arguments are based upon better use of faculty talents, large group, small group, and individualized instruction, resulting in more effective instruction and more learning by pupils in the subjects already being offered. But if genuine individualization of instruction and learning are to take place, there must be differentiation of objectives, content and materials. To date, no reliable research data are available regarding the merits claimed for team teaching or the resulting academic progress of students who have been taught by teacher teams over a period of three or more years. Neither are there any comparative data on the relative effectiveness of different patterns of team organization or the extent to which objectives and content are modified for different groups of pupils.

The idea of inter-grade grouping of pupils for various components of the instructional program is as "old as the hills." The concept was revived with new dimensions when the first edition of the Goodlad and Anderson book appeared in 1959.[27] Since then many others have published books on nongradedness. Nearly all writers agree that the chief purpose of a nongraded program is greater provision for individual differences, thus providing each pupil with tasks with which he can expect to be successful, can make steady forward progress without time or other pressures, and therefore enjoy better mental health and less school anxiety. Nongradedness is an empty shibboleth unless it is accompanied by extensive procedures for adapting instruction to individual differences. Genuine nongradedness, if it is applied to all or most of the curriculum areas, forces a revision of such other facets of internal organization of the school as policies and practices in grouping pupils, the use of basal texts and other instructional resources, marking and reporting to parents, and the basic philosophy undergirding the program of the elementary school. Although the authors of books on nongrading in the elementary school say little about the implications for curriculum change, it seems clear that genuine nongradedness cannot avoid some differentiation of content and materials and the expectations for pupils of different abilities. The underlying philosophy of a school program which embraces the elements of the so-called Procrustean Bed cannot accommodate nongradedness.

Nongradedness has acquired so many different meanings that it is impossible to know to what extent nongradedness in the true sense has been developed in the elementary schools of this country. Various versions of it have no doubt been incorporated in a good many schools, judging by the number of national, regional and state conferences at which special sections have been scheduled since 1962.

The confusion in the definition of nongradedness is also responsible, at least in part, for the conflicting findings of research. Approximately 40 evaluation studies have been reported in the literature. In some studies the findings favor the nongraded program; in others the graded classes are favored; whereas the majority of the studies show no difference in children's achievement or mental health among pupils in graded and nongraded classes.[28]

As part of the zeal for higher pupil achievement, the past ten years have seen more attention in the literature to departmentalization in the elementary school. This interest accompanied the agitation for better academic preparation and more academic specialization in teacher education programs, and certification requirement changes to force these changes in preparation programs. Only very meager data are available for ascertaining whether schools actually responded to the pronouncements in the literature.[29] Recent research confirms the findings of earlier studies: there is no difference.[30] The curricular corollary of departmentalization is subjects taught in isolation from each other, the abbreviated or non-use of unit method, and usually a great reduction of community resources in the instructional program. Theoretically departmentalization is a perfect match for "the structure of the disciplines" approach to the selection of content, but may at the same time crimp the chances of utilizing the accompanying desire for "discovery learning" and "problem solving" methods.

The forces that were pushing for greater adaptation of instruction to individual differences were also encouraging extension of ability and/or achievement grouping, with its accompanying multiple track program. The curriculum implications are similar to the ones discussed under meeting individual differences. The findings of former studies comparing children's achievement under ability vs. heterogeneous grouping schemes have been re-affirmed in recent research: there is very little if any difference.[31]

Part of the campaign for greater academic achievement by students included recommendations for a longer school day and a longer school year. No data are available on how many school districts lengthened the school year, but a study by the American Association of School Administrators and the Research Division of the National Education Association, involving reports from 326 school systems with enrollments of 12,000 or more, concluded with the comment that there was no trend in the direction of a longer school day. In fact, the majority figures showed no change since 1958-9. Only 77 out of the 326 districts had reported an increase, the average being 30 minutes per day.[32] This report said nothing about what the schools did with the extra time added to the length of the school day; hence no conclusions can be drawn about curriculum changes, although one would anticipate that an additional 30 to 60 minutes per day might open up the possibility for many kinds of curriculum change.

Cross Currents

Today, as in any era of change, there are many disagreements about what the schools should teach. Goodlad has been a consistent observer and critic of what is happening in the current curriculum revision movement. His main concern has been over the new discipline-centered approaches. In 1966, he commented on the potential imbalance in the curriculum.[33] Since science and mathematics had assumed priorities, would the social studies, humanities and the arts be squeezed into a secondary role? Would the many separate disciplines result in a piecemeal curriculum? What will happen if those subjects not included now, such as anthropology, economics and psychology, were to be added to the elementary school curriculum? At present, there is little effort to synthesize or merge content from related subjects; in fact, synthesis is anathema to the scholars who are now writing programs. He also called attention to the fact that federal influence has increased in recent years over what children and youth will study in school.

In 1968, Goodlad described important differences between former and present curriculum revision periods.[34] Using the period from 1930 to about 1950 as the first era and from 1950 to 1968 as the second era, he called attention to several differences. He complained that no group in the latter era is seriously discussing the commonplaces which ought to be in the curriculum. The earlier era had a political orientation, geared to the improvement of local communities and society as a whole; the latter era focuses on knowledge of subject matter. During the former era, curriculum revision was treated at the ideological level, the role of the school in society, the improvement of man himself, mental health, character and personality; not so in the recent era. During the first era, rigid programs based on textbooks were frowned upon; flexibility and teacher-pupil planning, and unit method were encouraged. Now the scholars prepare fully-packaged teacher-proof materials for use in classrooms and thereby bypass the curriculum-making role of state departments, local school districts and the individual school.

But there are other issues. The discipline-centered programs recommend inductive method, problem-solving, discovery learning, pupil manipulation of realia, and pupil experimentation. This kind of teaching takes time. How many subjects can be taught this way in a school day? Will half the school day be devoted to inductive method in two subjects and the remainder of the time assigned to the remaining subjects taught by deductive method and rote learning? Can inductive procedures be used successfully in a departmentalized program or under team teaching? To date there has been little discussion of the relationship between the new programs and the organization for instruction.

Programmed learning raises several questions. Can the inductive method, as recommended, be written or computerized successfully for individual learning? How much of a school day can a 6-year-old or an 11-year-old be expected to work diligently with individualized learning materials? Will programmed learning function satisfactorily under departmentalization or team teaching? If the new programs call for specialization in teachers, the latter questions raise all kinds of issues for the principal who must institute the best organization for accomplishing the accepted educational methodologies.

The last word has not yet been heard about the curriculum-decision roles of nationally supported groups and local boards. The potential conflict here is highlighted by the demands of parents in disadvantaged neighborhoods. The issue is twofold. Who shall be the final decision-makers? Shall the curriculum be oriented to the backgrounds, problems and aspirations of students or be devoted to "knowing the disciplines" and "how scholars work?" The latter issue was highlighted in the Ocean Hill-Brownsville area of New York City, and is evident in noticeably different programs for the disadvantaged. For example, Bereiter and Englemann recommend a highly structured daily and weekly program for removing the language deficiency of disadvantaged preschool children, even to the point of omitting the other usual activities found in a program for 4- and 5-year-olds.[35] Their goal is to remove the language deficiency and thereby prepare these pupils for successful participation in the school programs. Fantini and Weinstein, on the other hand, are strong for a curriculum oriented to the local situation and societal improvement.[36] A few quotations will clarify their position. "Education is being viewed increasingly in society as the instrument for social renewal for developnig the Great Society" (p. 151). "The first step in exchanging the uniform curriculum for one which matches pupil reality is to move from a pre-packaged, rigidly scheduled and uniform curriculum to one flexible enough to be geared to the unique needs of individual schools within a system" (p. 340). "Too often teachers assume that the words they use are related to the child's world, when, in truth, they have little or no relationship to him . . . The cardinal rule could be 'Experience first; we'll talk later' " (p. 347). "The real difference between this approach and older ones is that in a social-action curriculum actual participation — rather than mere awareness — is the key" (p. 357). The ideologies of George S. Counts, Harold Rugg and the Progressive Education Association of the 1930's are cast in new garments in the Fantini and Weinstein recommendations.

Except in special instances, the general curriculum of the public schools has never been related directly to current social problems or the community. An exception existed for those fortunate enough to participate in certain vocational education courses. In view of present student unrest and disenchantment with an irrelevant curriculum, what chance for survival will the new discipline-centered programs have?

Two final questions. What effect will discipline-centered prepackaged programs and programmed courses have upon the creativity and unique talents of individual teachers and the teachers' struggle to achieve true professional status? What will happen to students?

Some Concluding Observations

A broad look at current activities aimed at revision of the elementary school curriculum provides several generalizations. The activities are numerous, diverse, uncoordinated, and frequently in conflict with each other regarding method, content and goals. All seek to improve teaching and learning in subject fields already being offered in the elementary school. The societal climate for school improvement is strong. Hence, several programs are likely to emerge in each subject area, each different from the others although not necessarily better than the others. It is too early to know which programs will emerge as the most chosen ones, but *none* will be a panacea. It is unfortunate that human relations and citizenship continue to be the neglected fields.

REFERENCES

1. *The Changing American School.* Sixty-fifth Yearbook of the National Society for the Study of Education, Part II. Chicago: The University of Chicago Press, 1966.
2. Lawrence A. Cremin. *The Transformation of the Schools.* New York: Alfred A. Knopf, 1961.
3. Curriculum. *Review of Educational Research,* Vol. 39, No. 3, June 1969. In particular Chapter 1 by Arno A. Bellack and Chapter 6 by John I. Goodlad.
4. Ellsworth Collings. *An Experiment with a Project Curriculum.* New York: The Macmillan Co., 1923.
5. Carleton Washburne. *Adjusting the School to the Child.* New York: World Book Company, 1932, and Washburne and Marland, *Winnetka.* Englewood Cliffs, N. J.: Prentice Hall, 1963.
6. Elsie R. Clapp. *Community Schools in Action.* New York: Viking Press, 1939.
7. Ruth Cunningham. The Importance of People, a series of interesting narratives about teachers, pupils and teaching published in *Educational Leadership,* Vol. 4, during 1946.
8. Ned A. Flanders. *Interaction Analysis in the Classroom,* Ann

Arbor, Michigan: University of Michigan, School of Education, Revised edition, 1964.

8a. James R. Campbell & Cyrus W. Barnes. Interaction Analysis: A Breakthrough? *Phi Delta Kappan, 50:*587-591, June, 1968.

9. Arno A. Bellack *et al. The Language of the Classroom.* New York: Teachers College Press, Columbia University, 1966.

10. Phillp W. Jackson. *Life in Classrooms.* New York: Holt, Rinehart and Winston, 1968.

11. Educational Policies Commission. *The Purposes of Education in American Democracy.* Washington: National Education Association, 1938.

12. Nolan C. Kearney. *Elementary School Objectives.* New York: Russell Sage Foundation, 1953.

13. Gordon C. Lee. The Changing Role of the Teacher. Chapter 1 in *The Changing American School, op cit.,* pp. 20-25.

14a. Hugh Hartshore. *Studies in the Nature of Character* (Character Education Inquiry). New York: The Macmillan Co., 1928.

14b. Howard V. Meredith. *A Brief History of Character Education.* Iowa City, Iowa: University of Iowa Extension Bulletin No. 290, 1932.

14c. Kenneth L. Heaton. *The Character Emphasis in Education.* Chicago: University of Chicago Press, 1933.

15. *The Activity Movement.* Thirty-third Yearbook, Part II, National Society for the Study of Education. Chicago: The University of Chicago Press, 1934.

16a. Bernard I. Bell. *Crisis in Education.* New York: Whittlesey House, 1949.

16b. Mortimer Smith. *And Madly Teach.* Chicago: R. Regney Co., 1949.

16c. David Hulburd. *This Happened in Pasadena.* New York: The Macmillan Co., 1951.

17a. W. C. Ryan. *Mental Health Through Education.* New York: The Commonwealth Fund, 1938.

17b. Paul A. Witty & C. E. Skinner. *Mental Hygiene in Modern Edution.* New York: Farrar and Rinehart, 1939.

17c. *Mental Health in the Classroom.* Thirteenth Yearbook, Department of Supervisors and Directors of Instruction. Washington: National Education Association, 1940.

18a. William E. Vickery & Stewart G. Cole. *Intercultural Education in American Schools.* New York: Harper and Brothers, 1943.

18b. Celia B. Stendler & William E. Martin. *Intergroup Education in Kindergarten-Primary Grades.* New York: The Macmillan Co., 1953.

19a. Henry J. Otto. *Social Education in Elementary Schools.* New York: Rinehart and Co., 1956.

19b. Alice Miel & Peggy Brogan. *More than the Social Studies.* Englewood Cliffs, N. J.: Prentice Hall, 1957.

20a. *Large Was Our Bounty.* 1948 Yearbook, The Association for Supervision and Curriculum Development. Washington: National Education Assn.

20b. *Conservation Education in American Schools.* Twenty-ninth Yearbook, American Association of School Administrators. Washington: The Association, 1951.

21a. Edward G. Olsen. *School and Community* (1945) and *Community and School Programs* (1949), both published by Prentice-Hall.

21b. *The Community School.* Fifty-second Yearbook, Part II, National Society for the Study of Education. Chicago: The University of Chicago Press, 1953.

22a. Mario Fantini & Marilyn Gittell. The Ocean Hill-Brownsville Experiment. *Phi Delta Kappan, 50:*442-445, April, 1969.

22b. Irving A. Yevish. Decentralization, Discipline, and the Disadvantaged Teacher. *Phi Delta Kappan, 50:*137-138, 178-181, November, 1968.

23a. *Education for the Gifted.* Fifty-seventh Yearbook, Part II, National Society for the Study of Education. Chicago: The University of Chicago Press, 1958.

23b. Henry J. Otto, *et al. Curriculum Enrichment for Gifted Elementary School Children in Regular Classes.* Austin, Texas: The University of Texas Press, 1955.

24a. *Adapting the Schools to Individual Differences.* Twenty-fourth Yearbook, National Society for the Study of Education, Part II. Chicago: The University of Chicago Press, 1925.

24b. *Individualizing Instruction.* Sixty-first Yearbook, National Society for the Study of Education, Part I. Chicago: University of Chicago Press, 1962.

25. John E. Nixon & Ann E. Jewett. *An Introduction to Physical Education.* Philadelphia: W. B. Saunders Co., Seventh Edition, 1969, Chapter 11.

26. John I. Goodlad, *et al. The Changing School Curriculum.* New York: The Fund for the Advancement of Education, 1966.

27. John I. Goodlad & Robert H. Anderson. *The Nongraded Elementary School.* New York: Harcourt, Brace and World, Revised edition, 1963.

28. A comprehensive summary of the research may be found in Henry J. Otto *et. al. Nongradedness: An Elementary School Evaluation.* Austin, Texas: The University of Texas Press, 1969.

29. Departmentalization in Elementary Schools. *Educational Research Service Circular,* No. 7, October 1965.

30. Homer O. Elseroad. *Report on a Research on Departmentalized Organization in Grades 4-6.* Rockville, Md.: Montgomery County Public Schools, 1965.

31a. Walter R. Borg. *Ability Grouping in the Public Schools.* Madison, Wisconsin: Dembar Educational Research Services, 1966.
31b. Dorothy Westby-Gibson. *Grouping Students for Improved Instruction.* Englewood Cliffs, N. J.: Prentice-Hall, 1966.
31c. Miriam L. Goldberg, *et al. The Effects of Ability Grouping.* New York: Columbia University, Teachers College Press, 1966.
32. *Educational Research Service Circular,* No. 6, 1965.
33. John I. Goodlad *et al., op. cit.,* Sec. IV.
34. John I. Goodlad. Curricuulm: A Janus Look. *Teachers College Record, 70:*95-107, November, 1968.
35. Carl Bereiter & Siegfried Englemann. *Teaching Disadvantaged Children in the Preschool.* Englewood Cliffs, N. J.: Prentice-Hall, 1966.
36. Mario D. Fantini & Gerald Weinstein. *The Disadvantaged.* New New York: Harper and Row, 1968.

13

Poverty Children and Reading Curriculum Reform: A Broad Perspective

Carl L. Rosen

Millions of young Americans confront educational disaster as a result of school failure associated with reading underachievement. However, no other group of pupils represent a greater crisis and challenge to public education than do children from diverse poverty environments who, partially as a result of difficulties in reading, are being systematically and continuously recycled back into the same life of privation and segregation as their parents and grandparents before them. The comments and reports of massive reading retardation and school underachievement of these children are abundant.[3,4,13,18,26] Over ten million children from rural and urban poverty in thousands of towns, villages, settlements and urban ghettos across the nation — black, white, Mexican-American, Puerto Rican, Indian, etc. —

CARL L. ROSEN is professor of education at Georgia State University.

are in schools that are not providing them with appropriate educational experiences.

This paper is concerned with those children who, because of their racial, ethnic, linguistic and social class circumstances are all too often unsatisfactorily educated by a system that is not responsive to their needs. This paper is predicated on the assumption that this society and its institutions can, through change and modernity, make massive contributions to the betterment of the human condition. Middle class America must be willing to make the admissions and amends that are critical prerequisites to all citizens' obtaining the freedom and opportunity so often sloganized in our society. Educational institutions represent a primary means of achieving such freedom and opportunity.

This paper will review the traditional in education, analyze the present, and offer some considerations for future educational curriculum reforms which appear to be relevant to this topic. Within this context it should be pointed out that the difficulty is not in refraining from criticism but in being neglectful of one's conscience—and shame. It is indeed less hazardous to be loyal or silent regarding respected and hollowed public institutions than it is to be critical. The former behaviors should not necessarily be considered a greater sign of loyalty and responsibility than the latter, in spite of the ominous tenor of our times to the contrary.

The Tradition

The traditional public school has for generations perceived itself as a type of provider of a so-called free school with a common educational curriculum.[10] This type of school places the major burden of responsibility for achievement upon children, their families and the environment. If the child is willing and able to avail himself of these opportunities, he could, through educational success, so the thinking goes, move into the good life. By catching hold of this educational life-preserver, the child of poverty is considered to have been given an *opportunity* to change his circumstances. The opportunity offered by this school requires that the poverty student eventually break from his sub-culture and adjust his dress, language and behaviors to the social customs and expectations of the school, which are presented to him as being both superior to and more desirable than those of his family and community. In this manner, generations of poor children have indeed been able, partially through such schools — or perhaps in spite of them — to achieve an economically and socially superior status to that of their parents. Today some are still succeeding through such a process in improving their material standing in society. However, questions can be raised as to the price paid by such individuals and the effects of various forms of assimilation and acculturation on people and eventually on society.[19] Today, the majority of poverty children, crowded into ghetto slum schools in large urban areas or attending schools in rural poverty sections of the United States, have an infinitely more difficult state of affairs in operation. The far different past legacy of these people and the present mechanical, depersonalized and insensitive racist society perpetuates a poverty caste for people who are only a few generations removed from slavery and violent suppression.

The schools of many such children maintain educational curricula that are unilaterally decided upon and adopted via state departments of education and school district central offices. Typically universal for all children in a community, regardless of their special backgrounds or circumstances, various educational courses of study are prepared and sequenced by textbook publishers for the national market. Billions of dollars are spent on the purchase of textbooks which are rigidly utilized in standard curricula. As a result, schools today continue to confuse teaching in these programs with learning as they devote their entire day to getting young people through textbooks via guides, schedules and routines.

A term commonly used to assess the outcomes of such textbook teaching — achievement — is typically measured by a mixture of arbitrary teacher judgments in the various subject areas and administrative tinkering by means of intermittently conducted, massed standardized testing. Despite the expenses involved in such testing, little use if any is made of test results for teaching purposes. In the case of assessing reading growth and abilities, few teachers in slum schools and, for that matter, in most schools are skilled in observing and measuring the reading growth and needs of their pupils. Reading instructional approaches are all too often based exclusively upon single commercially published programs. These materials are presented according to a rigid schedule, regardless of whether the children are prepared for such an experience or sufficiently fluent and masterful enough to move on to more difficult and advanced sequences.

This system of *covering* textbook materials almost always seems to necessitate the need to eliminate, suppress, manage and control much of what constitutes healthy, natural child behavior. Activity, movement, talking and use of natural language, pupil interaction, play, curiosity and special interests must become secondary to the teacher's daily schedule of textbook consumption around the curriculum. Based on such notions as maintaining class order, discipline and teaching self-control, which some of these schools associate with patriotism and Godliness, teachers and principals frequently and sometimes crudely and brutally commit grotesquely insensitive acts. The motives of such people can range from confused and misconceived, good-intentioned paternalism to bigoted, racially and culturally superior attitudes that often mask their need to dominate, master and control other human beings. In various ways and in too many schools, children are thus forced and habituated to be silent, remain seated, look at and be interested in only that which the teacher wishes them to be concerned with and which is *on the schedule*. Behaviors divergent from expectations are perceived as being signs of basically inferior home environments or manifestations of immaturity or maladjustment. Consistent discipline and ordered and structured school days are confused by educators with regimentation, conformity and sometimes brutal suppression of the individual child's needs. The typical school sees these children as requiring such discipline.

Teachers operating in the center of activity serve a heavy educational fare from various teachers' manuals, textbooks and workbooks in the different subjects. Like priestesses, they ritualistically present the contents of these commercial materials and, like efficiency experts, learn to manage and control conditions conducive to bringing children through these materials in the allocated time. While little of what they teach seems to be learned, they continue to provide reading instruction around the use of basal reading programs with little if any divergence, creative inclusion, or individualized attention to children's personal needs. These practices constitute serious misuse of such materials. The consequences of such practices universally result in underachievement and disinterest among the children and feelings of hopelessness among teachers. Very soon these experiences lead to convictions regarding minority children's inabilities to learn that result in even *further* underachievement.

A number of basal reading programs literally blanket the nation's schools today. Many school workers have come to perceive these materials as carrying built-in assurances of linquistic, contextual and sequential infallibility. The world of basal readers is often white, neat, clean, neutral, orderly and suburban. Many questions are being raised regarding the suitability of such content for black, Puerto Rican, Mexican and Indian descended children in our society. The linguistic style of basal readers, while difficult to categorize in any manner in the earlier stages of such programs, becomes middle class English as the linguistic content matures. The possibility that various groups of poverty children might have other linguistic styles is neatly discounted by simply and prejudiciously considering such children to be linguistically immature or crippled[14,28] since they are silent or imperfect in their use of standard English in the classroom.

Introduced to the white man's or Gringo's school in such a fashion and to the process of reading in as rigid, unrealistic and inconsistent way as this, it is small wonder that poverty children seem to massively underachieve under present conditions. To explain away this situation, schools find it more convenient to deplore the home conditions of the children, which are judged by school standards and labelled as "crippling" or "deprived." Rather than objectively and dispassionately analyzing their own inadequate professional performance, many schools continue to displace responsibility or attempt to improve educational conditions in their own manner by launching all-out assaults on the behavior, customs, attitudes, language, beliefs and habits of minority children, assuming that these variables are central phenomena interfering with learning. As achievement gaps widen in the upper grades, esoteric terms such as "cumulative deficit effect" are coined and often substituted for sound objective attempts to improve conditions for learning.

In the shock over being obviously unable to succeed with poverty children, teachers sometimes bear down upon them even more heavily. Inability of the students to read with comprehension in increasingly more advanced textbooks, as well as disinterest of the older students in a frequently irrelevant and absurdly unreal curriculum (along with growing student harrassment, resentment and aggressive behavior toward these school conditions) result in strongly suppressive forms of discipline quite common in our schools today. Physical manhandling, bullying, haranguing and brow-beating young people into conforming and listening, even forcing verbal and written responses to notions such as honor, patriotism, freedom and gratefulness through effort and responsibility for the educational opportunity offered by the school, are no doubt major contributions to the contempt, anger and rejection of many of these values by young people today. The insight and understanding of students, frequently far superior to most of the school workers who are bullying them, often results in their self-separation from the school, its type of people and the values that hold society together.

Little patience or tolerance is shown for the teacher or principal who significantly attempts to question and modify educational conditions. Just as obedience is expected of pupils and students, so too is subservience to hierarchy, conformity and loyalty to the system expected of its employees. Strong-line establishment biases permeate educational leadership, which tragically shows little, if any, committment, compassion, or understanding and sensitivity to the problems of the poor. Operating sometimes with cynical contempt for democratic concepts of leadership or utter ignorance of the nature of the school as a public institution, many administrators are able to per-

petuate themselves by using minority peoples and financial resources to present a facade of community representation, minority
participation and school modernization.

Schools and colleges of education have been training centers
for school workers of every type. Perhaps no other nation in
the world views the role of training teachers, administrators and
specialists for their public educational system with as low a
regard as ours. The school or college of education is an "academic leper colony"[6] in the parent college or university under
which it operates. Despised, ridiculed and otherwise treated
with contemptuous disdain by other departments and faculties,
the typical school of education is too often a grossly exaggerated
facsimile of the very conditions existing in public schools. From
the stereotyped, encrusted and rigidly segmented teacher training
programs to the dreary and often mediocre staffs, the typical
school of education frequently provides the routinized model
and humdrum, unimaginative atmosphere that is so ingrained a
pattern of public education. In this way teachers are trained and
then certified to malpractice elsewhere. Restraint, neutrality,
objectivity and scholarly pursuit, certainly worthy and vital
virtues in any profession, are all too often used as shams for
a lack of personal values and commitment as well as disinterest
in the real world outside the college classroom.[37] Few of the
forgotten ideals, the lost and unfulfilled dreams, or the critical
and growingly tragic consequences of decades of injustice are
held up for future teachers, administrators and specialists to
ponder over. Instead, many schools of education continue to
graduate workers who not only are unable to educate the new
middle class child for a totally different world, but also produce
individuals who are unsuited, unskilled and hence unable to
meaningfully educate poverty children for whom such maledu-
cation results in an even greater personal loss.

In spite of years of providing methods courses in the teaching of reading, the overwhelming bulk of teachers who either
teach reading or require students to read textbooks in their field
have a profound lack of even basic notions pertaining to such
experiences. One problem is that for years reading courses were
either not required or, as is more common today, inadequately

taught. Overfilled college classes, inexperienced or mediocre faculty, isolation of instruction from direct experiences with children, and many other inadequate instructional procedures have contributed toward the maintenance of ignorance regarding reading instruction among teachers, administrators and specialists. Indeed, many reading specialists, both at the college and public school level, can be found who make few if any contributions, given their superficial professional training. Very few in the field of reading have committed themselves to studying and contributing to the improvement of educational opportunities for poverty children.

The "Great Society" Years

The Civil Rights Movement in the 1950's set into motion a period that subsequently was to result in a unique era of federal activity in education. As a result of initial thinking in the Kennedy Administration, the Johnson years began with the outward manifestation of commitment typified by a legislative program for a "War on Poverty." The Economic Opportunity Act, the Elementary and Secondary Education Act, and the National Defense Education Act launched a series of activities in education, among other areas, that in its scope and turbulence left few educators and institutions untouched. The vestiges and remnants of this short-lived period, with its widespread programs and activities, the momentum of which has the educational establishment reeling, surround us today. Some are beginning to pick at the fragments and debris of these past projects and programs, attempting to develop and circulate more comprehensive and systematic assessments. This section will comment on the past era.

In the last several years, hundreds of millions of dollars of federal money, along with large contributions from various private foundations, have been turned over to diverse groups and institutions for so-called innovative programs and projects in education. Individuals of every age group, from pre-school to high school dropout, adult jobless and illiterate, were target populations for various projects. Diverse workers, including public school teachers and administrators, college and university personnel and other community residents, participated in various ways in projects throughout the nation. Designed with the major intent of contributing to the improvement of education for urban black children and young adults, federal funding to a lesser degree was provided for various programs involving Mexican-American, Puerto Rican and Indian children as well. Broad in geographic scope, as well as in the diverse special fields included, activities ranged from specific attempts to provide educational services for poverty children, such as Title I Remedial Reading Programs, to more multi-faceted programs such as Job Corps, Head Start, Youth Corps and VISTA volunteers. Disciplines such as science, mathematics and social studies were included, both in omnibus programs and specific projects. Training institutes for teachers in many of these disciplines were funded for summer sessions and occasionally for a full year. Dropout prevention, Upward Bound and Talent Preservation programs aimed at remediating variously hypothesized conditions affecting young people were operationalized. Projects were developed both within public educational institutions and outside such structures. Some programs involved reciprocal and cooperative endeavors between various institutions. Workers from many disciplines allied to education, such as medicine, dentistry, sociology and psychology, were variously involved, and aides, tutors and volunteers were utilized as well.

An awareness of the somewhat flawed beginnings of this era has already contributed to a partial understanding of what has happened as a result. It appears, according to one report[24] to which this entire section is indebted, that this was a period of dominance characterized by a professional class of individuals who, with missionary zeal and certainly well-intentioned motivation, apparently confused their desire for rapid change and their self-righteous assertions of what should be done for and about poor minority people, with the possession of information both as to what the basic questions were and the methodology for their solution. Interacting in this "mix" was an executive and a legislative branch of government that seemed concerned with action, not planning; with operations, not clearly defined goals; and with structures, not functions. Apparently, the consuming motivation was the need for visible action, not the need for careful designing of such programs nor the inclusion of conditions necessary for the objective assessment of results. The untested assumptions of the reformers, along with the less than altruistic motivation of the Administration during these years, seems to have resulted in various educational projects and programs, many of which might be considered lofty and naive, and quite a few, sloppy and irrelevant.

Earlier conditions were *so* poor, however, that few programs of this era were complete failures. Many were far from the successes they were promised to be, in spite of the grandiose and heady publicity that invariably seemed to precede their inception. Partial results from some programs and projects are becoming available. Evaluations of projects such as Higher Horizons, Upward Bound and Head Start have provided preliminary data which indicate that reform and change resulting from various local enterprises were far from total successes.[20,27,34,36] Many variables and outcomes which should have been studied were not always included, and definitive data are far from easily available; but the information suggests that reform in education, along current lines of thinking, will be far more difficult to realize than many assume. Underestimating or not accounting for difficulties, suggesting results more positive and immediate than were probable under the circumstances, attempting to legislate and purchase educational change, working from the limited knowledge available and being unaware of these limits, ignoring the need to explore many alternatives, to include in decision-making participation of minority peoples — all of these eventually led to the unfortunate conditions and less than outstanding results characterizing the events of the period. This is not a condemnation of the valiant efforts attempted during this period.

Many forms of dysfunction prevailed. In some geographic areas, mimeographed lists of "canned" objectives were made available that could conveniently be copied and included in quickly drawn-up project proposals. Institutions nurtured a class of professional project writers who became skilled in putting proposals together with less than direct concern with what specific groups of children required. Massive expenditures for the typical educational equipment and materials were made with few attempts to purchase materials on the basis of their suitability and appropriateness for poverty children or the availability of staff for their effective use. Monies and educational equipment purchased for ghetto schools found their way into more affluent schools. Remedial reading programs funded primarily for poverty children often systematically eliminated such children from eligibility for services on the basis of absurdly arbitrary and technically fallacious criteria. Many remedial programs which work with poverty children utilize approaches that require serious reappraisal. Much of the funding for various educational projects were funnelled into salaries and positions for middle class white professionals. Some public institutions used government projects to unabashedly further their own needs and goals, which were not always directly or indirectly related to the education of poverty children.

These internal contradictions had a negative impact on such activities. A method for soliciting innovation without a valid set of original premises in a population of potential educational "innovators" who, more often than not, have demonstrated their past inability to deal openly and effectively with such problems, and a federal bureaucracy unready to administer such a massive program resulted in something close to a grotesque parody of the ghetto "hustle." Smooth operators, grabbing off chunks of the action with urbane, sophisticated aplomb were the order of the day. A new class of hustler became the casual commuter to and from Washington, D.C.

Much should be learned from these events and the mistakes made during this period. A single theoretical orientation regarding the educational needs of the poor was uniformly adhered to and well suited to the opportunity structure of the reformers and their institutions. To place the blame for reading underachievement upon the child's environment neatly fit the theoretical biases and needs of these reformers. To label and stereotype masses of children was all too efficient in identifying target populations for project proposals. There were too many children, too little time, and far too many who wanted to ride the "gravy train" for such considerations. Gradually, the people for whom all of this was originally planned seemed to fade from concern.

Having begun with the grandest of promises, the bureaucracies over-predicted results. By avoiding an open and objective analysis of other theoretical alternatives, by sidestepping vital issues pertaining to the participation of the poor in such planning, and by not being willing or able to see the contradictions and incompatibility of such behaviors, the conditions for failure were built in from the onset. A final misfortune of the period is the difficulty of deriving information, objectively and empirically, from the careful internal analysis of specifics within the various programs and projects of this era. Funding was frequently provided with little detailed prior requirements pertaining to their scientific assessment.

Considerations for Reform

At present, uncertainty prevails, as confused and somewhat desperate school administrators face new and more intensive pressures from the ghetto poor, or in rural areas from opposite forces. Unable to emotionally or intellectually face the realities of race, ethnic and social class, often with little commitment to anything but staying in the job and maintaining the kind of school system which had been satisfactory in the past, too many of these bureaucrats continue to hopelessly separate the poor, and sometimes the affluent as well, from their antiquated educational institutions. Many of these administrators look backwards with nostalgia to that era when fanfare and rhetoric were an adequate enough smokescreen to obscure their inability to make realistic and meaningful changes of direct benefit to minority children of poverty circumstances. A good deal of their thinking regarding how to cope with this educational crisis continues to be based upon the need for increasing financial inputs to their schools through massive governmental support, without providing information as to how such funds will be utilized to intensify the influence of education relative to the needs of poverty children.[10] The spectacle of these same people continuing to call for federal funding, with no evidence or signs of making their institutions more responsive to the needs of various poor children, is a sign of the serious and critical nature of conditions today.

This paper does not presume to be able in some final way to articulate the exact nature of procedures that must be undertaken to right the wrongs that our society has committed, and therefore, reform our educational system overnight. An attempt however, will be made in this final section to present a series of considerations believed to be part of what is necessary to understand and hence plan for *the reform of our educational institutions.*

A. Cultural Bias and Racism

With well over 200 years of history, most white middle class Americans take pride in the shift our country has made from an emerging but weak democracy in a world of powerful authoritarian states to the most technologically advanced industrial nation in the world. This position, however, has not come without its price. Our country quite early in the process pushed aside or ignored many of the earlier dreams and hopes for a just society and worthwhile life for all of its people. Our dramatic economic growth has come about through the ruthless exploitation of peoples, raw materials and the neglect of basic human values.

After generations of subjugation and suppression of minority peoples in our society—blacks, Mexican-Americans, Indians and others — we are being told that we are a racist society, that we have in fact suppressed and subjugated these people, and that now they are preparing to free themselves from such conditions. In striving for this state, they do not ask but rather put our society on notice that they will obtain the necessary powers to do so. They are talking of political, economic, social and psychological power to "be" and "become" a people first and eventually contribute, for the first time, as equals in our society.[9] That the United States is not quite as open, free, just and equal a society to all its peoples as we have been trained to believe comes as a shockingly disloyal and untrue statement to most Americans. However, if people who are shocked by such possibilities would be willing and open-minded enough to observe their own environments, it would be a simple matter to note the deeply imbedded nature of prejudice, bigotry and bias that pervades the attitudes and practices of many Americans. The imbeddedness of such behaviors regarding issues dealing with race, culture, language and ethnic and social class is all-pervasive. Our public schools are but a reflection of such a society. The workers who contribute to the functions of such social structures carry their biases with them into their schools and classrooms. Poverty children who do not achieve in such schools are seen as deficient and deprived of a culture and language; hence, are unable to learn. Schools exhibiting such cultural biases are seen by many middle class people as valiant defenders of proper educational procedures. It is quite common to hear school personnel reason that these children have crippling environments[35] and that they, therefore, must be changed from what they are, as a result of their backgrounds, to what we think they *ought to be*. Our society must recognize these issues and the vicious circle of underemployment, inadequate housing and ineffective education which perpetuate these conditions from generation to generation.

B. An Alternative Hypothesis

The deficiency-deprivation model has dominated both thinking and practice in the area of educating minority children from poverty environments for some time. On the basis of universally observed underachievement in reading, such children have been said to be in one degree or another, linguistically, cognitively and intellectually deprived and disadvantaged. Thus, educational strategies of a *remedial* or *compensatory* nature have been continuously applied to these children. A central theme of this paper is that such strategies have been grossly over generalized and malapplied in undifferentiated fashions — when they have actually been made to reach some of the children of the poor.

Research has been published in which observed differences

are noted between minority children and middle class children in various psychometrically determined characteristics.[7,11,33] Some commentary seems to be in order regarding such studies; one criticism might be that these differences are more a reflection of the cultural bias of the measuring instruments used than manifestations of so-called deprivations or deficiencies. Stated differently, one linguist pointed out that while one group of researchers was measuring how well such children mastered environmental tasks—not of their own environment—another group might very well ask how have these children learned and mastered tasks related to their own culture, language and environment.[2] The practice of generalizing from observations of cultural differences to hypothetical environmental causes of such differences without collecting data to support these generalizations seems also to be narrow and unscientific. Indeed, the exclusive focus on the children's home environments as a cause of poor test performance or on genetic factors rather than on the middle class biases of the test instruments and researchers themselves[8] suggests reasoning that is not without the element of bias. Generalizations regarding the influences of heredity and environment on such test performance may or may not be true or part of the truth. It is more likely that answers will be equivocal. The responsibility for verifying or refuting such assumptions, however, rests upon the scientists who must first collect and then account for data. Suggesting, in addition, that such measured differences imply discarding the notion of equal development of minority children through equal educational opportunity is somewhat premature in light of the criticism of the measuring instruments used in such studies.

A growing number of observers are questioning the deprivation-deficiency model and are suggesting careful study of an alternative hypothesis — that of cultural differences — as an explanation for the school underachievement of minority children.[3,16] The model of cultural differences suggests that a conflict of cultures might be a useful alternative explanation for the educational underachievement of poverty children. A number of linguists have reported studies and observations of black children's language system.[1,12,30,31,32] Evidence seems to point to the existence of a well-ordered and highly structured non-standard dialect of English which differs from standard English in terms of the sound system, grammar and vocabulary. In the view of several of these linguists,[3,32] such differences create an interference effect in learning to read for some black children whose vernacular is this dialect rather than standard English. An instrument designed for assessing such dialectal differences has been reported in the literature.[2] It has also been noted that such linguistic differences are a factor of some importance in the reading underachievement of various groups of Spanish and Indian speaking children, whose vernacular is a language other than English.[16,29] Many other so-called bilingual children might be experiencing difficulties in reading associated with this phenomenon.

Our schools, apparently assuming that all children should speak standard English as they enter school, introduce all children to reading in English, regardless of what dialect or other language happens to be spoken at home. The interference effect of this type of procedure, in terms of learning to read, as well as communicating with teachers and learning in other subjects, could be critical. Requiring children to read a language they do not speak or understand seems indefensible. A few studies are available dealing with the vernacular teaching of reading with populations of Indian and Puerto Rican pupils.[21,23] The results of these studies strongly support the value of introducing pupils to reading first in their mother tongue. It would seem important for a series of studies to be conducted with differing populations of black children to explore the influence of introducing various children to reading first in so-called Black English on the subsequent growth in reading abilities. The latter approach might prove to be more appropriate for certain of these children than remedial programs in English and English reading. Timing — which approach should come first for different children — is a major research issue.

Broader implications than bilingual and/or bidialectal teaching of reading and language instruction are consistent with a model of cultural differences. It would seem that linguistic differences, whether they be dialectal or a language other than

English, might better be thought of as reflections of subcultural differences that require a new look at both the context in which learning takes place — the teacher, school and format of instruction, as well as the content of instruction, the subjects, topics and sequencing that children will be encountering. It would seem that a bicultural learning experience requires uniquely oriented schools, specially trained teachers, and content developed specifically for various minority children of poverty backgrounds. This appears to be a consideration of some importance.[5,15,22] Many will question the economic efficiency of such educational explorations. Others will seriously criticize the "separistic" possibilities inherent in the model. A major misconception of all adversaries is their failure to perceive the alternative as a short-term initial approach.

Generalizations so often applied to black, Mexican, or Indian descended children — their inability to attend, their lack of interest, application and motivation — might be shown to be in this context, more an effect of unsuitable and inappropriate school learning conditions than a direct cause of the overly stereotyped factors of home neglect, family disorganization and neighborhood decay. The implications of the model of differences are such that perhaps rather than remaking and remodeling minority children of poverty into an image of what the middle class sees as necessary for learning, it would seem that a new primary school, teacher and curriculum are in order. This school must be attuned to *their* environment, which has its own reality and integrity independent of middle class society. Minority subcultures are complex, distinct and functional for poverty children. Value judgments about them depend on who is looking at what, and from which side of the fence. Since few if any whites are effective in a black ghetto and few if any Gringos are effective in a Spanish ghetto, focusing a primary school in such a manner on the nature of its community and people indeed requires a different makeup of leaders, teachers and community participants and educational content. Much testing of these assumptions, however, remains to be done.

C. Reforming the Educational Establishment

The professional educator need not always consider himself a mere creature of society and its prejudices. He could strive toward becoming an educational leader and agent of change in his community and institution. While many structures in the educational system continue to provide rewards for personal and professional conformity, while many still demand subservience reminiscent of forms of government other than our own, still others are striving towards democratization and modernity. A growing number of leaders, although still too few, are becoming aware of the changes needed in our institutions if our country and way of life is to move forward. Schools must be shaped by leaders to become more responsive through focusing on *people;* not on forms, structures and self-perpetuation.

The bottled-up feelings of powerlessness and hopelessness of poverty people might demand a form of catharsis other than that obtainable through institutionalized change, if this is not forthcoming soon. Our leaders and specialists in education can begin the process, however, by analyzing their practices and procedures against a number of new scales and measuring devices. Their prejudices, biases and ethnocentrism have made them ineffective in having a direct and significant influence on educational matters dealing with minority poverty children. Immediate steps, therefore, should be taken to democratize decision-making authority over the destinies of poverty children.[9] The contradictions between community representation in schools and leadership positions and American notions of democracy and self-determination should no longer be permitted to go unrecognized and unrepaired.

A new form of leadership is in order. Educational institutions with encrusted traditions and neutral or non-existent value systems which inhibit creative talent must be readjusted. Circular behaviors resulting from underlying paternalistic and racist patterns must be identified, and such leaders must be helped to find less sensitive situations. The forces operating on all workers must be identified, and conditions must be established which will permit interracial, interethnic and interprofessional

communications. Color and ethnic and social class are life realities—they cannot be overlooked, denied, hidden, suppressed, or
otherwise toyed with by leaders of the future.

Modern and more objective systems must be considered for
the recognition and training of new leaders in education, representative of all people in our society. Interdisciplinary activities
with community participation are necessary so that doors are
opened to the development of different and more creative types
of leaders. Their training must result in a break from authoritarian models and the misuse of institutionalized power. People
of minority and poverty backgrounds must be trained as leaders
to operate in environments to which they are sensitive. They
must be given the freedom to create conditions that will result
in achievement for their children. Trainees from diverse backgrounds should interact and together learn to define problems,
coordinate resources, facilitate change processes, and solve
problems so as to remake education for poverty children, eventually remaking education for all. A new bidialectal, bilingual and
bicultural emphasis requires leadership that is aware and open
to all the realities of minority status and life in our society. Mainstream status as a goal might be attainable for many different
peoples by following unique paths of education. Maintaining the
integrity of subcultures while moving into mainstream America
requires leadership and curriculum planning of a uniquely high
and creative caliber.

D. Civilizing Public Education

Crucial to all human learning and direction is the need for
children to be in an environment sensitive and concerned with
values and ideals that first begin with enhancing their own
life conditions as individuals. A mass society, with sprawling
slums, suburbs and a rampaging mechanical technology has
created a school in its very image. Separated from the people
and its community by decades of promulgating its omnipotence
and infallibility — such schools have been dealing with children
as if they were analogous to raw materials which are pounded,
beaten, molded and shaped into products to be consumed by

society, rather than human beings who should be learning to become free citizens in a democracy. Reform will require getting back to basics that have long since passed us by.

A regimented, conformity-oriented and brain-washing school must be considered as operating counter to the survival of a democracy whose form of government is based on the assumption of an educated citizenry. Schooling for too many children and young people in our society is a grim experience. Teachers themselves reward children by freeing them from having to be in their classrooms or from assigned work. The triumph of mechanical technology over human needs in our schools, the reverence for textbooks, equipment and devices, and the way children are scheduled into classes and processed through them — must be reversed if some relevant degree of civilization is to return to our schools. All children require redress.

Prudence, responsibility, spontaneity, creativity, eagerness to learn, pride in scholarly accomplishment, quest for a contributing way of life in one's society, and pride in one's people are not middle class values; they are human needs.[17] Our schools often do violence to such needs by over-ordering, managing and controlling human beings. In this regard one might consider whether the reported underachievement in reading and other school subjects of many young people might possibly be a response to such environments rather than manifest behavior.

E. Reforming the Training of Teachers

Exciting possibilities await the schools of education fortunate enough to have leaders with vision to plan and prepare in the present for the public schools of the future. The identification of key faculty and community leaders and workers; an energetic, flexible and sophisticated group of professionals and lay people are required. Interdisciplinary communications and participation is necessary for the development of new models for teacher training. Emphasis on the recognition and development of tough, alert, sensitive, questioning, skilled and resourceful young people must be maintained. The stultifying and banal segmenting of methods classes away from the realities of the community must be reconsidered, as individuals are helped to develop into teachers who can maximize learning opportunities for young children. Skilled in an understanding of the nature of language and the conditions necessary to enhance learning and intellect by means of language, these new teachers should be able to explore more creative and individualized approaches toward the development of pupils who can communicate. It is necessary to train teachers to consider the teaching of reading not as a separate discipline with its own unique technology but rather as a language experience and an outgrowth of relevant learning experiences. These new teachers should be skilled in basing reading instruction on both the communication skills and background of children with whom they will work. Beginning with strengthening understanding and pride for one's self and one's own people by using natural content that connects the school with children's real worlds, people and linguistic styles, teachers might see readers develop as a matter of course. Children must be educated who can move easily from one dialect to another and who can communicate fluently in various language modalities. To do this, these teachers should either come from or know the child's subculture so well that they are part of their students' world. Training models must focus on such concepts.

These teachers must be skilled in helping children find out what they can do — their talents, abilities and liabilities — by becoming sensitive observers of individual abilities, needs and growth in all areas of child development. They must become facile in developing learning contexts that permit children to think about and solve problems for themselves. The new teacher must learn to completely subjugate curriculum, textbooks, equipment and other media to the needs of the children whom they are guiding. They must also be capable of showing children how to become masters of this technology, how to use such devices wisely, justly and purposefully. The entire city should become a learning laboratory for children. The artificiality of the school as a learning facility must be recognized. All of these assumptions require scientific exploration.

F. Research and the Reform Movement

Research stands as the basis for moving toward the more useful questions and answers needed if educational reform is to be realized. In spite of the positive rhetoric associated so often with the values of research, school people frequently become intoxicated by the notion that some new reading program or kit of materials or programmed collection of reading skills will result in a solution for severe and complex educational ills. The history of reading instruction is an example of the muddled results that accrue from unsophisticated and enthusiastic faith and the search for panaceas. The research of the new period must maintain the critical spirit so necessary to separate the need for inquiry and the search for truth from the pressing social needs for action and immediate reform. The latter can be entered into in such a way that vital information can be forthcoming for the adjustment of such projects to their betterment. Practical changes in upgrading and maximizing innovative action programs can be realized through highly skilled and well-designed assessments and analyses. The search for truth through scientific method is a cumulative, long-term and separate process that cannot be mixed up with applied action-oriented research.

Correct answers to educational problems, however, must be based upon relevant questions raised by individuals who are not only scientifically trained but experientially suited to be sensitive to many of the issues and nuances involved. These researchers must be able to bring insights into experimental designs of multiple phenomena important to their questions. The research establishment, almost exclusively made up of people of middle class backgrounds,[25] is too predisposed, in general, to mainstream concerns to meet research demands in the area of poverty children. Immersed in middle class characteristics and the instruments for their measurement, many workers continue to show insensitivity to the necessities of useful research with poverty children. A serious need exists for an all-out, but well planned, national program for the recruitment, training and placement in key positions of minority people in fields of research and development. The current leadership, overwhelmed with fears of controversy over racial issues, tends to seriously inhibit possibilities for research in these areas.

The almost universal reliance in reading research on the quantitative assessment of variables requiring qualitative differentiation, as well as the continuous pursuit of the accumulation of research articles around atheoretical approaches, suggests that much of current research in reading is possibly make-believe science making. Greater attention must be paid in the future to the development of theoretical models of reading, the deeper exploration of the reading process itself, the careful study of changes in reading maturity at key points in a child's learning cycle, the interacting influences of learning environment with a child's characteristics, as well as the development of more sensitive techniques for observing reading growth and needs. Most important of all, however, is the need to identify differences in minority children, to explore the effects of adjusting schools to such differences, and to assess the results of such changes for the purposes of developing a new but differentiated model of public education for these children.

Conclusion

A Frankensteinian, massed, technological society has resulted in an educational system that appears to be unable to humanely educate young children. Its mechanical efficiency is a mark of its ineffectiveness. The system is particularly inappropriate for minority children from poverty backgrounds. In this system, the educational establishment develops all too frequently into a managerial class which seems to be more concerned with perpetuating its opportunity structure than with providing leadership in moving its institutions into more effective and responsive postures for educating human beings. The ordering, controlling and manipulating of the destinies of children about whom little is known and in many cases little care is evidenced should no longer be tolerated in our society.

Educational leaders, therefore, must make many far-reaching decisions in an unprecedented, increasingly chaotic environment, where social, political and international policies are more often being settled in the streets than around conference tables. While a democracy cannot afford to permit any individual or group to unilaterally nullify legally established and legitimate institutions and leaders, it cannot afford to ignore the conditions basic to such events. The old clichés of law and order, which every American stands behind, can no longer be hauled out conveniently to suppress the aspirations of people. The history of mankind has well demonstrated this.

Major changes are in order in our society. Chief among them is the need to reaffirm this country's basic committment to justice, equality and opportunity for all. The schools of this country should take the first steps in moving toward these goals by realizing major reforms in their operations. Some of the considerations underlying such changes have been briefly discussed in this paper. A major question which remains at this point is, *will there be enough time?*

REFERENCES

1. Bailey, B.   Toward a New Perspective in Negro English Dialectology. *American Speech, 40,* 1967, pp. 171-177.
2. Baratz, Joan C.   A Bi-Dialectal Task for Determining Language Proficiency in Economically Disadvantaged Negro Children. *Child Development, 40,* September, 1969, pp. 889-901.
3. ....   Teaching Reading in an Urban Negro School System. In J. Baratz & R. Shuy (Eds.) *Teaching Black Children to Read.* Washington, D.C.: Center for Applied Linguistics, 1969, pp. 92-116.
4. Barton, Allen.   Social Class and Instructional Procedures in the Process of Learning to Read. In C. Y. Melton & R. C. Staiger (Eds.) *Twelfth Yearbook,* National Reading Conference. Milwaukee: The NRC, Inc., 1962.
5. Bell, Paul.   The Bilingual School. In J. A. Figurel (Ed.) *Reading and Inquiry.* Proceedings of the International Reading Association, *10,* 1965, pp. 271-274.
6. Bernstein, Abraham.   *The Education of Urban Populations.* New York: Random House, 1967, p. 67.
7. Bernstein, Basil.   Language and Social Class. *British Journal Sociology, 11,* 1960, pp. 271-276.
8. Burton, Jean L.   Intelligence and Intelligence Testing. In M. Cowles (Ed.) *Perspectives in the Education of Disadvantaged Children: A Multidisciplinary Approach.* Cleveland: World Publishing Co., 1967, pp. 97-125.

9. Carmichael, Stokeley & Charles V. Hamilton. *Black Power: The Politics of Liberation in America*. New York: Vintage Books, 1967, pp. 1-98.

10. Coleman, James. The Concept of Equality of Opportunity. *Harvard Educational Review, 38,* Winter, 1968, pp. 7-22.

11. Deutsch, Martin. The Role of Social Class in Language Development and Cognition. *American Journal of Orthopsychiatry, 35,* pp. 24-35.

12. Dillard, J. L. Negro Children's Dialect in the Inner City. *Florida Foreign Language Reporter, 2,* 1967, pp. 7-10.

13. Flanagan, John C. *et al. The American High School Student*. Pittsburgh: Project Talent, University of Pittsburgh, 1964.

14. Frost, J. L. Developing Literacy in Disadvantaged Children. In J. L. Frost (Ed.) *Issues and Innovations in the Teaching of Reading*. Glenview, Illinois: Scott-Foresman & Co., 1967, pp. 264-274.

15. Gaarder, Bruce A. Organization of the Bilingual School. *Journal of Social Issues, 23,* April, 1967, pp. 110-120.

16. Goodman, Kenneth. Let's Dump the Uptight Model in English. *Elementary School Journal, 70,* October, 1969, pp. 1-13.

17. Goodman, Paul. *Compulsory Mis-Education and the Community of Scholars*. New York: Vintage Books, 1962.

18. Harlem Youth Opportunities Unlimited. In *Youth in the Ghetto*. New York: *HARYOU,* Inc., 1964.

19. Howe, Harold II. Cowboys, Indians and American Education. National Conference on Educational Opportunities for Mexican-Americans. Austin, Texas: Southwest Educational Development Laboratory, April, 1968.

20. Hunt, David E. & Robert H. Hardt. The Effect of Upward Bound Programs on the Attitudes, Motivation and Academic Achievement of Negro Students. *Journal of Social Issues, 25,* Summer, 1969, pp. 117-129.

21. Kauffman, Maurice. Will Instruction in Reading Spanish Affect Ability in Reading English? *Journal of Reading, 11,* April, 1968, pp. 521-527.

22. Mermelstein, Mariluz & Bernard Fox. The Sands Project. *High Points, 47,* March, 1965, pp. 5-10.

23. Modiano, Nancy. National or Mother Language in Beginning Reading: A Comparative Study. *Research in the Teaching of English, 2,* Spring, 1968, pp. 32-43.

24. Moynihan, Daniel P. *Maximum Feasible Misunderstanding: Community Action in the War on Poverty*. New York: The Free Press, 1969.

25. .... Sources of Resistance to the Coleman Report. *Harvard Educational Review, 38,* Winter, 1968, pp 23-36.

26. Mugge, Robert H. Education and AFDC. *Welfare in Review, 2,* January, 1964, pp. 1-14.

27. *Phi Delta Kappan, 50,* June, 1969. A Study of Head Start, from the *New Republic,* p. 591.

28. Raph, Jane B.   Language Characteristics of Culturally Disadvantaged Children: Review and Implications. In M. Cowles (Ed.) *Perspectives in the Education of Disadvantaged Children.* Cleveland: World Book Co., 1967, pp. 183-208.

29. Rosen, Carl L. & Philip D. Ortego.   Language and Reading Problems of Spanish-Speaking Children in the Southwest. *Journal of Reading Behavior, 1,* Winter, 1969, pp. 51-70.

30. Shuy, Roger W.   A Linguistic Background for Developing Beginning Reading Materials for Black Children. In. J. C. Baratz & R. W. Shuy (Ed.) *Teaching Black Children to Read.* Washington, D.C.: Center for Applied Linguistics, 1969, pp. 117-137.

31. Stewart, W.   Continuity and Change in American Negro Dialects. *Florida Foreign Language Reporter, 6,* 1968, pp. 11-26.

32. ....   On the Use of Negro Dialect in the Teaching of Reading. In J. C. Baratz & R. W. Shuy (Eds.) *Teaching Black Children to Read.* Washington, D.C.: Center for Applied Linquistics, 1969, pp. 156-219.

33. Stodolsky, S. S. & G. Lesser.   Learning Patterns of Disadvantaged. *Harvard Educational Review, 37,* Fall, 1967, pp. 546-593.

34. U. S. Commission on Civil Rights. *Racial Isolation in the Public Schools,* Vol. 1. Washington, D.C.: U. S. Government Printing Office, 1967, pp. 115-140.

35. U. S. Dept. of Health, Education and Welfare.   *The First Year of Title I ESEA: The States Report.* Washington, D. C.: U. S. Government Printing Office, 1966, p. vii.

36. Wrightstone, Wayne J. *et al. Evaluation of the Higher Horizons Program for Underprivileged Children.* New York: Bureau of Educational Research, Board of Education of City of New York, 1964.

37. Zinn, Howard.   The Case for Radical Change. *Saturday Review,* Oct. 18, 1969, pp. 81-82, 94.

14

A Systems Approach
to Curriculum Change
in Secondary Education

David S. Bushnell

School administrators are under pressure to bring about radical improvements in that change-resistant institution, the comprehensive high school. Many of the Cardinal Principles set forth by the Commission on Reorganization of Secondary Schools back in 1918 are as evident today as they were 50 years ago. Much of the form and substance of secondary school education is surprisingly similar to that practiced 50 years ago, even in the face of the dramatic new demands being made on it by society. Important advances in the concepts of inquiry, of learning readiness, of self-determination and of achievement motivation remain largely ignored. Only a handful of innovations have trickled down into a few adventuresome institutions. Why are so few in-

The preparation of this paper was supported through an appointment as an Advanced Study Fellow with the Battelle Memorial Institute, Washington, D.C.

novations finding their way into the classroom? What can and should be done about it?

Some years ago, Kurt Lewin observed that social institutions often behave like individuals in that they develop customary ways of behaving to insure an orderly progress towards institutional goals. Members making up such institutions are expected to conform to these customary behaviors or norms. Rules of dress, punctuality, peer group relationships, even attitudes of the individual members toward the institution itself, reflect this pressure for conformity. Deviant behavior is often rejected; the individual is made to realize that such behavior will not be accepted by the group. Of course, such norms are desirable in that they make it possible for members of the organization to work together towards some shared goal. How to effect changes in group norms was the subject of a Lewin study on altering the norms of eating. One conclusion of this study was that group commitment and participation in the setting of new norms were much more influential in changing behavior than individual attempts to change such norms.[1] It was this demonstration that groups can modify and reinforce each other's commitments to changing norms that led industrial psychologists to explore further the concept of participatory management.

Koch and French utilized this principle in an authoritative study on the productivity of girls in a pajama factory. By involving production workers in setting new production quotas resulting from changes in the design of pajamas, the investigators established a correlation between the level of group participation and the willingness to accept new production quotas. When such a procedure was employed by the investigators, the transition to a new set of production quotas was brought about without the usual evidence of resistance to change.[2]

A correlative characteristic of institutions is that when a change occurs within some segment of the institution, the entire system must change with it. Matthew B. Miles in his book *Innovation in Education*[3] makes the cogent observation that many experimental programs within a larger system fail because the change or innovation is perceived as creating too much disequilibrium in the system, thus preventing it from meeting its obligations in a well-ordered manner. Goodwin Watson, in the monograph *Concepts for Social Change*[4], stated:

> A change in teacher-pupil relationship is likely to have repercussions on teacher-pupil interaction, on parent-principal contacts, on pressure groups operating on the superintendent, on board members' chances for re-election, etc. Any estimate of resistance which considers only the persons primarily and centrally concerned will be inadequate . . . repercussions elsewhere may be even more influential in the survival of the innovation.

For this reason, small-scale and fragmented changes, such as many of those currently being tested in on-line school settings, are doomed to failure before they are even launched. What is needed is a more massive and coordinated approach to educational reform, where piecemeal efforts are linked together; with considerable time and attention given to the development of coordinate strategies for bringing about desired changes. To be successful, future innovations must not only be discussed in terms of what is to be changed but also in terms of how the change is to take place.

Dewey, Kilpatrick and even such contemporaries as Conant have failed to achieve their often elegantly stated objectives because of their failure to cope with the complexity of the change process. Perhaps for the first time a new approach to arraying goals and strategies which can assist decision-makers in analyzing choices open to them and preparing better ways of coping with the change process is now in the offing. This refers to the "systems approach."

Systems Approach in Education

It is difficult to imagine anything or anyone functioning apart from some kind of system. One has only to think of the human body as a series of interrelated systems and subsystems to gain a feeling for the comprehensiveness of this approach. The person or planner who applies a systems approach will usually view the institution or organism as a functioning entity. The basic elements are to set forth the goals in quantifiable terms, plan and present the various alternatives to achieving these goals, operationalize the plan to be carried out, evaluate the results, and feed back the evaluation into the system so that the operations can be appropriately modified or revised.

Morgan and Morgan, in their article on "Systems Analysis for Educational Change,[5] state that "the first step in applying a systems approach to education involves the specific definition of what outcomes or results are desired. It is against these specifications that the system, whether spaceship or educational program, is to be built. The next step is to analyze the many variables that will contribute to the performance of the system. What are the means and strategies that can be employed to produce the desired outcomes? This analysis of means can be complicated or relatively simple. It involves the study of relative costs of means, feasibility of their use, and the predictability of the results."

One of the first and most important tasks to be undertaken in systematically building a total curriculum with the necessary variety of materials and pathways for individual learning required by the schools of the '70's would be to convert where possible broad educational goals into observable behavioral specifications; i.e., a catalog of appropriately classified performance objectives that would describe with greater precision the levels of performance that each high school graduate should be able to achieve. This does not ignore the fact that some students could go well beyond the minimally sufficient level. However, it would define the minimum skills, knowledge and attitudes the educational program ought to develop in each student.

Why Performance Objectives?*

Apart from a growing discontent with the traditional ways in which educational goals have been stated, what compelling

---

*The writer acknowledges his indebtedness to his former colleague, Dr. Robert M. Morgan, presently Head, Department of Educational Research and Testing, Florida State University, for his contribution to the writer's thinking on the role of performance objectives in curriculum design.

reasons are there for going to the very great trouble of developing a full inventory of performance objectives?

First, in using the systems approach to curriculum design, the goals or objectives for the program must be stated in terms of *output specifications*. In education, these specifications can often be stated in terms of behaviors. Without them there is little basis for deciding which learning intervention or teaching strategy would be most effective. When decisions on the selection of teaching strategies have been made without performance objectives, there are no empirical means of determining the degree of their effectiveness. It is doubtless true that most decisions about changes in instructional practice are made without verification in terms of what someone *thinks* is the effect of the practice on what is hoped to be the result. Consequently, systematic program revisions are virtually precluded in the absence of measurable performance objectives.

A second reason relates to the need for *longitudinal validation* of the effectiveness of public education in preparing young people to cope with their social and economic environment after they leave school. Unless we know with what behavioral attainments a youngster enters the adult world, there is little basis for relating his success or lack of it back to his school experience. The selection of given sets of performance objectives is purely judgmental. People of wisdom must decide that one objective is important and reasonable and that other objectives are not. At least one important criterion for the selection of objectives is that they appear to relate to preparing a student for his adult roles — as worker, parent, or citizen. Such objectives tend to be selected in terms of their face value. That is, they look as if they ought to relate. Face validity is often misleading, and the appearance of relevance may not be supported by correlational analysis. Revisions in educational goals as a result of follow-up studies of high school students ought to be a widespread practice.

A third reason for requiring performance objectives is the need to assess the cost-effectiveness of educational programs. The American taxpayer will inevitably grow weary of continuing to vote for increased taxation for education with no tangible evidence of the effect that these expenditures have on the education of his children. With more precisely stated educational goals, it should be possible to associate behavior change with program costs. Student learning should certainly be the main, if not the only, basis upon which cost-effectiveness analyses should be made in education.

The most important reason, however, is the reliance of an individualized instructional program on a detailed, carefully sequenced set of performance objectives. If the schools are ever to provide learning experiences tailored to an individual student's measured progress and tied to what a student last learned, his step by step progress in mastering an instructional sequence must be measurable.

Prototype of the New School

The new, systematically designed school will be a learning center, flexible in construction, in curriculum and in schedule. School hours will no longer run from 9:00 a.m. to 3:00 p.m.; schools will be open from early in the morning — perhaps 7:00 a.m. — until 10:00 or 11:00 at night, 12 months a year. The programs of individual students, and their learning schedules, will be suited to their needs. Thus, a student may be working part-time but will have his education — his classes, lectures and self-study commitments — organized in such a way that it will not conflict with his job.

It goes further than that: a student's job and his classes will be coordinated. His formal education will carry him outside the school building part of the time so that "real-life" experiences can sharpen his sense of the relationship between himself and his community. Learning in the '70's will no longer be considered exclusively academic, but will still cover the important disciplines. All work performed by the student which helps him master new skills and develop his potentialities, as well as all work which at the same time prepares him to assume an adult role in his community, will be considered part of his education. In the school building itself, therefore, space will be allocated to various trades and industries, and instruction will be given by men and women who are technical experts in their field, but who, in addition, have been certified as special teacher-aides. In some communities, such classes may actually be held at an industrial plant.

In weaving together academic and vocational education, the new school uses practical matters as a way of providing insight into material that a substantial number of high school students would otherwise consider irrelevant. The occupational goals of young people, their desire for economic self-sufficiency, their need to be involved, to control their own destinies, and their desire to discover things themselves can provide the motivation for achievement in related subjects such as science and mathematics.

Each student will pursue his studies at his own pace or in groups by making use of a wide range of instructional techniques: audiovisual aids, self-study systems, programmed instruction and other self-pacing devices, educational television (closed circuit and public broadcast), computer-managed instruction, single-concept films, games and simulated real-world events, testing machines and many other instruments. While students may sometimes be studying alone, there will be specific periods set aside for them to meet as a group with teams of teachers who will help with tasks that have posed troublesome problems. (In this sense, individually prescribed instruction does not mean that all study is carried out on an individual basis by the student.) At the same time, older students from more advanced classes will be encouraged to join these groups as tutors so that they can pass along what they have already learned.

A student's standing at any given moment will simply reflect a realistic evaluation of the quality of work he has done up to that point: the level of skill that he has shown and the body of knowledge that he has absorbed. Although the competitive spirit will endure, it will express the student's search for ways in which he is superior; but his success will not be measured by how his performance compares with that of other students. Teachers in the '70s will evaluate a student in relation only to himself as he strives to achieve goals that he has selected with the help of the school staff. By periodically checking present accomplishments against those of the past, teachers gain a progress index which then becomes the basis for defining the next quota of work and, where indicated, a possible upgrading of aspirations.

To increase the individualized nature of any particular course of study, examinations will be available upon request at any time. If a student has finished a series of assigned work problems and believes that he has mastered all the necessary skills, he can go to the achievement center, where he can ask for an evaluation of his progress. On the basis of that evaluation, he may proceed to the next stage of study.

Since students in this new type of learning center will not be given passing or failing grades at the end of the year, there will be periodic evaluations of the individual's rate of progress. He will confer with counselor-teachers who are prepared with a complete and up-to-date record of his accomplishments made available through computers. At intervals throughout the year, each of the student's teachers will record on tape his subjective impression of the student's abilities and attitudes. These will be filed as part of his master profile. On the same tape will appear evaluations of his learning progress. These observations will be available to parents, who, in addition, will automatically receive periodic printed reports.

These are practices and programs which will, hopefully, characterize the new high school of the '70's. "Labor intensive" it will remain, but with increasing exploitation of technology and modern participatory management concepts. While students will enjoy greater freedom of choice and self-determination in terms of goals and instructional procedures, the teacher will still occupy the all-important role of catalyst in that complex process called learning.

REFERENCES

1. K. Lewin.   Group Decision and Social Change. In G. Swanson, T. Newcomb & E. Hartley (Eds.) *Readings in Social Psychology.* Rev. ed. New York: Henry Holt, 1952, pp. 459-473.
2. L. Koch & J. R. P. French, Jr.   Overcoming Resistance to Change. *Human Relations, 1,* 1948, pp. 512-533.
3. Matthew B. Miles (Ed.) *Innovation in Education.* New York:

Horace Mann—Lincoln Institute of School Experimentation, Teachers College, Columbia University, 1964.

4. Goodwin Watson.   Resistance to Change. In Goodwin Watson (Ed.) *Concepts for Social Change.* Published by Cooperative Project for Educational Development (COPED) National Training Laboratories, N.E.A., Washington, D. C., 1967, p. 20.

5. Robert Morgan & Jack Morgan.   Systems Analysis for Educational Change. *Trend,* Spring, 1968, pp. 28-32.

15

The Essence of Curriculum Reform in Higher Education

M. M. Chambers

What is needed in curricular change in education beyond the high school? Flexibility and freedom of choice are the touchstones. It is unfortunately true that at least until recently the advanced professional and scientific programs in most universities held rigidly to an almost total preoccupation with a prescribed professional course of studies that monopolized, not to say overloaded, the student's time, and left no room for any infusion of social science or the humanities.

For example, although the study of law, if properly regarded, is itself a noble philosophical contemplation of justice among men and a search for understanding of what is right and what is wrong in human relations at given times and places, law students have been required to spend about one-third of their time on

M. M. CHAMBERS is visiting professor of education at Illinois State University.

procedural law, mainly to master the complicated quirks of pleadings that will facilitate their winning of cases in a particular state or in the federal jurisdiction.

Of the two-thirds of the curriculum that consists of substantive law, perhaps three-fourths has been devoted to "private law," largely permeated by commercial concepts. Viewed at its worst, law study has been mostly acquisition of crafty techniques whereby the prospective practitioner may become able to prosper or to grow rich by virtue of the misunderstandings and misfortunes of ordinary men.

Another aspect is that craftily ambitious lawyers often attach themselves to large business corporations or large financial institutions such as banks and insurance companies with a view toward enriching themselves by the exercise of their legal expertise in behalf of their employers in their struggles against governmental agencies and in their legal controversies with "little people," who are usually unable to obtain the legal talent necessary to prevail against the big organizations. Unquestionably, too many lawyers, especially those of middle age and beyond, are stodgy, unimaginative "Establishment men" who do little to promote the progress of humane civilization. There are brilliant exceptions.

This picture, though dark, is by no means static. It is becoming brighter. The best law schools insist upon a philosophical and comparative approach, and abjure the teaching of local procedural law. (Graduates of the Harvard and Yale law schools who reside in New York frequently take an expensive and intensive "cram course" in New York City in order to pass the New York State bar examination). Some law schools have even loosened up the curriculum a bit to make room for a modicum of sociology, economics, government, or other social sciences. A combined curriculum leading to a J.D. in law and a Ph.D. in a social science field seems to be in the offing for those who want it.

It is a sad fact that an obsession with "scientism" to the exclusion of non-scientific subjects and of other modes of thought seems to produce inevitably a blindly reactionary or "status quo" attitude regarding social, economical and political problems. No better illustration is needed than the incredible ignorance, obduracy and obscurantism of a majority of middle-aged practitioners of medicine and dentistry when faced with modern social issues. Consider the half-century lobbying record of the American Medical Association, acquiesced in and at least tacitly supported by a heavy majority of practitioners of medicine.

The graduate education of teachers, and to an apparently growing extent, even that of social scientists, is permeated with a similar obsession which is perhaps better styled "pseudo-scientism" because in these fields there is comparatively little "hard data," and students and teachers must be content with endless questionnaires, most of which are actually "opinionaires," often sloppily constructed and loosely administered. Thus, each single coded response, perhaps piously intended to be a clean-cut and solid brick suitable for a scientific structure, is in reality only a slippery handful of soapsuds suitable for nothing but a confused mess. Apt were the words of Arthur M. Ross, a vice president of the University of Michigan and former United States Commissioner of Labor Statistics, when he said, "Specious quantification of the unquantifiable can be as mischievous as ignoring it."[1]

Excessive Scientism in Dealing with Imponderables

Pseudo-scientism not only seems to be inimical to original and imaginative forward thrusts in education and the social sciences, but also appears to conduce toward almost total denigration of the art of lucid literary expression. Most theses and dissertations are not only unreadable, but also fail to meet the elementary standards of writing skill. All emphasis by the graduate professors is on a "clean" job of statistical manipulation. This means there must be no hint of human interest, no suggestion of value judgments by the author, no injection of personal convictions. Nothing but cold objectivity (which is impossible on its face and can never be honestly asserted). With few exceptions, the "cleaner" the work is in these respects, the more useless it is as a contribution to knowledge, though it may be a good exercise in mathematics.

The education of teachers for the elementary and secondary schools, and even of teachers for the junior colleges in some states where "certification" is required for them, is constricted by state licensing requirements which include too many rigidly-prescribed, atomized and weaker-than-water courses in techniques, at the expense of substantive courses. This situation stems from the bygone days of the normal schools and teachers colleges, when "teacher-training" was a tightly-organized political racket in many states, closely controlled by the superintendent of public instruction and a ring of local bigwig school administrators and local politicos. This dark scene is also becoming lighter, but slowly.

Medical schools that once required sequences of courses in biological sciences as a prerequisite to admission are now content to ask only for a bachelor's degree in any field, provided it is from a good college and the applicant has made a good academic record. The relative preponderance of methods courses and substantive courses in teacher-education is being somewhat redressed. In graduate studies in arts and sciences the inflexible devotion to departmental "majors" and "minors" is being somewhat softened up by recognition of interdisciplinary studies so that "double majors" are now permissible in some graduate schools.

In the undergraduate colleges of arts and sciences the revulsion of students and a few faculty members against arbitrarily required courses and sequences, excessively mechanized testing and grading, and too general disregard for reasonable fair play and freedom of choice is not confined to any tiny minority of freakish habitual dissidents. It is shared by virtually all students except the vanishing docile conformers whose only aim seems to be to do as they are told and to believe everything they see in print or on television. It will bring change.

In vocational and technical education in junior colleges and technical institutes intended to lead immediately to wage-earning or salaried employment, the most glaring defect probably is that the programs include too little general education or none at all, thus denying the student his birthright of "two years of education beyond high school, with emphasis on intellectual growth," so eloquently advocated by the Educational Policies Commission in its famous statement of January 1964.[2]

Interaction Nourishes Independence and Originality

The critique of curricula in higher education could go on and on. It is best to pause and remind ourselves that teachers are much more important than curriculum as a factor in the quality of education. A "course," no matter how cut-and-dried or overstructured it may be, is always in large degree an expression of the individuality of the teacher. Its long-range consequences result largely from the quality of the interactions between student and teacher.

In elementary and secondary education there may be much need for "drill" in the use of standard procedures in language and mathematics, and in mastering the facts of history and geography. "But," says J. Douglas Brown, provost emeritus of Princeton University, "the one-way transmission of established data . . . should give way to *interactive* education, with constant, individualized response, as the student moves up through the university."[3] This is the way to "enhance understanding and sensitivity in respect to values, principles, judgments and insights."

Here, educational technology, with its frequently ingenious improvements, can be of some use to supplement and enrich the interactive work of student and teacher. The developers of educational technology should abstain, however, from half-baked claims that mechanical or electronic devices can supplant large numbers of teachers, rendering them superfluous and enabling one professor to instruct thousands simultaneously as against the dozens he formerly taught, with equal results.

It continues to be false to assert that any machine can be in any sense a substitute for human discretion and discrimination; though it may aid the exercise of those high qualities by speeding the availability of pertinent data; and though it may provide the student with novel ways of teaching himself many essential elementary facts or techniques. Higher education is much more than the acquisition of knowledge. If it were to be confined to that function, it could indeed be made much cheaper and much more perfunctory. This could easily lead to "more people being manipulated for more purposes by fewer manipulators" than ever before in history—an ugly picture.

Higher education becomes much less than its name implies if it fails to maintain its chief emphasis on individual independence in the assessment of values, the selection of purposes and the fulfillment of individual potentialities. The paramountcy of freedom of choice coupled with fair responsibility on the part of students and teachers conduces toward the self-respect and high morale which furnish the climate for discoveries of new knowledge and insights and the accretion of wisdom.

REFERENCES

1. Arthur M. Ross. The Data Game. *The Washington Monthly,* Vol. I, No. 1, February, 1969, pp. 62-71.
2. Educational Policies Commission. *Universal Opportunity for Education Beyond the High School.* Washington: National Education Association, 1964, 35 pp.
3. J. Douglas Brown. *The Liberal University.* New York: McGraw-Hill, 1969.

16

General vs. Specialized Education: Source of Institutional Tension

Philip C. Chamberlain

There should be little doubt that the premium today is on specialized education. The effect of this emphasis can be felt at all levels of education and is related to our need to work and function within an increasingly complex and intricate world. In the process we often overlook the fact that this premium is a relatively recent phenomenon and, as such, has drastically altered our concept of the distinction between specialized and general education. This alteration is most prevalent at the higher education level and has created a crisis of identity for many institutions, notably the liberal arts colleges.

The distinction between general and specialized education has been discussed by philosophers for twenty-five centuries, beginning at least with Aristotle's warning against learning to

PHILIP C. CHAMBERLAIN is associate professor of higher education at Indiana University.

play the flute too well lest other interests suffer for lack of attention. At the beginning of what might be described as the modern era, Francis Bacon observed that "amongst so many great foundations of colleges in Europe, I find strange that they are all dedicated to professions, and none left free to arts and sciences at large."[1] Despite his concern for arts and sciences at large, the type of education to which Bacon was referring as being dedicated to professions was not what we normally think of today as professional, but was, instead, the traditional education required as a prerequisite for entrance into the professions. The distinction between special (professional) and general education, therefore, was seen not as one of a kind but rather as ends for which the existing education was pursued. Moreover, education that was indeed specialized was most apt to be seen as vocational and not worthy of inclusion in the traditional pattern.

John Cardinal Newman during the later part of the last century stressed as illiberal any education that exhausted itself on particulars. Specialized education, therefore, had little claim for inclusion in the university curriculum. Although specialized education was seen as having value and importance to a changing society, and was necessary to be pursued, it was not seen as a function of traditional university education.[2]

American writers were also addressing themselves to this topic in the face of pressure for curriculum change during the last century. Frederick A. P. Barnard, for example, writing with respect to improvements in education which he believed practicable and necessary, said, "Nothing can possess a higher practical value, to any man, than that which makes him a man, in the fullest sense of the word."[3] He was, of course, referring to the importance of liberal or general education as the means for achieving that end. He went on to add that new additions to the curriculum were valuable insofar as they contributed to the amount of knowledge which a student possessed.

That the traditional distinction between general and specialized education existed in this country until very recent times also is indicated by the creation of the office of Superintendent of Instruction in many states during the late nineteenth and early twentieth centuries in response to the developing need for universal public education. The choice of terms was not accidental, for there was a perceived difference between education as then understood and instruction, the latter seen as being more in keeping with demands of a public seeking a more utilitarian educational experience.

In viewing our present premium on specialized education against this historical background, there is little doubt that the notion of liberal or general education, once the guiding spirit of American higher education, is no longer seen with the same precision or clarity. Indeed, it can be said that directional roles have been reversed.

In the past one hundred years the introduction of the elective system, the creation of the modern service oriented university, the gradual implementation of the Morrill Land Grant Act, the increasing technology and industrialization—all have forced hard decisions upon American higher education. Increasingly, educational emphasis has become more utilitarian, it has proliferated program offerings, it has moved away from the influence of the church, and it has permitted students to elect the programs of study they would pursue. The elective system brought to an end the concept of a fixed body of knowledge to be pursued for its own sake, for increasingly students were allowed to pursue courses of their own choosing, and most frequently the choices were made for utilitarian or instrumental ends.

Since interaction has continually characterized the relationship which has existed between American society and its educational institutions, the continuing and extremely complex changes which are occurring today are sure to have a significant impact upon the future growth and substance of the collegiate curriculum. Although, it is impossible to comment on all factors, it is appropriate to suggest some of the more relevant.

No greater force for curriculum change exists than the increasing number of students engaged in the educational process, particularly at the higher education level. And an increasing number of these in the future will be coming from disadvantaged backgrounds, as more and more youth of lower socioeconomic origins seek the benefits of higher education. These students come from a society which is becoming increasingly computerized, mobile and impersonal, and the rate of change within that society is accelerating. A phenomenon of this change is the dynamics of rising educational aspirations, for this is seen as a force in itself affecting the number of students who pursue higher educational levels. In essence, it would appear that the more education a student receives, the more he tends to want, usually of a different sort. The significance of this force for collegiate curricula is considerable, especially as it relates to the need for general and specialized education.

Paralleling increasing enrollments as a force for curriculum change has been the general shift of the population from a rural to an urban pattern. This means that the megalopolis will become the home for an increasingly larger segment of society. Equally important is the racial revolution, with its concentration of blacks in the largest cities. The challenge these population shifts hold for the curriculum is only now being realized, but we can be sure that in the future it will be bound to alter existing ideas as to the content and experiences associated with general and specialized education. Moreover, the progressive secularization of western culture is singled out by many as having an important impact on higher education and on liberal education in particular. Since many of our educational institutions were originally church-related, a religious orientation still pervades many of them. The growing secularism in American society thus creates a conflict in values.

Another significant factor altering the relationship of general and specialized education is the expanding role being played by the federal government in higher education. Clark Kerr has stated that the two forces which have molded the modern university, and indirectly all other educational institutions, have been those having their origin in the federal government. The first was the land grant college movement of the last century, and the second was the federal support of scientific research during and after the Second World War.[4] That the role of the federal government in higher education in the future will increase is widely predicted. Not so clear, however, is the meaning of this expanded role for the relationship of general and specialized education; for not all the nation's priorities in the future will be geared to scientific research.

In addition to the changes within society which have had great impact upon educational institutions, there has also been tremendous change within higher education itself. The advanced placement movement, which affects the general studies of the first college years along with the strong trend toward narrow specialization prerequisite to graduate and professional studies, have had considerable consequence for the balance between general and specialized education.[5] In many instances what was once spread over the four years of the college experience is now compressed into a period of a year or two. Much has been written concerning the problems for the curriculum at all levels of education as a result of these pressures. In essence, it is the assertion that the pressure upon the student to restrict his interests, accelerate his program, and move into advanced study at an earlier age is having a dysfunctional effect upon the structure of the curriculum and on the education of the student as well.

Within higher education, the increasing specialization of the curriculum due to the impact and dominance of the graduate school is resulting in specialization in the structure of the undergraduate college. The unity of the whole is being undermined by the tendency for faculty to have greater allegiance to their discipline than to their institution. The consequence of this redirected allegiance for the curriculum should be obvious, as the substance of general education recedes in the face of greater specialization. Little understood in the process of increasing specialization is the evident fact that the end of specialization is *more* specialization — with the consequence that the parts will further tend to become more important than the whole. The significance of this continuing change for general and specialized education is yet to be fully comprehended.

In brief, the present conditions brought about by the forces of change in society and particularly in higher education have drastically altered our understanding of the continuing role of higher education and of the distinctive difference between general and specialized education. Furthermore, there is no indication that a clear understanding of the difference between these forms of education is forthcoming when one considers the prevailing diversity of opinion as to the purposes of higher education.

However, there does exist in the literature some level of agreement as to basic generalizations concerning the nature of general and specialized education.

First, there is a consensus that general education is not limited to any one type of institution, but may be identified in a wide variety of colleges and universities, regardless of the type of specialization which is dominant. It would appear that it is not the institutional form which determines the nature of the relationship, but rather the nature of the educational program itself — and particularly the manner in which the educational experience is approached by faculty and students.

Second, there appears to be fairly wide agreement that general education is not to be identified solely by subject matter, just as it is wrong to associate this form of education with just one type of institution. It is not the subject matter which determines the character of the educational experience as much as the way it is approached. For most, this approach is characterized by a sense of historical perspective and by an appreciation of philosophical implications. In this regard, a general education experience is one that is essentially philosophical.

Third, with today's premium on specialized education in society, the role of general education takes on added and dynamic aspects in regard to emphasis on integration and generalization. This particular function increases in importance, also, with further constriction and fragmentation of the undergraduate experience. Williams Arrowsmith of the University of Texas states that the undergraduate still acts as if he were an integrated individual, and wishes his learning to have relevance and meaning.[6] The question of the relationship of general and specialized education in this context is not one of different ends to which each may be leading, but of the proper time and exposure to each in order to create the maximum balance for specialty acquisition and integration into the student's total educational experience.

Fourth, many take the view that general education may

often include preparation for a useful career and need not be contrasted with specialized education on the assumption that the latter is for servile ends. John D. Millett has voiced the opinion that there should be no conflict between general and specialized education. The conflict, he said, is a result of the fear that men will value knowledge by what it pays rather than by the intellectual satisfaction it brings. The challenge, therefore, is to find an appropriate balance between these emphases.[7]

Fifth, general education should be relevant to society; and, in order to accomplish this, it must acquire a posture of openness to that society and a responsiveness to its changing needs.

Sixth, there is widespread agreement that education, particularly general education, must be a continuing process, with formal class work merely marking the onset of this process. This importance is seen as particularly crucial in the face of increasing leisure time, resulting, ironically, from the increasing application of specialized education and its offshoot, technology. Failure to recognize the need for meaningful continuing educational experience throughout life could result in a greater distinction between what is meant by free time and what is thought of as leisure time; the former deriving its direction from others, while the latter being self-directed and suitable only for the free man.

The question of the relationship of general and specialized education in the future, in addition to its philosophical overtones, will undoubtedly have considerable influence on the structure of our whole system of education.

REFERENCES

1. Sir Francis Bacon. *Of the Advancement of Learning.* Everyman's Library. New York: E. P. Dutton and Co., n.d.
2. Cardinal John Henry Newman. *The Idea of a University.* New York: Holt, Rinehart and Winston, Inc., 1960.
3. Frederick A. P. Barnard. *On Improvements Practicable in American Colleges.* F. C. Brownell, Hartford: 1856.
4. Clark Kerr. *The Uses of the University.* Cambridge: Harvard University Press, 1963.
5. Francis H. Horn. Forces Shaping the College of Arts and Sciences. *Liberal Education, 50:5*-16, March, 1964.

6. Williams Arrowsmith. The Shame of the Graduate Schools. *Harper's Magazine 232*:50-51, March 1966.
7. John D. Millett. *The Liberating Arts: Essays in General Education.* Cleveland: H. Allen, 1957.

17

The Impact of
New Materials and Media
on Curricular Design

Abram W. VanderMeer

For the purposes of this essay, curriculum is defined as everything that is planned to happen to a learner with a view to enhancing, instigating, or modifying pre-determined behaviors. Obviously, this means that the curriculum is not defined by a set of textbooks nor by a printed course of study; it is much more than either of these. Nor is the curriculum limited to that which is presented to the learner or that which he is brought into contact with, although, of course, the importance of these contacts and encounters is very large. The methods by which these contacts are arranged, the interventions of the teacher in the relationship between the learner and the environment from which he learns (including all varieties of instructional materials) likewise constitute an important part of the curriculum and must

ABRAM W. VANDERMEER is dean, College of Education, The Pennsylvania State University.

be included in the definition thereof.

It might be reasonable to object to limiting the definition of the curriculum to *planned* or *intended* experiences, since it is perfectly obvious that learning takes place as the result of unplanned and unintended experiences also. While acknowledging this fact, the curriculum definition must exclude these unintended and unplanned experiences and learnings if we are to be able to manage the concept of the impact of media and materials on the curriculum. But, one might say, in the best of all possible classroom worlds, an infinite variety of instructional materials would be available instantaneously to every member of the group. Certainly then, individual encounters with these materials outside of those immediately and directly planned for would take place and learning would result. To this line of reasoning it must be rejoined that a rich array of instructional materials does not become available to learners except through *planning*. In summary, we define the curriculum for purposes of this essay as encompassing those experiences that are planned for the purpose of teaching people something.

How Is the Curriculum Determined?

In order to see how materials and media affect curriculum design, it is necessary to accept, as a point of reference, a model of curriculum design. Many such models exist, and there are varying degrees of similarity and compatibility among the models. Ralph Tyler has identified four elements in curriculum development; namely, establishing educational purposes or goals, selecting educational experiences that are most likely to lead to goal achievement, organizing these experiences to make them readily available and deliverable to learners, and determining the extent to which the goals are attained. Implicit in these four steps are a number of sub-steps or related elements. Presumably, the development of worthwhile educational goals involves an assessment of the needs of society in all of its various levels and types of groupings, and also the needs of the individuals who make up society. Both of these presuppose some philosophic assumptions concerning what is good and what is beautiful. By the same token, selecting educational experiences designed to attain the desired goals involves not only choices of which experiences (activities, encounters with content, etc.) are most useful, but also planning for a sequence or ordering of these experiences. Both a selection of experiences and their sequencing is based on some knowledge of the goals and of the characteristics of the learners who are presumably going to achieve the goals.

Organizing experiences involves not only considering what the learner shall do but also the content — intellectual or aesthetic — that must be involved. Here, in addition to considerations of goals and the peculiar characteristics of learners, consideration must also be given to the inherent logic of subject matter, sometimes referred to as the *structure of disciplines*.

Media and the Curriculum

The foregoing brief statement on the determination of the curriculum lends itself to the interpretation that primary emphasis may be given to the needs of society, and furthermore that goals are *imposed* on the learner rather than developed with or by the learner himself. It also is subject to the interpretation that, in at least one given instant in time in one particular set of circumstances, a valid notion of what is true, worthwhile and beautiful exists. Such an interpretation is not necessarily valid; it is possible that the implied assumptions do not necessarily pertain. But it is clear, likewise, that certain philosophic positions would tend to dispose one to such interpretations. In some systems of educational philosophy, for example, the notion of the temporal nature of valid goals is a central concept. Other positions in educational philosophy would, on the contrary, extend the concept of a "goal being valid for a given instant" to eternity; holding that though "we see now through a glass, darkly," eternal verities and values *exist,* and *can be found,* and that these verities are the structure and framework of the goals that should be sought. This philosophical position rejects that what is true, worthwhile and beautiful depends on the time, the place and the circumstances. To a greater or lesser extent, however, the extremes of philosophical positions that have been referred to here are alike in that they do emphasize a kind of conformity, a kind of notion that the group can determine, at least for the novice, what is good for itself and for its members.

A more modern philosophic position, existentialism, stresses the individual and his direct personal experience; the choices he makes as an autonomous individual. Choices made as an autonomous individual must be, of course, free choices. This philosophy stresses less what a person knows than what he can, or is able, to know. If an individual conforms to a group, it is because he, as a free spirit, has chosen to do so, presumably because he feels that conformity is instrumental to achieving his own self interests.

Some may see a relationship between the contrasting points of view regarding the philosophy or rationale that ought to overarch decisions about the curriculum as it has been broadly defined for the purpose of this essay, and the two major trends that have emerged in the context of the application of newer media and modern technology to education. As the late Jim Finn saw it ". . . two trends, at the moment, lead in opposite directions.

"The first is the trend toward a mass instructional technology, and is governed by machines and systems suitable for that purpose. Foremost, of course, is television, of which there are four instructional types: (1) broadcast on an educational channel, (2) broadcast on a commercial channel, (3) closed circuit of the Hagerstown - Penn State type in which live instructors are used either to supplement instruction or to provide direct instruction exclusive of classroom teachers, and (4) the Compton type in which filmed lectures are distributed by a closed circuit medium as replacement for classroom teachers. In all cases the desire is to reach more students with fewer teachers or to obtain 'quality instruction.'

"In opposition to this trend of mass instruction is a growing technology for individual instruction. This trend is the audio-visual wave of the future (for the moment). The most dramatic development here is that class of instruments and systems known as teaching machines. Actually, I would class all teaching equipment designed for individual and near-individual operation as being in the category of teaching machines. At present, then, there are approximately five types, listed here on an ascending scale of sophistication: (1) individual reading pacers and similar devices; (2) individual viewing and listening equipment for existing slides, filmstrips, motion pictures and recordings; (3) language laboratories of all types; (4) specially programmed printed material such as scrambled textbooks, etc.; and (5) true teaching machines of the Skinner or Pressey type containing carefully worked out verbal or pictorial programs with various and ingenious mechanical or electronic arrangements to test student reaction, inform him of his progress, errors, etc."

It is not within the assignment of this essay to reconcile the alternative philosophic views regarding the curriculum or the impact on curriculum development of the acceptance of these views. It is not within our province, either, to take sides as to the trends toward individualization or mass instruction. It is, however, germane to present purposes to point out what can be accomplished by media in curriculum design and delivery and, by implication, the impact of the media on curriculum design.

Curriculum Design: The Science of the Possible

It is obvious, in the short view, that in curriculum development it is useless to select goals that cannot be achieved. A little perspective from history, however, may add some insight to this conception. Consider, for example, how futile it would have been to attempt as a goal an understanding of the condition of the surface of the moon in 1960 as compared with what could be done in 1970. This is a matter of greater knowledge having become available; but it is likewise a matter of the miracle of television, which was able to show millions of people all over the world the first human step onto the moon's surface.

The thesis of this section is that the new media stimulate curriculum revision by making possible the attainment of goals that were hitherto unattainable or attainable only at the price of too great an expenditure of time and other resources.

The term "media" as used here refers essentially (1) to realities selected for instructional purpose, and (2) to various representations of realities with varying degrees of editing or embellishing those realities.

By way of illustrating the impact of media on the curriculum, and the relationships between these categories of media, examine the curricular implications of "a rose is a rose is a rose." Suppose it is decided (goal selecting) to teach or to cause children to learn how Mary's garden grows. The richest learning experience would involve learners in the planting of a garden, caring for it, and observation of the growth of the plants. All steps would be included from preparation of the seed bed to harvesting the crops. Actually, perhaps, what would be essential would be planting many gardens over many seasons, using many different preparation and cultivation methods and many different flowers and vegetables. Probably as far as the public school curriculum is concerned, however, it is rarely if ever necessary to have such a complete answer to the question put to Mistress Mary in the traditional nursery rhyme. It usually seems far wiser and more economical to stop considerably short of the wide variety and range of new and redundant experiences that would produce the most complete learning. Rather, some *representative version of the real experience* concomitant with some dependence upon internally or externally induced generalization is what is opted for. The gardening season and the school year don't match, so the teacher may be content to have the student simply start a garden. Or there may be no garden space, so seeds are planted in flats or earthenware pots right in the classroom. Or maybe the goal is to teach, or to have the children learn, the anatomy of the flower rather than the whole concept about how a garden grows. In such a case, all that is really needed is the rose itself, and the garden or pot in which it grew — the life cycle that it followed doesn't matter. In this case, perhaps a rose is not wanted at all, for a tulip has more clearly defined parts; and therefore it would be more effective to learn the parts of the flower by examining the tulip than it would by examining the rose.

The half-facetious previous paragraph illustrates one way

in which media relate to curriculum. Given an educational objective and a learner or a group of learners with particular characteristics, the appropriate medium is selected and used. To the extent that the medium is inappropriate, the goals fall short of achievement. If the medium is largely inappropriate, the goals may not be achieved at all. Recognizing the varieties of learners and learning styles, and the variety of media that are available, the preceding sentences should perhaps be stated in the plural form, but the principle is nevertheless here.

In many — probably most — instances, the realities of the environment are not effectively available for educational purposes. This may be because of the scarcity of realities in terms of time and place, because of the size or other characteristics of the realities, or because of the magnitude of the investment of time that would be required to bring realities into contact with the learners. This principle of economy of time has broader implications for the relationship between media and the curriculum, as will be seen later.

An important curricular goal that must be pursued, along with those goals related to the development of wide ranging knowledge and understanding, is the ability to handle ever more abstract symbolism. The ability to sum up a complex relationship in an equation, to present a many-faceted concept in a few words, to express pristine beauty in an abstract work of art is the epitome of educational achievement; and the ability to learn from, to derive the meaning of, these abstractions is equally important. But, in a very real sense, these goals are reached toward the end of the learning process. Without rich, meaningful experience with realities, abstractions cannot meaningfully be used, and what Edgar Dale terms "verbalism" inevitably results.

For reasons already noted, media that *represent,* as contrasted with *being,* reality, often make the greatest contribution, all things considered. Returning to the question of teaching the parts of a flower, should the teacher really prefer to base the learning experience on an encounter with a tulip? Why not, instead, use a picture? Why not, indeed, use a series of pictures showing, in some sequence presumably from the more obvious to the less obvious, the anatomy of the flower? Or, why not use the botanical equivalent of an anatomic model? The point is, all of these and other choices could be made and defended. In each case, something is gained in educational currency and something is given up. In the case of the picture, it is clear that it would be relatively easier to direct learner attention to the exact location and characteristic of the parts of the flower — easier that is than would be the case with each individual student having his own tulip to dissect. Clearly, what is given up in choosing the picture is the richness of the individual's sensing of the flower which, in its real state, has three-dimensionality, texture and odor — none of which could be provided in the still picture. On the other hand, the model, in the company of similar devices such as drawings, charts, or diagrams, has the power to eliminate what may be non-essential or even distracting details in the interests of presenting the essences of the structure itself. All flower pistils are not the size, color, shape, or texture of the pistil of the tulip. To use the tulip, therefore, as the central medium of instruction, risks teaching things that aren't so; or, at best, distracting the learner from the essence of the flower anatomy. On the other hand, the model or the diagram does not necessarily look like *any* flower. The abstract clarity of the parts is purchased at the price of realism. Richness of detail, typical of realities in instructional situations, is avoided or given up, according to one's judgment of the relative gains or losses resulting from choosing a more realistic medium or a more abstract one.

In the foregoing paragraph, consideration has been given to media which, in essence, edit reality. Some media, on the contrary, embellish reality in a variety of ways. Returning, for example, to the task of teaching the anatomy of the flower — if it is conceived that function is an important aspect of anatomy, two needs seem to emerge as conditions for the selection of media. The first of these is the need for making visible the invisible, and the second is the need for compressing time. The motion picture and television employ techniques that satisfy both needs. If it seems desirable to show how pollen develops on the surface of the anthers, drops on the sticky end of the pistil, transmits germ material to the ovaries, and combines in developing seeds, it would seem that an animated film clip would be indicated. In no other way could this process be actually or realistically demonstrated economically. There are literally hundred of valid curricular experiences that are made feasible if not made *possible* as a result of the introduction some decades ago of the process of photographic animation.

The second need referred to is that of compression of time. By varying the ratio between the intervals of *recording* frames in film and in television on the one hand and that of *projection* on the other, motion can be made to apparently speed up or slow down. Again, a film clip would be indicated in which, through time-lapse photography, the actual development of a flower from bud to mature seed could be shown in the process of a very short period of time.

Different varieties of media, it has been shown, have different characteristics that bear on their inherent capacity to record and present information. Media potentially influence the curriculum in terms of the manner in which the information is presented. Some media, like motion pictures and television, have their own pace, unity and fact density. The teacher, therefore, is very limited in what influence she can have on students *during* the presentation. Her influence is of necessity largely confined to what happens before and after the experience. She can help the students with what to expect, if she wants to, and she can help them to recall and organize what they saw and heard; but she cannot speed up or slow down the rate of development; she cannot change the order or sequence of events portrayed; and she cannot explain, enlarge, clarify or correct during the presentation without taking liberties with the integrity of the medium.

Other media, of course, have other characteristics that determine how they can be used. Sequence can't be changed in a filmstrip, but it can in a slide set. Recordings, tapes and radio programs require the teacher to decide what the students are going to *look at* while they listen. Pictorial prints may be too small for group use, etc.

Up to this point, consideration has been given solely to the cognitive dimension of learning. At this juncture, it would be well to take an excursion into the psychomotor domain and the affective domain. If through time-lapse photography the motion picture and television can compress time so that the events of educational concern can be shown in a much shorter time than it took for them to transpire, by reversing this technique (an over-simplification) the opposite effect can be obtained. As millions of football viewers who have enjoyed the "instant replay" can attest, the analysis of performance is rendered tremendously more effective by the use of slow motion photography. The use of "game movies" by coaches and the presentation of models of performance through tapes and films is illustrative of the contribution of those media to psychomotor learning. The "instant replay," of course, brings to mind the point that the use of videotape and other visual and auditory devices that may be used for the analysis of physical performance can also be used for the analysis of more complex performances in, for example, micro-teaching. Comparing the critique of a lesson taught by a novice teacher as based on observer notes on the one hand with the critique made possible on the other hand by use of videotape, it is easy to see the impact of the medium on the curriculum. The goals may have been the same in practice teaching before videotape, but the achievement most assuredly was not.

Many important elements of the curriculum that relate to the human condition and the problems and concepts of human relationships depend upon not only realistic portrayal but also upon emotional impact. Sympathetic understanding of psychological dependency could be much more easily achieved by seeing the movie "The Sterile Cuckoo" than perhaps by any other means. More realistic (less fictional) films and tapes designed to combine understanding and emotional impact are available for those parts of the curriculum for which media illustrative of such characteristics are indicated.

How the Media Are Used

In a very real sense the very existence of media themselves has added potential *content* to the curriculum. This content relates to the production of communications and the expression of ideas through media other than, or in addition to, the printed or spoken word. It also includes the study of the media themselves with respect to their individual styles and rhetoric. Courses and units in motion picture and television production, in photography and radio production are beginning, albeit in a very small way, to compete for student's time with courses in English composition and persuasive speech. By the same token, the art and rhetoric of the film and television are beginning to compete with the studies of English literature and of the styles of noted orators. In a very real sense, along with the technological and industrial revolution of the past century or more, there has been a communications revolution. The result has been an imperative need to widen the range of the *study* of communication, and thus a whole new and valid discipline has been made available to curriculum planners.

The introduction of a wider range of possible media has had a tremendous influence on that part of the curriculm that relates to the method of instruction and the style of learning. The lecture-textbook-recitation method, which has changed very little from the beginning of time, is now yielding to a wide range of learning experience, styles of learning and strategies of teaching in which the availability of varieties of media has played an important part. Returning once again to the illustration of teaching the parts of a flower, the teacher faces a number of methodological choices. Assuming that the choice has been made to use the real flowers, should one opt for a flower per pupil, or a flower for each group of four, or a single flower to be dissected and displayed for the entire class group? Obviously, if the teacher believes that "we learn what we do," she will need to consider the full interpretation and explication of the original curricular goals. It is likely, for example, that the total quantum of learning or understanding of the essential elements of the parts of a flower would be greater if a half hour were devoted to a demonstration by the teacher. There would likely be an important side effect, however, for while indeed the level of understanding of the concept may be generally raised, the students would also be learning to *watch* in order to learn. By way of contrast, if each student has a flower and has directions as to how to proceed to dissect it (and the whole matter of the degree of explicitness and detail of the suggestion is a moot question) it is quite clear that while the level of understanding of the specific content might be lower at the end of a given period of time, the students would have been learning, as a side effect, something about how to work alone and at their own pace with relatively little first-hand direction. In this case, the total quantum of knowledge of the flower might well be lower. Finally, the alternative of relatively small groups working together to dissect the flower would produce similar trade-offs in terms of general level of understanding exhibited by the class, and the type of methodological learning likely to be attributable to that portion of the curriculum.

Learner Needs and Instructional Media

Assuming, for the moment, that appropriate goals have been set as the starting point in the matter of teaching the anatomy of the flower, alternative choices of media will still relate to the inherent and persistent needs of individuals as they learn. The advertising slogan of the late '60's, "Please, Mother, I'd rather do it myself!" exploited a basic human need — the need for self-activity. The teacher who pays special attention to this need would have solved the problem of what media to use to teach the parts of the flower by choosing one flower for each student. It would be theoretically possible to produce the same degree of individual autonomy and self-activity through the use of computer assisted instruction. The price of choosing the computer would be the relinquishment of those characteristics already attributed to the reality itself. What would be gained would be the kind of structuring of the individual student activity that the teacher had in mind in providing instruction sheets, and that she would like to provide if she could spend full time sitting with each individual as he worked.

Another basic human need which is related to classroom activities using media is the need for interaction. Classroom situations in which the teacher is dominant need not *eliminate* interactive processes, but inherently such classroom situations focus the interaction so that the predominant pattern is inter-

action between individual student and teacher rather than between students and other students. While this interaction is
taking place, of course, the other members of the classroom are,
at best, interested observers. By selecting media that lend themselves to small group activity, the teacher can broaden the foci
of interaction three- to seven-fold.

Perhaps the obverse of the need for interaction is the need
for evaluative feedback. This may be considered as interaction
in a very special sense in that it presumes an interaction between
one who *needs to know* and one who *already knows*. Computer
assisted instruction, of course, has as one of its major attributes
the capability of providing immediate, and, to judge from the
results of much research, a highly satisfying feedback. While
CAI is perhaps the penultimate in the mechanization of evaluative feedback, the differentiated staffing patterns combined with
individualized packets of media materials that are characteristic
of individually prescribed instruction and similar teaching-learning strategies provide, in addition to mechanized feedback opportunities, a multiplication of human feedback potentials. This is
achieved by enlarging the number of adults with whom the child
can interact. Here, too, the media have made it possible. Individual learning stations fitted with projectors, record-players, etc.,
are an integral and essential part of such systems.

Individual learners appear to differ in accordance with
their preferences as to the sensory avenues that they use in
dealing with the outside world. Some appear to learn best through
the visual sense, some prefer the auditory sense, and others
prefer the tactile sense. Evidence of this is more abundant in
the case of students with learning disabilities than with average
students; however, this is not to say that normal children do not
display these same characteristic sensory preferences in perhaps
a less exaggerated form. The excellent results in remedial reading
that are achieved in some cases from introducing the tactile sense
(tracing letters and words that are written in sandpaper or as
grooves in slates or plaques) offers an example of catering to
the child who has strong tactile sensory preferences. Similarly,
college students vary widely in terms of their more effective
strategies in learning from lectures. Some prefer to take copious

notes which they can then review. Some prefer to underline the textbook, whereas others learn best by concentrating all their attention on what they hear in lectures. These learning strategies are probably to some degree related to preferences among vision, hearing and feeling. It should not be inferred that sensory preferences in dealing with the outside world should be considered as immutable and inalienable. A goal of the curriculum may well be to reduce the impact of differences among learners as to preferred senses, but if it is considered also that learning must proceed from where the learner is found, the impact of varieties of media on a curriculum is clear within the context of sensory preferences. Obviously, characteristics of media must be matched to characteristics of learners.

While, as has been noted earlier, the improvement of the learner's ability to deal with abstractions is a worthy aim of education, it is likewise clear that individuals of relatively lower maturity and relatively lower intelligence have considerably greater difficulty in dealing with abstractions than do their more fortunate peers. Edgar Dale has, for years, conceptualized the range of instructional media on a continuum from the more abstract to the more realistic in his "Cone of Experience." Research tends to show that, while students who belong in the upper ranges of ability are not greatly affected by the "realism - abstractness" of media, those in the lower ranges are. Another way of saying the same thing is that the individuals who make up the lower half of the distribution in terms of ability at the outset of experiments comparing the effectiveness of various educational media tend to account for a considerably larger proportion of the observed variance at the end of the experiment than would be predicted from the weight of their numbers. Presumably, the normal course of development in maturity and learning is along the lines of greater facility in dealing with abstractions. Again, the implication of the hypothesis that lower ability learners need more realistic materials is *not* that such materials must be provided to them forever, but rather that over the range of their development a beginning may be most effectively made with more realistic materials being emphasized in the curriculum.

Summary

The burden of this essay can be expressed in two major points. In the first place, it is argued that an increased variety of educational media and materials make it possible and feasible to achieve a wider range of worthwhile goals for the curriculum and, indeed, to achieve them with greater economy. In the second place, it is argued that the achievement of goals is conditioned by the selection of materials that are appropriate; that the degree of goal achievement is directly proportional to the appropriateness and the variety of media available to the teacher and the learner. Appropriateness of the media relates to the ability of the media to present, in the broadest sense, the material that makes up the content of the curriculum. Content and method have inherent characteristics that make particular, varied demands on media. Media, by the same token, have varieties of abilities for eliciting desired behavior in learners. Also, the appropriateness of media may be judged in terms of their ability to relate effectively to the learning styles and inherent needs of individuals. Finally, the teaching strategies and learning styles of teachers and students are satisfied in varying degrees by the various media. It follows, therefore, that since teaching strategies and learning styles are an important part of the curriculum, the availability of a variety of materials affects this aspect of education as well.

18

The Impact of the
Mass Media on Curricula

Richard W. Budd

There is no way to "know" the nature or magnitude of the impact of the mass media on education or on educational curricula. There is, of course, a plethora of visible traces which tell us that the products of the mass media wend their way into the classroom and, in some unsystematic manner, into the design of curricula. But a one-to-one relationship is not discernible, for a variety of simple reasons.

A major reason is that one is never quite sure what is meant when we talk about *the* mass media. Another is, assuming some solution for the first, that there is no useful way of sorting out the "impact" of a multitude of other institutions and events which most certainly in some way influence the process of learning. Still another reason centers on the nature of "find-

RICHARD W. BUDD is director of the Mass Communication Research Bureau at the University of Iowa.

ings" regarding the effects of the mass media. These data tend too often to be general and undiscriminating, and reflect a general confusion about levels of impact and about the difference between technology and the uses to which technology is put.

This lengthy introduction is simply another way of saying that what follows will not provide answers, but raise questions; it will be speculative rather than authoritative. This paper explores the issues, and attempts to arrive at a focus by tapping in at the point where the mass media and education seem to intersect and overlap in function. A basic concern will be the ways in which many educators have been seduced by and, to a considerable extent, incorporated into the mass media systems.

This paper will also be concerned more with the relationship between producers and consumers of mass communications (broadcast, film and popular print) than with the technologies (mass media) involved in delivering those products. At the same time, technology cannot be ignored as a powerful handmaiden to the functions carried out by the mass communicators. The specific effects of mass communications are also of less concern than viewing mass communication more generally as an environmental force which, in some manner, influences the ways in which we organize ourselves with respect to that environment (e.g., the ways in which we go about educating ourselves).

The functions of mass communication, as they are traditionally categorized, include: (1) surveillance of the environment; (2) correlation of the various sub-segments of the environment; and (3) transmission of the cultural heritage.[1] Entertainment is frequently mentioned as a fourth function, which quite likely is subsumed by, or subsumes, the other three. These functions are not inventions of modern society. They have existed as long as men have lived in organized societies. The functions were derived, in one way or another, from "needs" created by organized living and from the inventions, both cultural and institutional, man collectively created to help him deal with his environment.

The surveillance function allows man to become aware of events in his environment which he is unable to witness personally. Ideally, this consists of the raw data he must use in making decisions to improve his condition; which gives rise to the second function. Not only does man seek to know about events distant from him in time and space, but he wants to know what they mean to him in the context of his own existence. The mass communicators perform this function by putting together the "pieces," as it were, into some meaningful pattern. This may mean relating either events which are distant in time or space, or giving currency and shape to issues derived from one's own local environment.

As "transmittors" of the cultural heritage, the mass communicators act in a broad sense as custodians of the repositories for those communicational artifacts which give meaning and consistency to a society. This framework, which a society employs for viewing itself, is passed along and augmented by succeeding generations.

As noted earlier, the functions performed by the mass communicators are not new. What are altered, of course, are the technologies man has devised to dispatch these functions (which are currently referred to collectively as the mass media). The new technologies have served to increase the power of the mass communicator by making his messages more abundant and more accessible. It would perhaps be useful to maintain a distinction between technology (the mass media systems) and the mass communicators who employ the technology as a means of distributing their products. A great deal of the criticism aimed at the mass media today, particularly the medium of television, fails to make this crucial distinction. Obviously, there is considerable room for improvement in the products offered by the mass communicators. At the same time, much of the criticism reflects our own lack of strategy for coping with technology.

When we are bored by a public lecturer or offended by a bad dramatic performance, we walk out. When we pick up a book that fails to stimulate us, we put it aside. We have not yet learned, it would seem, to deal with a piece of electronic furniture in a similar manner.

Since both students and educators are, to a larger extent than we might wish, played upon and enter into play with the products of the mass communicators, the dynamics of the inter-action may be what is meant by the impact of the mass media upon education.

The confounding aspect of the issue at hand is one of the basic functions of education, which is the transmission of the cultural heritage. However, a second and equally important function is to foster the conduct of inquiry about the nature of the beast, about ways in which we have constructed our environ-ment. So while it may appear on the surface that the functions of mass communication overlap and are consistent with those of education, they may in fact be operating at cross purposes. It is at this juncture that the impact of the media is most felt by education, and, perhaps, in a way that may be detrimental to both.

An observation by Hugh Dalziel Duncan may help cut to the heart of the matter:

The reality in which we live is the reality of the named relations between the things of the world and man, as well as between man and man.[2]

The assumption presented here about what is currently occur-ring in the society is that there is too great a dependence upon the mass communicators for naming relationships which for-mulate our "realities," and too little being done by education to question both the communicators and the "realities" of their creation.

There has grown from all of this a basic dilemma. One of the functions of education is to help students acquire a frame-work for inquiring into the basic constructs that have been developed for explaining the environment. These constructs have to a great extent been defined and perpetuated by the mass communicators (with substantial reinforcement across media). How does the educator, then, immersed as he is in the environ-ment, overcome the problem of being *reactive* to already named problems rather than *proactive* with respect to the way the problems are initially named?

It is abundantly clear that modern educational curricula must take into account the mass media and their products. We could ignore them only through ignorance. We must, for example, at least acknowledge that the average child today spends as much time in front of his television set each week as he does in the classroom, and ask what that might mean. It is true that many educators already include in their curricula units, sections, modules, or courses centering on mass communication and the mass media. The present concern is not that the courses exist, but rather with the way in which they are conceived and the ends they are designed to achieve.

There are also programs of instruction using daily news-papers in the classroom, and courses centering on media crit-icism. The basic notion of such courses should be encouraged, but the execution of a number of such efforts fall short because of a rather basic, inherent flaw. The nature of the criticism such efforts are designed to cultivate at once implies that the designers — and by default the students — have fallen prey to the mass produced communication "realities."[3] In many instances, the general thrust of the criticism advanced addresses itself to the manifest product, to what is there (and seldom to what is not there or what else of completely different genre might have occupied the same time-space). This sort of reactive stance in respect to mass produced realities implies a prior acceptance of the realities being reacted to. It is perhaps a mistake for mass communicators to conceive of their role as that of educators. In the first place, they labor under far greater constraints; and consequently do not enjoy the same freedom educators do (or should). They are, as well, inextricably bound up in the para-dox of a closed system that cannot help but prevent them from serving a basic function of education, i.e., open inquiry into that system.

Lee Thayer most usefully conceptualizes a notion that might help explain the nature of the paradox. He draws a distinction between two communicational processes he calls *informing* and *in-forming*.[4] The distribution *per se* of messages or information via the media is subsumed under the function of informing the public. The particular selection and non-selection of information or aspects of information with consis-tency over time serves to in-form members of the society. This latter concept refers to the process of organizing oneself with respect to one's environment in service of innate or self-determined ends. The broad agenda-making role performed by the mass communicators would appear to be a way of establishing those ends. The specific information distributed through the mass media is selected or not selected, employing as criteria the predetermined ends. This process does not occur consciously or deliberately; but it does occur.

The paradox is that the process of mass communication is self-reflexive. The consequence of the way the mass communicators perform the informing function is that they at the same time serve the in-forming function. It is this sort of process that makes one believe the open conduct of inquiry so necessary to education cannot be performed by the mass communicators. Within their framework, inquiry into the relations between means and ends would appear to be effectively blocked. Not only are the ends defined by the mass communicator, but they seem to describe and justify their very existence.

At the outset, a complaint was registered regarding the confusion surrounding the use of the term "mass media." It might be useful for a moment to extend the term, as it has been used here, to include education itself. This would allow us to aim a number of the notions and criticisms advanced concerning the process of mass communication at the process of education. This further implies that as educators we must address ourselves to some fairly knotty questions. To begin with, the central question of this essay can be rephrased: What is the impact of "education" on learning? Have we defined our educational ends too narrowly (perhaps by subject matters), and allowed them to dictate our own inclusive-exclusive message systems (courses and content) in service of those ends? How successful have we been in creating environments in which our students are free to swing their axes into the relations between the means and ends of the educational process itself? What are our criteria for participation in the educational experience? Do we also aim our products at a level that is intended to include everyone and offend no one? Perhaps the analogy breaks down at one obvious point; educators are not nearly so adept at making education as exciting and attractive as are the mass communicators in the packaging of their products.

The main concern raised by all of this is how do we go about breaking out of the constraints — now for the most part hopelessly institutionalized — we have succeeded in placing upon ourselves? Is it too simple a solution to say we reconceptualize our methods and goals as educators? If we are uncomfortable conceiving of ourselves as mass media (in the technological sense), perhaps we ought to get out of that business.

As has been noted elsewhere[5], we must develop educational environments in which the problems exist by design, but are not already named, and where solutions to problems are not necessarily preconceived as right or wrong. This, in part, suggests that a main purpose of the educator should be to create an environment in which students can acquire the tools necessary for coping and adapting to the demands of a changing environment. This further implies that rather than teaching "knowledges" that tell our students what *the* world is *really* like, we help him cultivate those knowledges that help him to cope with events in *his* own world.

The implementation of such programs may not be as simple as it sounds, because they must be conciously designed to cut across the grain of the society that fosters them. To a certain extent, educators need the freedom to occasionally bite the hand that feeds them, to raise questions about basic and unquestionable societal values. David Riesman has expressed a similar point of view, noting that education is most effective when it assumes a "counter cyclical" stance with respect to dominant and accepted trends in the society.[6]

In a somewhat more direct manner of naming the problem, Postman and Weingartner suggest that educators need to develop methods of helping our students devise "shockproof crap detectors."[7] In giving this Hemingway term currency in their recent book, the authors write:

> One way of looking at the history of the human group
> is that it has been a continuing struggle against the
> veneration of "crap." Our intellectual history is a
> chronicle of the anguish and suffering of men who

tried to help their contemporaries see that some part
of their fondest beliefs were misconceptions, faulty
assumptions, superstitions, and even outright lies. The
mileposts along the road of our intellectual development signal those points at which some person developed a new perspective, a new meaning, or a new
metaphor. We have in mind a new education that
would set out to cultivate just such people—experts
at "crap detecting."[8]

We must reconcern ourselves with a more direct, although
related, effect of mass communication than those discussed
previously. As educators we need to be deeply concerned with
the context the popular press builds around the educational
process. The writer has frequently been disquieted by (and at
times a target of) the ways in which the mass communicators
have dealt with educational innovation. The in-forming of our
society in regard to educational values has, it would seem,
militated against change from the traditional and familiar form.
This one concern has unfortunately diverted attention, time and
energy of many educators away from their main function to the
lesser one of smoothing ruffled feathers. At a deeper level of
concern, innovative educators may even shy away from curricular changes that can potentially bring adverse publicity to
them and their institutions.

This is not to say this is always the case. There are a
number of enlightened mass communicators who are not only
aware of the necessity for freedom in education, but who see
the positive values in bringing educational criticism to bear on
societal institutions, including their own. Joseph Benti, who
anchors the "CBS Morning News," feels that the general public
has not been equipped to handle the flood of information they
are receiving, much less use it to develop a clearer picture of
their environment. But his concern does not end with the public.
He feels education could do a great deal for the producers of
mass communications. He cited some of the need thusly:

. . . when I talk to my friends at CBS about some of
the ideas that men like Schramm put forward. They've
never heard of Schramm, let alone his ideas. And

they've never really questioned the process they are responsible for. What is a message? What are you communicating? What in the heck is it you are doing? Who is the audience out there?[9]

Unfortunately, there are not nearly enough professional communicators raising questions about what they are doing, much less providing support for educators who are.

Before concluding, one more issue should be raised. The emerging adult,[10] used as referent throughout this essay, is probably one in late high school or an undergraduate in college. He is a young person who is seeking to find out who he is, what he feels, and how he relates to and is different from others in his society. In recent years, owing to our advanced technology, he has come more and more to rely upon institutionalized communication to help him find his answers. It is true that the media have provided him the opportunity to become aware of a wide range of events which would otherwise be impossible for him to know. At the same time, much of that communication occurs with a synthetic slickness that frequently tends to show life as it is not, not as it is. Such pictures of life stem from a programming foundry that venerates products such as "I Love Lucy" and a tour of the palace with Princess Grace, but expresses grave doubts about black sheep products such as "Harvest of Shame."

It seems that this sort of tacking down and glossy varnishing of human experiences does not serve a very useful function for the emerging adult seeking to sort out his own rough and unfinished experiences. Still another personal concern of the writer is that the amount of time spent alone watching television displaces slightly less than one-third of the average young adult's waking hours. Among other things, that time displaces the amount of time he might spend in direct human contact. The further question of how those thirty hours with TV affect the nature of the human intercommunication that does occur is perhaps unanswerable. But it does seem worth fantasizing about.

The point to be made is that our schools and universities may be among the last institutions where such direct and meaningful human contact might be ensured. Without question, such contact will still provide the opportunity to employ the mass produced trivialized behavioral models that do more to evade meaningful human interaction than promote it. But the educator, through controlling the environment, can ensure that meaningful encounters occur within a context that will allow the students to profit from them. This has been one clear justification for the use of basic encounter groups within the educational setting.

Of the many outgrowths of the ways in which the mass media and education come together, one of the most significant lies in the natural push mass communication puts on education to reach fuller potential. We often have difficulty seeing the relationship that way. Educators cannot afford to become mere extensions of the mass media, where it costs nothing to play in either purpose or competencies. Yet the failure to set demands of purpose, relevancy and competency is the very reason why education cannot help but be mass media. Granted being so removes a considerable amount of ferment and hassle from our lives. It is, in fact, considerably more comfortable because it serves to strengthen our certainties of what the world is like. It is most unlikely to help us, however, and quite likely to hinder us in conceptualizing a future whose only certainty is that it will be *different*.

REFERENCES

1. This particular category scheme was developed by Harold D. Laswell. The Structure and Function of Communication in Society. In L. Bryson (Ed.) *The Communication of Ideas*. New York: Harper and Brothers, 1948.
2. Hugh Dalziel Duncan. *Symbols in Society*. New York: Oxford University Press, 1968, pp. 103-104.
3. Thayer refers to communicational realities as one kind of verbal artifact. Such realities have no existence apart from that we talk about them. A fuller understanding of this and other integrally related notions can be found in Lee Thayer, Communication: *Sine qua non* of the Behavioral Sciences. In D. L. Arm (Ed.) *Vistas in Science*. University of Mexico Press, 1968; and *Communication and Communication Systems*. Homewood, Illinois: Richard D. Irwin, 1968.
4. The special context from which this usage is drawn is in Lee Thayer, Communication and the Human Condition, a paper prepared for

the VII Semana de Estudios Sociales, Mass Communication and Human Understanding, Instituto de Ciencias Sociales, Barcelona, Spain, November, 1969.

5. Richard W. Budd & Malcolm S. MacLean, Jr. Applying Communition Principles to Communication Education. In Lee Thayer (Ed.) *Communication Spectrum '70* (Proceedings: 15th Annual Conference of the National Society for the Study of Communication), 1968.

6. David Riesman. *Constraint and Variety in American Education.* Lincoln: University of Nebraska Press, 1956, Section III.

7. Neil Postman & Charles Weingartner. *Teaching as a Subversive Activity.* New York: Delacorte Press, 1969.

8. *Ibid.,* p. 3.

9. Joseph Benti. TV Speaks with Forked Antenna. *Iowa Journalist,* September, 1969, p. 13.

10. Richard W. Budd. Charting the Communication Patterns of the Emerging Adult. Paper presented to the Association for Education in Journalism, August, 1966.

19

Information-Processing
Models and
Curriculum Design

Robert C. Calfee

This paper[1] consists of three sections — (a) the relation of theoretical analyses of learning to curriculum design, (b) the role of information-processing models in analyses of learning processes, and (c) selected examples of the application of information-processing models to curriculum design problems. By *learning* is meant those changes in a student's state of knowledge which are the result of instruction. Learning is a theoretical construct, the measurement of which requires collateral specification of observable performance indices. These indices may be used to direct decisions during instruction (i.e., we can make decisions about *how* to teach on the basis of the student's performance history), as well as to evaluate the adequacy of a student's knowledge at the end of a given instructional program. *Instruc-*

ROBERT C. CALFEE is associate professor of educational psychology at Stanford University.

tion is being used in a general sense to refer to presentation of information of some kind, possibly initiated by the student, and possibly but not necessarily incorporating interactive feedback between student and teacher.

Contemporary analyses of learning aim at uncovering the mechanisms by which information is taken in or encoded, stored in memory, and later retrieved. The term "information-processing" in the title points up the emphasis on tracing the flow of information in the student, on the postulation of under-lying psychological processes (perceptual, attentional and stra-tegic as well as the associative processes more typically thought of as learning) and on the formulation of models strictly limited in their range of application to a specified set of behavioral phenomena. In this paper, *information-processing* and *learning* will be used more or less interchangeably.

There is little reason other than parsimony to assume that a single mechanism or process would adequately account for the phenomena variously referred to as learning. Depending on the nature of what is to be learned, how it is taught, and the resources and preparation of the student, different cognitive processes might well come into action. Consider, for example, experiments in which by varying instructions students are caused to adopt different "sets" or learning strategies.

In a typical instance, a student has to learn a list of *paired-associates,* such as the (spoken) names of the letters of the alphabet, or the English equivalents of German words. By appro-priate instructions, an experimenter can lead a student to try to learn the list by rote, or by forming mnemonic linkages or codes for each pair, or by constructing an organized or rule-governed structure for the entire list. Recent studies (e.g., Bower, in press) have shown how association strategies can be manipulated in this manner with dramatic results. We are still a long way from a complete understanding of the mechanisms behind such phenomena, but it is fairly clear that the single-process models of a few years ago provide little insight into this kind of result.

Learning Models and Curriculum Design

There are two major questions to be considered in curriculum design: *what* shall be taught and *how* shall it be taught. While it is not traditionally considered a part of curriculum design, a closely related problem is the matter of *evaluation* — how well the material in the curriculum has been taught by the teacher using the resources available, and how well it has been learned by each student. Evaluation has typically represented the performance of the individual student relative to his peers. While considerable research has sought to compare the effectiveness of different instructional systems (the combined *what* and *how* referred to above), all too often the observed differences have been so negligible as to be of no practical consequence. It has proven much easier to assign grades to *students* than to *curriculum designers* and *teachers*.

Models of the learning process have a potential bearing on each aspect of curriculum design mentioned above. By revealing the component processes in classroom learning, task analyses can be carried out in a rational fashion. Long-range or terminal curriculum goals involve value judgments that cannot at present be evaluated scientifically. However, once such goals have been established, learning models can be used (at least in principle) to determine what must be learned to achieve those goals, and to search for the most efficient ways of presenting the necessary instructional materials.

Learning models also provide a means of examining the procedures used to evaluate instruction. Test performance can be used in various ways: as a means of "candling" students (e.g., kindergartners with a high score on reading readiness tests are put on a "high" track in first grade, those with a low score are placed on a "low" track); for predicting success at a later point in the instructional sequence; and in some cases as feedback for the entire instructional system — teacher, curriculum and student. Learning models provide a means of examining the skills required to do well on a test. It seems reasonable to ask that a test designed to evaluate a particular curriculum segment be primarily sensitive to the information in that segment and only slightly dependent on other knowledge available to the student. For example, a test of reading achievement should *not* depend on a child having a detailed knowledge of rural America (cows, horses, barns, hay, and the like). It also seems reasonable to ask that a test be diagnostic, in the sense that it provides information about the deficiencies of the student (or instructional system) which have produced unsatisfactory performance.

For example, suppose one wanted to develop a test to measure the effects of an instructional segment designed to teach students to write complex sentences containing dependent clauses. A common problem in this task is that students produce incomplete sentences consisting only of dependent clauses. If a student submits an essay (a kind of test) with one or more incorrect sentences of this sort, the difficulty may be traced to several sources: the student may have neglected to reread his essay carefully after completing it; the student may not have known how to correct such an error even though he detected it; or the student may not have understood the basic concept that a dependent clause is not a proper sentence. In order to carry out the assignment, all of these abilities have to be in good working order — possession of adequate criteria for self-evaluation of test performance, ability to correct errors when they are detected, and attainment of the appropriate concept. If an incomplete sentence appears in a student's essay, we can only conclude that there has been a failure at one or more of these points in the system.

This analysis of the test requirements suggests ways of expanding the test procedure to allow more precise specification of the deficiency. For example, if a student has learned the concept (i.e., the difference between complete and incomplete sentences), then he should be able to point out complete sentences when he is shown examples of each. This task requires only that the student have attained the concept. Another way of determining whether or not a student has learned the concept is to ask him to reread his essay and point out any incomplete sentences. In either event, if the student is unable to identify incomplete sentences, there is no need to conduct further tests. At the other extreme, if a student can point out and correct his errors, then the source of the original mistake can be attributed to inadequate monitoring by the student of his own writing. This kind of sequential testing procedure, aimed at exact specification of sources of failure, is a natural outgrowth of information-processing models.

The preceding remarks are admittedly optimistic, given the miniscule contribution of learning theories in the past to curriculum design, particularly to the *how* of instruction. In practice, theoretical models have been of limited usefulness, to say the least. There are undoubtedly numerous reasons for this state of affairs, but the most important may be that learning psychologists have attempted to provide answers where a more valuable function would have been to raise questions. That is, learning models may make their greatest contribution to curriculum design in the future by prompting a behavioral analysis of curriculum, by asking *what a child must know* and *what cognitive skills he must have acquired* before we decide he has learned some part of the curriculum.

Information-processing analyses tend to focus on the relation of performance to the internal representation of the knowledge that is acquired. For example, suppose we want to teach a child the addition table, the sum of all pairs of integers from one to ten: How should this table be taught? In part, the answer to this question requires an analysis of the input or stimulus discriminations that are needed, the responses that must be added to the student's vocabulary, likely sources of inter-item interference, etc. — the traditional tools of the learning theorist's trade. However, the answer should also say something about instructional or training procedures, and about the effect that the choice of a particular procedure is likely to have on *what* the student learns. Thus, a "drill" procedure might lead to rote memorization which, in spite of its bad reputation, could be the most desirable form of learning in certain instances. By rote memory is meant a type of storage akin to what is known as "table lookup" in computer programs. When using this kind of memory storage, the student is able to respond to a relatively small number of inputs rapidly, accurately, and with a minimum of intermediate processing. As an alternative, memory might take the form of a generative rule or algorithm by means of which the output is reproduced. As an illustration, the binary numbers 00, 01 and 11 correspond to the decimal numbers 0, 1, 2 and 3, respectively. There is a rule for transforming any binary number to decimal form; in the present instance, a two-place binary number ij, is equal to $(i \cdot 2 + j \cdot 1)$ in decimal. The rule is completely general and can be expanded to apply to binary numbers with any number of places. On the other hand, if a computer programmer worked with binary numbers frequently, it would be to his advantage to learn by rote the decimal values of a limited set of binary numbers. For these numbers, he could then produce the decimal equivalent *without thinking,* (i.e., without employing a conversion rule), with a consequent improvement in speed and accuracy.

A parallel choice faces the curriculum designer in deciding how to teach the addition table. On the one hand, a child can be taught a counting algorithm (in its most common form, this algorithm involves fingers and toes as markers), one simple rule by which the one hundred entries in the table can be generated. This algorithm has the virtue of simplicity, of being easy to teach, and one might even argue that it gives the student an insight into the nature of addition. Teaching the addition table by rote, in contrast, would rely on drill and repetition — "one and one are two," etc. The counting algorithm would not be mentioned; in fact, it might even be desirable to arrange the instructional procedure so as to obscure the nature of the counting operation. If drill and repetition produce more rapid and accurate access to the sums in the addition table, this could be an important advantage when the sums are needed in other more complex operations, such as long multiplication. The disadvantage is the relatively slow rate of learning. Incidentally, an innate wisdom may be seen in the efforts of elementary teachers to discourage children from counting on their fingers. While there is nothing inherently wrong or improper about counting on your fingers, it may be instructionally and psychologically inefficient.

In summary, a learning theorist can serve a useful role in curriculum design by analyzing performance demands on the student during and after instruction. He has at his disposal theoretical and experimental tools which allow him to evaluate performance, and to develop methods for improving instructional efficiency based on analysis of the underlying processes. The curriculum can thereby be analyzed according to commonalities based on these underlying processes, as well as substantive content.

Next, we consider recent developments pertinent to processes that constitute learning.

The Present Status of Learning Theory

Learning theory has seen considerable ferment in the last two decades. The comprehensive theories of Hull, Tolman and others, which attempted to deal with learning and motivation in a general way, without regard to task context or subject matter, have lost the popularity they once enjoyed. It has even become fashionable to attack "simple-minded" stimulus-response (S-R) models. Of more significance has been the development of a new class of models, usually referred to as information-processing models. Where S-R models tended to focus on the elements that constitute the hardware of a computer, the newer models are more closely related to computer software, to programs, executive systems, operating systems, and so on. The contrast between these two approaches can be seen by comparing two recent books on human memory, one by Adams (1967), the other by Norman (1969). The Adams book represents a concerted and creative use of associationistic principles, including mediation, to account for the various phenomena that interest learning theorists. Norman considers many of the same data, but his interpretation is quite different. The discussion to follow will focus on the substance of the new developments; for a discussion of the differences between the S-R and information-processing approaches, the references above may be consulted.

Information-processing analyses of human behavior attempt to describe the transformation of information in the organism over time. These descriptions generally involve an interplay of attentional, perceptual, storage, retrieval and decision processes. Evaluating the contributions of these several processes has depended on the development of theoretical and experimental techniques which permit the operation of internal processes to be inferred from observable behavior.

Particularly significant has been the proliferation of extremely simple behavioral models which have functioned as microtheories within limited domains. In place of the comprehensive theories of a few decades ago, psychologists have increasingly turned to the formulation of simple models designed to accommodate a small but specifiable set of behavioral phenomena. A broad range of experimental data has proven amenable to this treatment: learning (Hintzman, 1968), recognition memory (Wickelgren & Norman, 1966), concept identification (Trabasso & Bower, 1968) and memory and perception tasks in which reaction time is the primary variable (Sternberg, 1968). Some models are both conceptually and mathematically simple, such as the one-element model for learning and concept identification (Atkinson, Bower & Crothers, 1965), some are conceptually simple but involve more difficult mathematics (Bower, 1967; Atkinson & Shiffrin, 1968a), and some entail more or less complex conceptual treatments which turn out to be mathematically simple (Sternberg, 1968). New applications for "old procedures," such as analysis of variance (Sternberg, 1968; Anderson, 1968) and information theory (Garner & Morton, 1969) have also been developed.

An interesting distinction has been drawn (e.g., by Atkinson & Shiffrin, 1968b) between the *structural* and *functional* elements of information processing. Structure refers to those features of the system that have more or less permanent operating characteristics; the fact that short-term memory capacity is limited to about seven chunks of information (Miller, 1956) is an example. Function refers to those features which depend on how a student uses the cognitive resources available to him. For example, the amount of information in a chunk depends on the coding strategies employed by a student.

The role of language in information processing has been increasingly emphasized — the wonder is that theories of human learning (and curriculum design) could have arisen which paid so little attention to language. The reasoning in such theories (explicit in Skinner, 1957, and Staats, 1968; and implicit in Osgood, 1963; and others) has been that (a) S-R associative links are the basis of all behavior including cognition, and (b) language can be understood as complex concatenations of such links. Statement (a) may be true, but (b) does not necessarily follow. A number of psychologists (e.g., Miller, 1965) have argued for some time against (b), and other "conversions" have been observed lately (e.g., Deese, 1969; also see Osgood, 1968, for some thoughtful comments on the problem). While it might be possible to describe language behavior by a model based at the lowest level of analysis on S-R links, the structure of the model — the description of how observable behavior is related to such elements — would almost certainly be nonlinear. Miller (1965) states this for sentences: "The meaning of an utterance is not a linear sum of the meanings of the words that comprise it." The principle may be extended: the meaning of a word is not the sum of the associations to that word, and so on.

The point of these remarks is that the ability of a model to handle language behavior may be an index of its adequacy and representativeness. As noted previously, theories of curriculum design have tended to be more *content oriented* than *behaviorally oriented*. The remarkable corollary of this state of affairs is the relatively little attention given to the relation between curriculum design and the language system of the student.

Applications of Information-Processing Models to Curriculum Design

Three examples will now be presented in which simple behavioral models will be used to separate the cognitive processes intervening between input and response. In each case, the model is an obvious oversimplification, but this has little bearing on the usefulness of the model as an explanatory tool. In other cases, the nature of the simplification dictates the limits within which the model should be applicable. Finally, "stripped-down" models provide a norm or reference, deviations from which can suggest the direction that changes should take.

A Decision Model for Recognition Tests. The first example concerns the role of decision processes in recognition-test performance. Suppose a student is being taught to factor algebraic expressions. For simplicity, assume that there are two classes of such problems, C_1 and C_2, and two methods of solution, M_1 and M_2 (e.g., quadratic equations consisting of "simple" factors, and those where there are no simple factors, in which the general quadratic solution must be employed). To make the problem interesting, it will also be assumed that the difference between C_1 and C_2 is of such a nature that it is difficult to explain to the student. Instruction is carried out in inductive fashion; a series of problems are presented to the student, some from C_1 and some from C_2, and the student is asked to state which method, M_1 or M_2, is more appropriate for each problem. He is then told whether or not his choice is correct.

In analyzing performance in this task, a reasonable starting point is the assumption that two processes intervene between input and response. First, there is a process of interpretation and identification of each problem as belonging to C_1 or C_2, or as indeterminant. The corresponding internal states will be referred to as C_1', C_2', or C_0', respectively. For simplicity, suppose that c, the probability of a correct identification, is the same for both classes of problems, so that the probability that a problem is seen as indeterminant is $1-c$. Second, there is a decision process; after "identifying" the problem, the student then decides whether to chose M_1 or M_2. The assumption will be made here that if the student identifies the problem as C_1 or C_2 he will respond appropriately, and if he is uncertain, he will choose M_1 with probability d and M_2 with probability $1-d$.

The possible sequences of events are represented in FIGURE 1, where internal unobservable events are enclosed in solid blocks. The rules of probability theory can be used to generate a variety of predictions, the most significant of which are presented at the bottom of FIGURE 1. The term $\Pr(M_1|C_1)$ is the probability that the student choses M_1 when a problem is from C_1, and $\Pr(M_1|C_2)$ is the probability that he choses M_1 when the problem is from C_2. (This analysis is formally identical to what is known as signal detection in psychophysics; Green & Swets, 1966; Atkinson, Bower & Crothers, 1965, Ch. 5). The model predicts that these two probabilities will be related to each other, as shown in FIGURE 2, which also presents graphical interpretations of the identification parameter c and the decision parameter d.

The instructor is primarily interested in c, the probability that a student correctly identifies the solution class of a problem. Ideally, this probability should be close to 1 at the end of instruction. It is often assumed that performance mirrors the internal states of the subject in a direct fashion; if a student choses M_1 or M_2, it is because his internal identification states are C_1' or C_2', respectively. This assumption greatly simplifies evaluation of the student's performance, since correct responses reflect correct identification. However, if the student is sometimes uncertain, then there are several factors that might lead a student when uncertain to be biased in his choice of one method or the other. Under certain plausible conditions, the student's performance may be perfect because of his bias, even though he is completely unable to identify the class of problems.

One factor that can affect response bias or d is the relative frequency of occurrence of problems from the two classes. For example, suppose that one problem class is much more likely to be presented than the other. This situation is found frequently in algebra texts, in which most or all of the problems in a section can be solved by a single method. Whether or not the student can identify the class of a problem, his best bet if uncertain is to try the method that is *au courant* for that section. This strategy will produce quite adequate performance. The inadequacy of this strategy shows up only at the time of a final exam, when all classes of problems are equally represented. If the student cannot identify the problem class (i.e., if c is small), and if problems from C_1 and C_2 are equally likely to occur, the student will be wrong about half the time, no matter what his decision strategy.

A second factor affecting the decision process has to do with the costs and gains of the different outcomes. In the algebraic factoring example, M_2 will always produce a correct solution, since the general quadratic formula always works. On the other hand, if simple factors can be seen directly, the computations are much less onerous and calculation errors are less likely. Thus, a lazy student might decide to choose M_1 when he was uncertain because of the less work involved, while a compulsive student might select M_2 because a correct solution was guaranteed.

Two students are displayed in FIGURE 2, representing different identification and decision parameters. To the extent that the model is reasonably adequate, this method of portraying a student's performance permits separate evaluation of the role of identification and decision processes for each student. For example, by visual examination of the graph we can state that student A is less accurate than B in identifying the class of a problem, and that A is slightly biased toward M_1, while B is very biased toward M_2.

The analysis also points up potential inadequacies in curriulum design procedures. In this example, if a particular response is likely to be correct for all problems in a set, the student can do well by deciding to employ this method, regardless of whether he can identify the aspects of the problem set which differentiate it from other problem sets. A better design would be achieved by always including problems from two (or more) classes in each section, so that the student cannot perform well simply by varying his decision strategy.

An Additive-factor Model. The second example is modeled after Sternberg's (1968) *additive-factor* method. Suppose a student is presented with information which he is to remember for a period of time, after which a recognition test is to be administered. The information may be presented in one or more modalities — visual, auditory, tactual, and so on. Similarly, the test procedure can incorporate various modalities. Thus, in teaching a child to point out the letters of the alphabet as each is named, visual or tactual modalities or both could be employed (i.e., the child might see the visual form of the letter, or touch the form). The question can be raised: how is performance determined by choice of modality and combinations of modali-

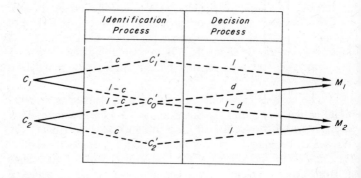

$$Pr(M_1 \,/\, C_1) = c + (1-c)\,d \qquad Pr(M_1 \,/\, C_2) = (1-c)\,d$$

$$Pr(M_1 \,/\, C_1) = c + Pr(M_1 \,/\, C_2)$$

FIG. 1. Flow diagram of events in recognition task. Student is shown problem from C_1 or C_2, and must choose method M_1 or M_2. Two-process model assumes identification process in which class of problem is correctly identified with probability c (internal states C_1' and C_2') or not identified (internal states C_0') with probability $1-c$, and decision process in which student decides to chose M_1 with probability d and M_2 with probability $1-d$ when uncertain about class of problem. Statistics derived from the model are shown below flow diagram.

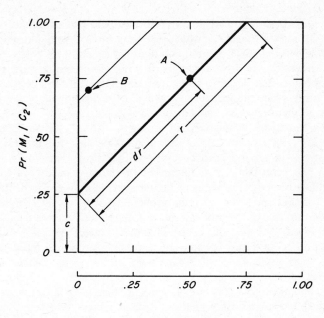

FIG. 2. Graphical interpretation of model in FIG. 1. Student's perform-ance, measured by $Pr(M_1|C_1)$ and $Pr(M_1|C_2)$ jointly, locates student in the square above. Heavy 45° line describes student A. Point at which line intersects vertical axis provides an estimate of c. The line is traced out as decision probability d ranges from 0 to 1. Estimate of d is pro-vided by location of student up the line relative to length of line r. For student A, $c=.2$ and $d=.67$; this student can identify the class of a problem only 20% of the time and chooses M_1 67% of the time when uncertain. For student B, $c=.70$ and $d=.15$; 70% of the problems are identified, and when uncertain the student chooses M_1 only 15% of the time. (Cf Atkinson, *et al.*, 1965, Ch. 5, for complete description of this technique.)

ties? Similar questions have been raised frequently about "auditory-visual" vs. "auditory" or "visual" instruction, or radio vs. television instruction.

To begin the analysis, we will postulate two processes — *storage* and *retrieval* — which will be identified with the independent variables of presentation and test modality, respectively. In order for a correct response to occur, information must be properly stored during presentation, and retrieval must be satisfactorily accomplished during testing. (The likelihood of being correct by chance is assumed to be negligible.)

Details of the analysis are shown in TABLE 1. First, let us consider the implications of the assumption that the processes combine in an independent fashion. Specifically, assume that (a) the probability of a failure in the storage process is the product of the probabilities of failure given each of the presentation modes employed; (b) the probability of failure in retrieval is the product of the probabilities of failure given each test mode employed; and (c) the probability of a correct recognition is the product of the probabilities of successful storage and retrieval.

The probabilities of a failure in storage given *visual* and *tactual* presentations are $s(v)$ and $s(t)$, respectively, and *mutatis mutandi* $r(v)$ and $r(t)$ are the probabilities of a failure in retrieval test modes. If visual and tactual presentation are combined, then a failure in storage will occur only if *neither* of these inputs are successful; the probability of this event, assuming independence as in (a), is $s(v)s(t)$. Hence, the likelihood of successful storage in the visual-tactual presentation condition will be $1-s(v)s(t)$. Similarly, (b) implies that the likelihood of successful retrieval in the visual-tactual test condition is $1-r(v)r(t)$.

For a correct response, both storage and retrieval must be successful. From (c) these are also assumed to be independent, so that if i and j are the presentation and test conditions,

$$\Pr(\text{Correct}|\text{Presentation } i, \text{ Test } j) =$$
$$\Pr(\text{Storage}|\text{Presentation } i)\ \Pr(\text{Retrieval}|\text{Test } j).$$

The full set of probabilities implied by these assumptions is shown in the expected performance matrix in the middle of TABLE 1. The equation above also implies that:

log Pr(Correct|Presentation i, Test j) =
log Pr(Storage|Presentation i) + log Pr(Retrieval|Test j).
In other words, the assumption of independent combination of processes implies a multiplicative relation between the component probabilities, and hence an additive relation between the logarithm of these components, as shown at the lower part of TABLE 1.

Suppose an experiment has been conducted following the experimental design in TABLE 1, employing log Pr(Correct) as the dependent variable. To the extent that the assumptions of independent storage and retrieval processes is an accurate description of performance, then analysis of variance of the data should show only main effects of the presentation and test variables. No interaction is expected since the predicted values at the bottom of TABLE 1 are additive combinations of the row and column components. The test of this additive-factor model does not require explicit estimation of any parameters, and the power of the test is the power of the analysis of variance procedure under a particular alternative hypothesis.[2]

The major implication of the model is that performance when measured on the proper scale is the simplest possible combination of presentation and test variables — the effect of one variable is not dependent on the level of another. Thus, if *visual-tactual presentation* and *visual test* conditions produce the highest average performance levels, the combination of these two conditions will be optimal.[3]

A simple way of making a more powerful experimental test of the additive-factor model is to increase the number of dimensions in the design. For example, suppose that in the visual mode an associative or mnemonic cue is added to the visual stimulus (e.g., the letter form is embedded in a familiar context such as a drawing of an apple for *a,* a butterfly for *b,* etc.) Two new presentation conditions, *visual-associative* and *visual-tactual-associative,* would be added to the three in TABLE 1, so that the experimental design would become a 5 x 3 factorial. The power of the test for presence of an interaction would increase with the greater degrees of freedom in the analysis of variance.

The effect of combined modalities within presentation or test conditions must be considered apart from the question of how presentation and test modes combine. In the preceding discussion, it was assumed that combinations of modalities contribute independently to the operation of a process; if $s(v)$ and $s(t)$ are the probabilities that storage does *not* take place in the visual and tactual presentation modes, respectively, a failure of storage in the visual-tactual mode occurs only if *neither* mode results in storage. The probability of this event is $s(v) \, s(t)$, and hence the probability of storage given in TABLE 1 as $1-s(v)s(t)$. I have not been able to think of a simple way of applying an additive-factor analysis in the evaluation of the assumption of independence-of-modalities. An alternative approach would be to estimate parameters from the single-mode conditions, and predict the multiple-mode condition. This approach would be quite adequate if the storage and retrieval processes actually combined in an independent fashion. Specifically, if there were no interaction in the analysis of the logarithms of proportion of correct responses, then the proportion of errors in the *visual-tactual* presentation mode should equal the product of proportions of errors in the *visual* and *tactual* presentation modes, and a similar relation should hold for test mode.

The prediction of independent combinations provides a useful norm against which to test other hypotheses. For example, one might argue that when a student is presented information in more than one modality, only one of the modes actually will be effective, whichever is the more likely to produce successful storage. This alternative hypothesis would predict that the proportion of errors in the combined visual-tactual condition would be equal to $s(v)$ or $s(t)$, whichever was less. The effect of combining modalities would therefore be less than predicted by the assumption of independence. On the other hand, it might be assumed that for combined modalities the whole would be greater than the parts, i.e., that performance would be better in the combined modality condition than predicted by independence. Once again, by introducing additional modality combinations a stronger experimental test of alternative hypotheses would be achieved.

Response-dependent Teaching Strategies. The third example has its origins in the "all-or-none" controversy about the effect of repetitions on the formation of associations in rote learning (Estes, 1960; Underwood & Keppel, 1962). Briefly, the controversy took the following form: Consider learning situations in which the material to be learned can be broken into more or less independent segments, each consisting of a block of information (the "stimulus") about which the student must learn something (the "response"). While most of the experiments on this problem actually involved learning of paired-associate nonsense syllables (e.g., VAC as the stimulus, DIB as the response), the analysis is in principle applicable to any curriculum with the properties just specified.[4] It is also assumed that each segment will probably have to be presented several times before learning is complete.

It had been generally assumed that in such tasks, each time a segment was presented for study, there was an increment in associative strength between the stimulus and response. Learning occurred as a consequence of a gradual accretion; "practice makes perfect" in a slow but sure fashion.

The all-or-none hypothesis asserted that most repetitions or study periods generally produced no permanent change in performance. However, during each study period on a given segment, with some probability an effective code would be established between the stimulus and response, associative strength would jump from a negligible value to a maximum value in a single trial. Hence, following each study period, learning was *all* (an effective code had been established) or *none* (none of the preceding study periods had been effective).

It is not germane at this point to review all of the details of the controversy surrounding this question. The fighting was fierce, and so many compromises occurred during the battle that it is now difficult to tell who won.

One point that was relatively well established was the existence of marked *response dependencies* in associative learning. A response-dependency exists when the student's response to a segment provides significant information about his state of learning on that segment. This characteristic of the learning process proved to be a critical distinction between all-or-none and incremental models of associative learning. In its strongest form, an incremental position implies that the only relevant index of amount of learning is amount of practice or number of study periods — the responses are irrelevant. The contrasting all-or-none position is that the only relevant index of learning is found in the student's responses; specifically, if a student is tested on a segment and his response is an error, then no learning has occurred up to that point, regardless of whether the segment has been previously studied once or a hundred times. The data indicated that both indices were important, as one might predict, but response information was substantially more significant than the amount of practice. The adage applies in a slightly modified form — if you don't succeed (on a segment), you'd better try again.[5]

A number of theoretical investigations (Groen & Atkinson, 1966; Karush & Dear, 1966; Calfee, in press) have focused on optimal instructional strategies based on the all-or-none or incremental models, a distinction basically parallel to repsonse-dependent and response-independent processes, respectively. These investigations have explored a variety of interesting technical details, but the gist of the results is straightforward — if the student's performance is a good index to his state of learning for a segment, this information should be used in apportioning study time to the various segments. For example, the all-or-none model implies that learning is optimized if the following decision strategy is employed in selecting segments for study—present for study that segment with the fewest successes since the last error. An optimal decision strategy based on the incremental model, assuming equivalent rates of learning for every segment, would be to equalize the number of study periods.

By way of illustration, suppose a lesson consists of three segments, S_1, S_2 and S_3, which have been studied five, ten and twenty times respectively. Assume further that the last incorrect response for S_1 was just prior to the fourth study period on that segment, and that the last errors for S_2 and S_3 were prior to the seventh and twentieth study periods for those segments. A decision based on a response-dependent model would be the choice of S_3; since the immediately preceding response was incorrect, the odds are high that this segment is unlearned, and hence could benefit from study. The fact that the last three responses to S_2 were correct would be evidence that it may well have been learned and hence nothing would be gained by studying it. The single success on S_1 since the last error is weaker evidence that it has been learned, but the odds would still favor presentation of S_3 over S_1. A decision based on equalizing the total amount of study time on each segment would be to choose S_1 for study, since it has been relatively neglected.

As applied to curriculum matters, a response-dependent decision strategy amounts to a policy of oiling the wheels that squeak the loudest. In other words, the instructor uses the students's response history to determine those instructional segments that are least likely to have been satisfactorily learned, then directs the student to work on those segments. While this strategy may seem sensible, it is not widely employed, nor is it always desirable. A critical analysis of teaching procedures would probably show that most teachers (and students) employ a policy of uniform distribution of study time or, more likely, of spending more time on those segments which are the easiest for the student. For example, phonics instruction is frequently omitted for beginning readers on the lowest track, because it is quite difficult for them.

On the other hand, it should be noted that there are other important conditions on the optimal decision strategy that were not raised above. One of these conditions is the form of the gain function; i.e., what is the value of studying a particular segment. The usual assumption has been that the largest gains in performance come early in the learning process, and while this holds true for most laboratory learning tasks with college students as subjects, it may not hold for classroom learning and student populations. Such a gain function could lead to "get what you can while the getting's good" strategies in which a large number of segments are presented a relatively few times, as opposed to presenting fewer segments a large number of times.

There are other criteria of optimality than maximizing average performance. One would be to maximize the number of segments on which performance exceeds a critical minimum level (e.g., select segments so that on a final criterion test, every segment has at least a 50-50 chance of being correctly answered), or a type of *minimax* criterion, in which the strategy would minimize the maximum "loss" so that the poorest segment in the set would reflect the least possible loss consistent with over-all performance on a final criterion test.

This example has illustrated the application of learning process models in the derivation of instructional strategies. This type of analysis calls explicit attention to the interrelation of instructional decisions, costs, gains and criteria for evaluation of an instructional strategy, and emphasizes the role of learning models in developing such strategies.

Summary

The information-processing approach to theoretical analyses of learning provides an answer to the question: *how should we do research to determine how to teach?* This is a more modest goal in some ways than earlier efforts to give a general answer to the question: *how should we teach?* Information-processing models are developed for application to a limited set of experimental conditions. Within those contexts, they constitute a powerful means of identifying the effects of independent variables on underlying cognitive processes.

The models that have proven most useful have tended to be quite simple, measured by the number of parameters required to describe the process, or by the form of the functional relations. The use of standard statistical models such as analysis of variance to represent psychological processes is an important step. To the best of my knowledge, Anderson (1962) was the first to recognize the potential of this technique. As Sternberg (1968) has observed, the adequacy of the additive-factor technique depends on the appropriate choice of independent *and* de-

Description of Underlying Processes

Storage Process	
Presentation Mode	Probability of Storage
Visual	$1-s(v)$
Tactual	$1-s(t)$

Retrieval Process	
Test Mode	Probability of Retrieval
Visual	$1-r(v)$
Tactual	$1-r(t)$

Expected Performance Matrix
Probability of Success

Test Mode	Presentation Mode		
	Visual	Tactual	Visual – Tactual
Visual	$[1-s(v)]\cdot[1-r(v)]$	$[1-s(t)]\cdot[1-r(v)]$	$[1-s(v)s(t)]\cdot[1-r(v)]$
Tactual	$[1-s(v)]\cdot[1-r(t)]$	$[1-s(t)]\cdot[1-r(t)]$	$[1-s(v)s(t)]\cdot[1-r(t)]$
Visual-Tactual	$[1-s(v)]\cdot[1-r(v)r(t)]$	$[1-s(t)]\cdot[1-r(v)r(t)]$	$[1-s(v)s(t)]\cdot[1-r(v)r(t)]$

Logarithm of Probability of Success

Test Mode	Presentation Mode			
	Visual	Tactual	Visual – Tactual	Row Component
Visual	$\log[1-s(v)] + \log[1-r(v)]$	$\log[1-s(t)] + \log[1-r(v)]$	$\log[1-s(v)s(t)] + \log[1-r(v)]$	$\log[1-r(v)]$
Tactual	$\log[1-s(v)] + \log[1-r(t)]$	$\log[1-s(t)] + \log[1-r(t)]$	$\log[1-s(v)s(t)] + \log[1-r(t)]$	$\log[1-r(t)]$
Visual-Tactual	$\log[1-s(v)] + \log[1-r(v)r(t)]$	$\log[1-s(t)] + \log[1-r(v)r(t)]$	$\log[1-s(v)s(t)] + \log[1-r(v)r(t)]$	$\log[1-r(v)r(t)]$
Column Component	$\log[1-s(v)]$	$\log[1-s(t)]$	$\log[1-s(v)s(t)]$	

TABLE 1

Additive-Factor Analysis of Effects of Presentation and Test Modality on Storage and Retrieval Processes During Learning of Alphabet Names. See Text for Discussion.

pendent variables. The proof of the pudding is in the eating, however, and the strongest support for these techniques lies in the success that has been achieved in providing concise descriptions of data by this means.

Examples of the application of information-processing models to curriculum problems were given in the previous section. The models do not necessarily say what the best teaching method will be in any particular instance. Although theoretically optimal teaching techniques have been derived for certain classes of learning problems (and the next decade should see substantial theoretical and empirical extensions of this work), so many external and internal variables affect learning that it seems unlikely that we shall ever find a completely general answer to the question of "what is the best way to teach." However, information-processing models do provide a means of specifying precisely what a student has and has not learned following instruction and a means of identifying the effects of variation in instructional method on each of the cognitive processes which combine to produce the observed behavior.

References

Adams, J. A. *Human Memory*. New York: McGraw-Hill, 1967.

Anderson, N. H. A Simple Model for Information Integration. In R. P. Ableson, R. Aronson, W. J. McGuire, T. M. Newcomb, M. J. Rosenberg & P. H. Tannenbaum (Eds.) *Theories of Cognitive Consistency: A Source Book*. Chicago: Rand McNally, 1968.

.... On the Quantification of Miller's Conflict Theory. *Psychological Review*, 1962, *69*, 400-414.

Atkinson, R. C., Bower, G. H. & Crothers, E. J. *An Introduction to Mathematical Learning Theory*. New York: John Wiley, 1965.

.... & Shiffrin, R. M. Human Memory: A Proposed System and Its Control Processes. In K. W. Spence & J. T. Spence (Eds.) *The Psychology of Learning and Motivation: Advances in Research and Theory*. Vol. II. New York: Academic Press, 1968(a).

.... Some Speculations on Storage and Retrieval Process in Long-Term Memory. Technical Report 127. Institute for Mathematical Studies in the Social Sciences, Stanford University, Stanford, California, 1968(b).

Bower, G. H. A Multicomponent Theory of the Memory Trace. In K. W. Spence, J. T. Spence & N. H. Anderson (Eds.) *The Psychology of Learning and Motivation: Advances in Research and Theory*.

Vol. I. New York: Academic Press, 1967.

.... Mental Imagery and Associative Learning. In L. Gregg (Ed.) *Cognition of Learning and Memory*. New York: John Wiley, in press.

Calfee, R. C.   Further Analyses of Optimal Procedures for Associative Learning. *Journal of Mathematical Psychology*, in press.

Deese, J.   Behavior and Fact. *American Psychologist*, 1969, *24*, 515-522.

Estes, W. K.   Learning Theory and the New Mental Chemistry. *Psychological Review*, 1960, *67*, 207-223.

Garner, W. R. & Morton, J.   Perceptual Independence: Definitions Models and Experimental Paradigms. *Psychological Bulletin*, 1969, *72*, 233-259.

Green, D. M. & Swets, J. A.   *Signal Detection Theory and Psychophysics*. New York: John Wiley, 1966.

Groen, G. & Atkinson, R. C.   Models for Optimizing the Learning Process. *Psychological Bulletin*, 1966, *66*, 309-320.

Hintzman, D. L.   Explorations with a Discrimination Net Model for Paired-Associate Learning. *Journal of Mathematical Psychology*, 1968, *5*, 123-162.

Karush, W. & Dear, R. E.   Optimal Stimulus Presentation Strategy for a Stimulus Sampling Model of Learning. *Journal of Mathematical Psychology*, 1966, *3*, 19-47.

Miller, G. A.   Some Preliminaries to Psycholinguistics. *American Psychologist*, 1956, *20*, 15-20.

.... The Magical Number Seven, Plus or Minus Two: Some Limits on Our Capacity For Processing Information. *Psychological Review*, 1965, *63*, 81-97.

Norman, D. A.   *Memory and Attention: An Introduction to Human Information Processing*. New York: John Wiley, 1969.

Osgood, C. E.   On Understanding and Creating Sentences. *American Psychologist*, 1963, *18*, 735-751.

.... Toward a Wedding of Insufficiencies. In R. T. Dixon & D. L. Horton (Eds.) *Verbal Behavior and General Behavior Theory*. Englewood Cliffs, N. J.: Prentice-Hall, 1968.

Skinner, B. F.   *Verbal Behavior*. New York: Appleton-Century-Crofts, 1957.

Staats, A. W.   *Learning, Language and Cognition*. New York: Holt, Rinehart and Winston, 1968.

Sternberg, S.   The Discovery of Processing Stages: Extensions of Donder's Method. In W. G. Koster (Ed.) *Attention and Performance II*. Amsterdam: North-Holland Publishing, 1969.

Trabasso, T. & Bower, G. H.   *Attention in Learning*. New York: John Wiley, 1968.

Underwood, B. J. & Keppel, G.   One-Trial Learning? *Journal of Verbal Learning and Verbal Behavior*, 1962, *L*, 1-13.

Wickelgren, W. A. & Norman, D. A.   Strength Models and Serial Position in Short-Term Recognition Memory. *Journal of Mathematical Psychology,* 1966, *3,* 316-347.

---

1. The preparation of this paper was made possible in part by Grant MH12637 from the National Institute of Mental Health. Dennis Bunde first suggested the extention of Sternberg's additive-factor approach to probabilities, and deserves credit for the idea. Thanks also go to Jane Marantz for a helpful critique of earlier drafts.

---

2. As Sternberg (1968) points out, interactions may also reflect the fact that there is but a single process underlying performance, and that the experimental factors affect this process in an interactive fashion, or interactions may result from inappropriate identification of experimental factors with underlying processes.

---

3. As an alternative hypothesis, assume that retrieval is dependent on the extent to which presentation and test conditions are equivalent. Specifically, if the visual stimulus is present both during presentation and test, then the likelihood of retrieval is $1-r(v)$, but if the visual stimulus is present only at test, then likelihood of retrieval is $1-r'(v)$ with the implicit assumption that $1-r'(v)$ is less that $1-r(v)$; and *mutatis mutandi* for the tactual retrieval parameters $r(t)$ and $r'(t)$. The pattern of results in this second model is more complex than in the previous model; an interaction is predicted such that entries along the main diagonal will be greater than predicted by the main effects, and cross-modal entries (e.g., *visual* presentation and *tactual* test) will be less. The notion here is that retrieval is facilitated to the extent that during testing there is a reconstitution of the original presentation.

---

4. The importance of this remark should not be overlooked. Rote association has typically been identified with drill-type material such as foreign language vocabulary, initial reading vocabulary, or addition and multiplication tables. The present discussion certainly applies to these problems, but is also applicable to any subset of curriculum which can be partitioned into independent "chunks" or segments. Independence is defined to mean that the learning of any particular segment is not affected by whether any other segment has been learned, so that the instructor is free to select any segment for presentation without worrying about interactions with other segments. A great deal of introductory material in fields such as history, geography, chemistry, psychology, etc., may well satisfy this requirement; much of mathematics does not, since some segments are prerequisite to the learning of others (e.g., addition, subtraction and multiplication must be learned before long division can be introduced).

---

5. The existence of response dependencies is not strong evidence *per se*

that learning is all-or-none, but only that the simplest form of the incremental model is inappropriate. For example, if some segments are fairly easy to learn, and others are quite hard, the responses will serve to identify these classes of segments differentially, whether learning is all-or-none or incremental. In the discussion that follows, the response-dependent character of a learning process is significant, not whether learning is all-or-none, incremental, or a combination of the two.

20

Computers, Instruction and the Curriculum

Max Jerman

The cries heard in the Halls of Education today include the one which claims that for education to be effective it must "meet the needs" of each person by individualizing instruction. The computer appears to offer the only serious hope of accomplishing this objective.

Nevertheless, many school teachers and administrators, particularly those not closely related to some operational computer center or CAI program, have no clear idea of the current state of the art. They often are disappointed to learn that the computers pictured as operational in science-fiction movies or popular articles are not off-the-shelf items. Others feel that unless the computer is used to its fullest capacity in a creative sense, educators are not doing their job. These people object to em-

MAX JERMAN is research associate at the Institute for Mathematical Studies in the Social Sciences at Stanford University.

ploying a computer for the routine tasks that fill the average school day, such as giving tests and drills, and grading papers. Rather, they contend that unless a computer is programmed to interact with each student individually and take into account personality and aptitude variables while generating curriculum appropriate to his specific needs in terms of his educational achievement and background, its capability is being misused. There are, however, several viable modes of instruction.

Modes of Instruction

1. Drill and Practice

The drill-and-practice system is based on the hypothesis that the classroom teacher assumes responsibility for the sequential development of the conceptual content of the course of instruction.

There are at least two approaches to the construction of drill-and-practice CAI programs; the concept block approach and the concept strands approach. In the first, the content of the year's work in a subject area is subdivided into logical units on specific concepts or topics. The units of instruction are arranged in a sequence intended to optimize learning. However, all teachers do not follow the same sequence of instruction. Also, students may find some units either easier or more difficult than desired or expected. The CAI program, therefore, must be flexible enough to permit the sequencing of units to suit the needs of any individual, group, or class as determined by the classroom teacher.

The teacher then is at all times the master of the flow of topics. The first level of individualization is teacher-directed, in the sense that he controls the order of topics. The second level of individualization is computer-directed, since the computer automatically adjusts the difficulty level and branching structure for each student. The capability of adjusting the level of difficulty provides motivation in that each student is able to achieve a degree of success at whatever level of difficulty he is capable of working.

To be most effective, drill-and-practice work on basic skills and concepts should follow the initial introduction of a concept in the classroom by two to four weeks. The sequence of events is something like the following: Topics are first introduced in class by the teacher. With the introduction of each new topic, the teacher develops concepts and raises skills to an acceptable level by concentrated practice. Then, as the teacher moves on to a new topic, the drill-and-practice system through constant and individualized review at appropriate levels of difficulty fixes the concepts and increases computational skills.

Teaching with a drill-and-practice system. Perhaps the most effective technique with which a classroom teacher can gain maximum benefit for his students from a CAI drill-and-practice system is to prepare a list of instructional objectives, in behavioral terms, for each course. In mathematics, for example, each type of problem the student will be expected to complete successfully should be the object of a behavioral description.

In the workshops conducted for teachers in the Stanford drill-and-practice program in elementary school mathematics (Jerman and Suppes, 1969), the first step toward planning and preparing statements of instructional objectives is to define the end-of-year objectives. Although teachers do not commit themselves in writing to achieve these objectives for their classes, they do establish goals for their classes of the types of exercises they would like their students to complete successfully by the end of the school year. For a surprising number of teachers, the preparation of behavioral objectives is a new experience. Ideally, the statements of behavioral objectives should contain three parts: (1) an example or description of the type of exercise the student is to perform; (2) the conditions under which he is to perform the exercise; and (3) the criteria for successful performance. Stated another way, teachers state what task they will accept from the student as evidence of his successful mastery of each skill or concept.

Perhaps the most disturbing feature of this exercise for teachers is that they must begin with statements of end-of-year objectives rather than following the text page by page. At first, teachers are discouraged from using their classroom texts. Rather they are encouraged to specify the mathematical content, instead of simply teaching the text. Once the end-of-year objectives are written, including examples of each exercise, the teacher prepares lists of exercises for each grading period. By first defining the end-of-year objectives, the teachers have less of a tendency to aim too high or too low in their expectations than when they plan the year from first to last. Once the statements of objectives for each grading period have been written, the teachers are introduced to the available concept units on-line to their students. They then select the appropriate units to support their planned program of classroom instruction and are free to select any unit from any grade level and to schedule them in the order desired.

A daily class report furnishes information on each student's performance and progress to date.

The exact content of each lesson is provided in printed form for reference so that the teacher may see exactly what kinds of problems the student is working on.

The last line of the report gives a distribution of the number of students working in each concept unit for that particular class.

Teachers are able to group the students in their classroom into different computer classes for the purpose of having different groups of students work on different sequences of review-and-practice lessons on the CAI system. The students are unaware of any grouping. They simply sign on each day and are given a lesson. They pride themselves in having lessons that are different from those given other students.

This brings us to the second type drill-and-practice system — the concept strands — which provides a higher level of individualization and furnishes more specific information to the teacher about the difficulties children may have. The curriculum content is organized by concept strands rather than units. Each strand begins at the lowest appropriate level and extends in a logical sequence to the highest level. Each student's lesson consists of a mixture of exercises from each appropriate strand according to his own achievement level. A detailed description of this type of program is given elsewhere (*ET*, August, 1969).

A student in this program is limited only by his own learning rate. The sequence of exercises in each strand and the strands themselves are preset. The teacher may not alter the sequence. Some teachers become uneasy at the prospect that some students may "get ahead" of the rest of the class, while others encourage able students to advance as rapidly as possible. Of course this may mean that a teacher is required to work on a more individual basis by providing an introduction to each new topic for students *who* need it *when* they need it.

The classroom organization is usually little affected, from an outside observer's point of view. Students are scheduled to take their lessons at the same time each day and generally operate independently in going to the terminal when it is their turn.

Perhaps the greatest impact of a drill-and-practice CAI system is on the teacher. Daily reports provide a continuous flow of information on the achievement of each student. When the daily report data are checked against the defined objectives, the teacher has a clear indication of each student's success as well as areas where some students may need extra help. Time does not permit many teachers to provide the individual attention necessary when students simultaneously work at many different points in the curriculum. Then, too, some teachers simply do not know how to work individually with students to help them overcome existing learning difficulties.

To help both the teacher and the students it may be necessary to reshape the traditional teacher-classroom role. As more and better CAI programs are developed, schools can be expected to be organized around a seminar-type instructional program where the function of the teacher is (a) to introduce a concept, (b) send the students to work at instructional terminals, and (c) synthesize the concepts and handle individual problems in a subsequent seminar session. The teacher in the seminar session would have the advantage of knowing by means of a computer-generated class report how well each student performed on the set of developmental or practice exercises at the instructional terminal following the introduction to the topic. Specific and general difficulties could be covered at the beginning of the seminar and the next topic for study introduced.

2. Tutorial

To many people, tutorial instruction in the sense of a programmed text they may have seen or used is what first comes to mind when they hear the term "CAI." This concept, no doubt, is behind the often-heard question "Will CAI replace the classroom teacher?" Like drill-and-practice programs, tutorial programs serve specific purposes and are most effective when used in conjunction with a well-trained teacher.

Teaching with a tutorial system. The value of having well-defined behavioral objectives is not attenuated when a tutorial program rather than the teacher assumes the responsibility of instruction for a topic or course. The teacher must be thoroughly familiar with the content of the program, and must be prepared to assist students with any questions that may arise. In cases where the instructional program is relatively advanced, the teacher may learn along with the students when the topic is also new to the teacher. For example, in the Stanford logic and modern algebra program, bright students in the fifth grade and above are introduced to topics that normally are not taught as part of the regular mathematics curriculum in most schools. Few elementary school teachers have had a formal college course in logic. In this kind of situation, it was found that teachers who stayed several lessons ahead of their students were able to answer most of their questions with the aid of a handbook containing sample solutions. Such programs offer many schools enrichment and acceleration opportunities that otherwise might not be available.

Since tutorial programs are often prepared for use on multimedia systems or systems with expensive terminals, they are expected to produce a significantly greater amount of learning. Simply having several media available at an instructional station, i.e., films, audio, CRT, keyboard, light pen, etc., does not automatically guarantee a better program or a higher level of learning. This is not so say, however, that a multimedia student terminal is not desirable. All of us wish more features were available at reasonable prices. The teacher must define both his objectives and the content of the CAI program as well as the organization of program to provide instruction. To be able to judge the quality of instruction, a teacher must resist the glamour of a pretty terminal and judge the value of the program on the basis of student achievement and attitude. This presents a more difficult task with tutorial programs than with drill-and-practice programs. The key to a good tutorial program as well as to any other program is the amount and kind of student involvement it produces. Experience at the Stanford Laboratory has shown that elaborate hardware alone does not maintain student interest or attention for long. Only the programs can do this.

Administratively, tutorial instruction is no more difficult to schedule than drill-and-practice. If anything, it is simpler. The major share of the administrative chore, however, is borne by the teacher who must plan and schedule the instructional sessions.

The teacher who used tutorial programs with their classes in enriched or conventional subject areas did not change significantly their own patterns of behavior. Hopefully, however, as more programs become available in the future, teachers will introduce seminar-type class sessions and place more emphasis on individual problems. After years of discussing the role of the educator as a professional, we now are beginning to have the tools at hand to do the professional job of teaching each person as an individual. One of the things that makes a doctor's work effective is the test data he gathers on our physical processes. He knows how our bodies function in critical areas and is able to prescribe treatment. Educators have been handicapped by a lack of up-to-date, reliable data for each student and have had to rely on yearly tests, periodic daily work, and experience. With daily reports on each student's performance, teachers soon will be in a position to make a professional diagnosis and to make a prescription for each student on a one-to-one basis, just as doctors and lawyers who are labeled professionals do now. This technology will increase rather than decrease the importance of the role of the classroom teacher — by demanding more of him in both knowledge of curriculum content and in his ability to instruct on an individual basis. Also, we know from experience that it is easy to give a teacher more data about students' performance than he can accommodate.

The problem of getting programs on the market has been

one of who makes the first move. On the one hand, curriculum developers, faced with the high cost and the large commitment of time necessary to produce a good program, want to see the customer "sign on the dotted line" before they make an extensive commitment. On the other hand, customers respond by saying they will not sign until they see the finished product and have an opportunity to test its validity. To break this deadlock, someone must make the first move. It would seem that both sides must take a step forward together.

3. Student Research

This mode of instruction allows the student to enter data and solve problems on instructional terminals. At least two areas are included here. The first is on-line computation such as that developed by Culler and Fried at the University of California. The second is simulation. A number of developmental programs in operation for various types of simulation are described by Hickey (1968).

The on-line computational area can also be subdivided into two categories. The most popular is problem solving. Many secondary schools are participating in some time-sharing network, such as Dartmouth's. Students learn to solve problems new to them, such as studying the behavior of some functions in mathematics. Students gain insight and an opportunity to work with functions in a way that was not possible previously. A second area is research in prediction. A high school boy recently submitted a program in the annual AEDS competition which predicted the time at which the ice on a river in Alaska would break in the spring thaw. This program involved research of the breakup dates of ice over many years, together with associated weather conditions. Variables were formulated, defined and entered in the program only after they were carefully checked and appropriately weighted.

Recently in the Midwest, a computer program was tested that was designed to predict which type of corn would produce the highest yield and best quality under various conditions. Years of research data had been summarized and variables formulated that appear to influence the growth and quality of corn. Now these data are used to suggest new hybrids and care.

For these applications, a time-shared system may offer the most for the least cost. However, as greater numbers of students perform research and as the complexity of programs submitted increases, it soon becomes advantageous to have one's own computer. When a system is used to execute problems after CAI hours and before EDP operations in the evening, it quickly becomes cost-effective through maximum usage. Add the Dial-A-Drill component to reach out into the surrounding homes during evening hours and one has a saturated system with low-cost-per pupil instructional programs and EDP operations.

The number of teachers who use a computer for research with their classes is small. There appears to be no consistent pattern except for the numbers of offerings which emphasize the learning of computer programming itself. Surely it will not be long before a pattern emerges as communication between various user groups improves.

4. Computer-Mediated Instruction

The concept of mediated instruction is very close to that of multimedia instruction — with one important difference. For the computer to mediate instruction, the sequence of topics must be under computer control, even when the student is off-line. Although it appears that no computer-mediated instructional systems are in operation at the present time, at least as described here, this approach could offer a high degree of individualization at a relatively low cost per pupil. The function of the system visualized is to (1) introduce a topic; (2) test; (3) prescribe appropriate off-line materials for study; (4) review the off-line material; (5) retest; (6) report to the teacher; and (7) introduce a new topic, etc.

Students are given either tutorial or drill-and-practice work, depending on the topic and situation at the beginning of each session. If they meet criteria on the set of exercises in the introductory lesson, they proceed directly to the next lesson. If they fail to meet criteria on any scale of the set of criteria exercises, the students are directed to off-line sources of information. The source may be a textbook or a film. Perhaps the student will be directed to his teacher first, then to some source for further information. When the off-line material has been studied, the student returns to the terminal and receives a review on the material he has studied and retakes the criteria test. The report to the teacher includes information on the pretest score, a prescription for off-line work, review results, and a posttest score.

Adults or mature young people who wish to learn a specific task or to make up specific deficiencies in their educational background would benefit most from this approach. For example, those who wish to take the GED examination for a high school equivalency certificate could take a sample test that contains a separate scale for each subject area contained in the examination. A separate score on each scale could be calculated automatically by the computer. Students who score below the acceptable level on any scale could be directed to off-line sources for more information or an explanation. When ready, they could return to the terminal for a review of the material they were to have covered. A passing score on the review lesson would permit the student to work in another area which was below passing or to retake the test. In some cases, the off-line material might be another CAI program operating independently from the mediated system. In other cases the off-line material could be programmed texts or conventional material.

Large Systems Versus Small Systems

At the present time, a large system is capable of operating 200 terminals simultaneously in a CAI mode. But this picture could change quite rapidly. A small system may be simply an expansion of an existing EDP facility or a small, stand-alone computer dedicated to CAI.

The cost figures on each system may be misleading. A large system may sound expensive but actually provide instruction at a lower cost per student hour than a smaller system that sells or leases for a lower price. The decision must rest on the quality of the programs available on each system as well as on the budget.

One advantage of a large system is that it usually can provide multiple services, such as CAI and EDP, which make the system cost effective on a 24-hour-a-day basis. A second advantage is that no more staff members are required to operate a single large system than several small ones, and the task of operating the system and generating reports is facilitated by having a larger computing capacity. However, the major disadvantage of the large system may be the telephone-line costs to a large number of remote users. Also, if the system breaks down, everyone is without CAI. On the plus side, when a large system goes down the manufacturer is more apt to send repairmen immediately.

The chief advantage of a smaller system is its low operational cost. But the EDP services during evening hours may be less encompassing, or not available at all. Some small systems currently on the market can be used for CAI only, and only one program can be in operation at any one time. These may or may not be important factors in choosing a system.

Selection of the Proper Program

The computer offers numerous opportunities to curriculum designers, but the questions that must be answered are still the basic ones: What is to be taught? What are the characteristics of the audience? What is the most efficient means of instruction? What is the relationship of the program to the objectives set for the students for the year? What evidence is there that the program will be successful?

All these questions and more need to be considered by anyone about to become involved in a CAI program. Finally, even though the point has been made several times, it bears repeating again — the only basis for judging CAI must be on the quality of the instructional program and not on the complexity of the hardware or the lack of it.

References

Atkinson, R. Computer-Based Instruction in Initial Reading. *Proceedings of the 1967 Invitational Conference on Testing Problems.* Princeton, N. J.: Educational Testing Service, 1968, pp. 464-470.
Atkinson, R. & Hansen, D. Computer Assisted Instruction in Initial

Reading: the Stanford Project. *Reading Research Quarterly, 2,* 1966, pp. 5-25.

Atkinson, R. & Wilson, H. *Computer Assisted Instruction: a Book of Readings.* New York: Academic Press, 1969.

Grant, C. B. S. CAI in Typing—an Unfilled Need. *Data Processing Magazine,* August, 1969, pp. 44-45.

Hickey, A. *Computer Assisted Instruction: Survey of the Literature.* (3rd ed.) Newburyport, Mass.: ENTELEK, Inc., October, 1968.

Hansen, D. *et al.* Research and Implementation of Collegiate Instruction of Physics via Computer Assisted Instruction, Vol. I. Technical Report No. 3, November, 1968, Computer Assisted Instruction Center, Florida State University.

Jerman, M. & Suppes, P. A Workshop on Computer Assisted Instruction in Elementary Mathematics. *The Arithmetic Teacher, 16,* 1969, pp. 193-197.

Jerman, M. Promising Developments in Computer Assisted Instruction. *Educational Technology, 9,* August, 1969, pp. 10-18.

Prince, J. A Practitioner's Report, Results of Two Years of Computer Assisted Instruction in Drill-and-Practice Mathematics. Progress Report No. 3, June, 1967 to May, 1969, McComb Schools, McComb, Mississippi, May, 1969.

Suppes, P. Stimulus-Response Theory of Finite Automata. *Journal of Mathematical Psychology, 6,* 1969, pp. 327-355.

.... & Morningstar, M. Computer Assisted Instruction. *Science, 166,* 1969, pp. 343-350.

Winer, M. *et al.* An Evaluation of the 1968-1969 New York City Computer Assisted Instruction Project in Elementary Arithmetic. Prepared by the City University of New York for the New York City Board of Education, July, 1969.

21

Accountability and Curriculum Reform

Leon M. Lessinger

A growing number of people are becoming convinced that we can hold the schools — as we hold other agencies of government — to account for the results of their activity.

In his Education Message of March 3, 1970, President Nixon stated "From these considerations we derive another new concept: *accountability*. School administrators and school teachers alike are responsible for their performance, and it is in their interest as well as in the interests of their pupils that they be held accountable."

The preamble to the agreement between the Board of Education of the City of New York and the United Federation of Teachers for the period September, 1969 - September, 1972, under the title *Accountability,* says "The Board of Education

---

LEON M. LESSINGER is Callaway professor of urban education at Georgia State University.

318

and the Union recognize that the major problem of our school system is the failure to educate *all* of our students and the massive academic retardation which exists especially among minority group students. The Board and the Union therefore agree to join in an effort, in cooperation with universities, community school boards and parent organizations, to seek solutions to this major problem and to develop objective criteria of professional accountability."

Many more pronouncements and program activities of a similar sort to these quoted above from key groups and important decision makers could be added. Clearly, a new educational movement is under way. We are entering the age of accountability in education.

The call for accountability in education is a summons to review and reform the educational system. The concept rests on two foundations: demonstrated student learning and independent review. These legs of accountability can have substantive effects upon the school curriculum and operation. This paper attempts to describe some of the more important of these potential impacts.

If schools are to be accountable for results, a new approach to their basic mission becomes mandatory and a new educational tradition will begin to emerge. Let us see why.

In the first place, emphasis will shift from teaching to learning. A growing research literature shows that, with respect to learning, teaching can be independent or influential, and that learning can take place without teaching. So independent is this relationship that some have termed it a teaching/learning paradox. This suggests that the present and traditional methods of requesting resources for education as the principal bases for accrediting schools will undergo basic change. Instead of equating quality in terms of resources allocated, such as kinds and numbers of teachers, space available, materials for use and books in the library, the independent variable will become *student accomplishment*. This will lead to a revised educational commitment for the nation.

In principle, the American educational commitment has been that every child should have access to adequate education

— this is the principle of equal educational opportunity. This commitment has been translated into dollar allocations for the people and the "things" of education. When a child has failed to learn, school personnel have assigned him a label — "slow," or "unmotivated," or "retarded." Accountability triggers a revised commitment — that every child shall learn. Such a revision implies the willingness to change a system which does not work, and find one which does; to seek causes of failure in the system, its personnel, its organization, its technology or its knowledge base, instead of focusing solely on students. This revised commitment can be properly called the principle of equity of results.

The second major effect of accountability on school curriculum reform centers on a technology of instruction and the notion of better standard practice. Without accountability for results, educational practice is unverified, and good educational practice is not identified. Technology is more than equipment, although equipment may be a part of technology. Technology refers to validated practice — the use of tested means to produce desired ends. When the author was a child, his father, a medical doctor, treated sore throats by swabbing them with a black substance called Argyrol. This caused gagging and was most unpleasant. Medical technology of that day suggested the medical practice of throat "painting" as good practice. It was the standard practice for treating sore throats. Today, given a better technology, the improved practice is the use of antibiotics. The use of Argyrol, a standard practice once, would today be malpractice. If cure and results were not the criterion, there would be little impetus for improved technology and better medical practice. The same logic applies to education.

The generation of an improved technology of instruction is allied to another benefit of accountability. Since World War II, several fields have been developed to enable leaders of very complex enterprises to operate effectively and efficiently. These emerging fields include: systems design and analysis, management by objectives, contract engineering (including warrantees, performance contracts, incentives), logistics, quality assurance, value engineering and the like. The coordination of these fields around educational concerns for an improved technology of instruction may be conveniently called *educational engineering*. Engineering has traditionally been a problem-solving activity, a profession dedicated to harnessing and creating technology to the accomplishment of desired ends, the resolution of difficulties and the promotion of opportunities. The American educational system is experiencing continuing and growing criticism and even overt challenge. Virtually everyone agrees that something has gone wrong and that something dramatic ought to be done about it. Engineering accountability into public education can be that dramatic "something."

The process of change in education starts with the design or location of good practice and ends with the installation of that good practice in the classrooms and learning centers of the nation, where it becomes standard practice. Educational engineering is the field designed to produce personnel with competence in this change process. Accountability for results in education is mere rhetoric without an engineering process to sustain it.

The "eye" of accountability lies in the phrase "modes of proof." Recognition of an expanded notion of assessment of results is the third major effect of accountability on school reform. For too long we have confused measurement of results in education with standardized achievement testing of the paper and pencil, normal curve based variety. Limited to this useful but restricted means of assessment, the pursuit of accountability would be frightening and even potentially destructive, for not everything in education can be (or ought to be) quantified in such a manner. But accountability in education, like accountability in other governmental enterprise, can make use of "evidence" from a variety of modes of attaining evidence. One thinks immediately of hearings, of juries, of expert witnesses, of certified auditors, of petitions and the like. Education can make use of all these modes, and can use such means of acquiring evidence as videotape and pupil performance in simulated real-life situations, to mention a few. To argue that scientific measurement is limited to narrow so-called objective tests is to display ignorance of the rich field of assessment, limited experience with science, and an inability to forsee the rapid development of creative output instruments and strategies which money and attention can promote.

The outside review component of accountability, another spur to school curriculum reform, can bring education more closely in line with the mainstream of science. Science relies for its very existence on qualified, independent review and replication. Thus, literally nothing is established in science unless and until it can be demonstrated by someone other than he who claims discovery or invention. The scientist defines a problem clearly, separates complex problems into their individual components, and clarifies their relationships to each other. He records data in a communicative and standard form and ultimately accepts an audit from objective peers by seeking publication in a journal. Scientists are neither better people nor better scholars than educators; they do not pursue more "scientific" or intrinsically "better" problems than teachers. They are simply subject to better monitoring by a system that both encourages and mobilizes the criticism of competent peers throughout their lives. Education, on the other hand, substitutes the gaining of a credential or license at a single point in a career for a continuing process of independent review and mandated accomplishment replication. Accountability addresses this lack by insisting upon techniques and strategies which promote objectivity, feedback of knowledge of results and outside replication of demonstrated good practice.

Outside review tied to public reporting probably explains the popularity of the emerging concept of accountability to the public at large. Schools in America serve and are accountable to the citizenry, not the professionals. Since the public served is in reality many "publics," each of whom have legitimate needs for information, accountability can lead to an opening up of the system to bring in new energy and support.

All of us in the business of formal education need to be reminded that we have promised each family sending its children and each community employing our services that we will do all within our power and competence to have each student succeed. Failure to deliver on promises is a test of our integrity.

22

Humanistic Education

Alfred S. Alschuler

In the Symposium, Alcibiades praised Socrates by saying, "He is exactly like the busts of (the god) Silenus which are set up in the statuaries' shops, holding pipes and flutes in their mouths; they open in the middle and have images of gods inside them. When I opened him (Socrates) and looked within at his serious purpose, I saw divine and golden images of such fascinating beauty that I was ready to do in a moment whatever Socrates commanded." Silenus was a minor Greek diety, a follower of Dionysus, disconcertedly homely, and nearly human. Usually he was seen drunk, sitting precariously on the back of an ass, yet he was renown for the unsurpassed wisdom and knowledge of past and future that emerged, as with Socrates, in any dialogue. Silenus was a popular god, for he symbolized the universal desire

ALFRED S. ALSCHULER is director of the Program on Humanistic Education at the State University of New York at Albany.

to be discovered and valued for one's inner virtues. All of us want to be a Silenus and to have our Alcibiades. "His words are ridiculous when you first hear them," continues Alcibiades, "but he who opens the bust and sees what is within will find that they are the only words which have a meaning in them, and also the most divine, abounding in fair images of virtue and extending to the whole duty of a good and honorable man." As Humanistic Educators, we are Alcibiades for our students, opening them up, discovering their inner virtues and drawing forth (literally, "educating") the "good and honorable man."

Only a small number of events in a lifetime radically change the way a person lives — a deeply religious experience, getting married or divorced, having a child, the death of parents, involvement in a serious accident. These dramatic, singular events transform a person's outlook, relation to others and view of himself. By comparison, daily learning experiences in school are undramatic, regularized and designed to promote steady, small increments in external knowledge rather than rapid changes in motives, values and relationships. Obviously we do not want to create regular apocalyptic events that drastically change students' personal lives. However, the ultimate teaching goal of Humanistic Education is to develop effective strategies and humane technology for educating inner strengths as profoundly as these rare life-changing events.

Uniquely Human Learning

Inchoate work in Humanistic Education exists. Scattered across the United States a handful of individuals working in isolated independence have created programmatic approaches to the discovery and enhancement of inner strengths. These Humanistic Education courses respond directly to previously unanswered student questions about setting goals, clarifying values, forming identity, increasing their sense of personal efficacy and having more satisfying relationships with others. The array of humanistic education courses include training in: achievement motivation, awareness and excitement, creative thinking, interpersonal sensitivity, affiliation motivation, joy, self reliance, self esteem, self assessment, self renewal, self actualization, self understanding, strength training, development of moral reasoning, value clarification, body awareness, meditative processes and other aspects of ideal adult functioning.* The variety of virtuous sounding titles testifies to the extent of developmental efforts underway, and also reflects the absence of a definitive description of ideal end states. In spite of this diversity, most of these courses share four general goals, in addition to their unique and specific emphases.

First, most courses attempt to develop a person's *imagination* by using procedures that encourage a constructive dialogue with one's fantasy life. In Synectics training, a creativity course, students are asked to "make the strange familiar" by fantasizing themselves inside a strange object, or to "make the familiar strange" by fantasizing about a common object. In other creativity courses, remote associations are encouraged in order to attain a new, useful and creative perspective on some problem. In other courses, students are taken on guided tours of day dreams and night dreams and on fantasy trips into their own body. In achievement motivation courses, students are encouraged to fantasize about doing things exceptionally well and are taught how to differentiate between achievement imagery and plain old task imagery. Later in the course, these achievement images are tied to reality through careful planning and projects. These procedures often bring previously ignored aspects of one's personality into awareness. Usually this is a joyful, enhancing experience in contrast to psychoanalytic dream analysis and free association, which are oriented to uncovering unconscious con-

---

*Descriptions of a number of these courses along with a comprehensive bibliography are contained in *New Directions in Psychological Education*, A. S. Alschuler, *Educational Opportunities Forum,* whole issue, January, 1970, State Education Department, Albany, New York. The three most well developed sets of curriculum materials exist for: 1) *Teaching Achievement Motivation,* by A. Alschuler, D. Tabor, J. McIntyre, Education Ventures, Inc., Middletown, Connecticut, 1970; 2) "Urban Affairs and Communications," T. Borton and N. Newberg, specialists in Humanistic Education, Philadelphia Board of Education Building, Philadelphia, Pa.; 3) "Value Clarification," see *Values and Teaching,* L. Raths, M. Harmon, S. Simon, Columbus, Ohio: Charles Merrill Books, 1966.

flicts. The implication is that most adults don't make constructive use of their fantasy life and have forgotten how to enjoy fantasy in a childlike but healthy way.

Second, most courses try to develop better *communication skills* by using non-verbal exercises, such as silent theater improvisations, free expression dance movements, meditation, the exaggeration of spontaneous body movements and a wide variety of games. In sensitivity training and encounter groups, non-verbal exercises are used to increase channels of communication. Some personal feelings can be expressed more effectively in motions than in words. Other times, dance and theater improvisations are used because they increase one's expressive vocabulary and are simply joyful experiences. As with constructive fantasizing, proponents of these methods believe that this type of expression, communication and learning is underdeveloped in most people.

A third goal common to these courses is to develop and explore individuals' *emotional responses* to the world. In most courses, how people feel is considered more important than what they think about things. Without these emotional experiences, ranging from laughter and exhilaration to tears and fear, the teacher is likely to consider the course a failure. For example, if an adolescent is scaling a cliff in an Outward Bound course and does not feel any fear, he will not increase his self confidence through his accomplishment. In Achievement Motivation courses, strong group feelings are developed to help support the individual in whatever he chooses to do well. In all of these courses, there is a shared belief that affect increases meaningful learning and that the capacity for the full range of affective responses is a crucial human potentiality often underdeveloped in adults. As a result, a wide range of techniques to enhance affect have been created.*

A fourth goal emphasizes the importance of *living fully and intensely* "here and now." The emphasis takes many forms. In

---

*Human Relations Education: A Guidebook to Learning Activities, prepared by the Human Relations Project of Western New York, reprinted by the University of the State of New York, the State Education Department, Curriculum Development Center, Albany, New York, 1969.

Gestalt awareness training, the goal is philosophically explicit. In most courses, it is subtle and implicit. Usually courses are held in retreat settings which cut people off from past obligations and future commitments for brief periods of time. The isolated resort settings dramatize the "here and now" opportunities. In general there is little emphasis on future "homework" or past personal history as an explanation for behavior. A vivid example is Synanon, a total environment program for drug addicts, which promotes "self actualization," and in the process cures addiction. Synanon requires the addict to kick drugs immediately upon entering the program. Other "bad" behavior which stands in the way of self actualization is pointed out as it occurs. Historical explanations for bad behavior are considered excuses and are not tolerated. In other Humanistic Education programs, the games, exercises, group process, etc., are model opportunities to explore, discover and try out new behavior "here and now." The assumption is that if a person can't change "here and now," where the conditions for growth are optimal, he is not likely to continue growing outside and after the course.

The existing procedures for developing new thinking, action and feelings in the "here and now" constitute humane methods for educating inner strengths. These methods make it possible to create, without trauma, the sequence of uniquely human learning that occurs during and after rare, dramatic, life-changing events.

In most of these naturally occurring events there is a strong focus of attention on what is happening "here and now." Whether it is a mother's labor during birth, the taking of marriage vows, the shock of realizing your arm is broken, or the ecstasy of a religious vision, the intensity of the experience crowds out familiar reactions. One characteristic that sets these experiences apart is the simultaneous intensity of radically new thoughts, actions and feelings. Usually these experiences break established relationships, as when a parent dies. Often they disrupt habitual patterns of living, or dissolve longtime beliefs. Whether the experience is revealing or traumatic in nature, it breaks basic continuities in a person's life. After the peak of the experience has passed, there is a period of some confusion and puzzlement, during which the person attempts to make sense out of what happened and to establish meaningful new continuities. This attempt takes many forms, from conversation with friends to meditation and prayer. Even if the experience is never fully understood, in time the consequences become clearer — how relationships are altered, what goals and values are different, and what new behaviors occur. After a while these changes seem more familiar and practiced. For example, new roles become less confusing. As the newness of being a parent wears off, the role becomes an integral part of a person's life, with its own rich set of relationships, behaviors and meanings. Similarly, in time, the traumatic loss of a loved one results in new relationships, behaviors and meanings that we internalize in our way of living.

This sequence of learning can be conceptualized as a six-step process and used as a guideline in planning Humanistic Education courses and sequencing existing humanistic procedures.

1. Focus attention on what is happening here and now by creating moderate novelty that is slightly different from what is expected.
2. Provide an intense, integrated experience of the desired new thoughts, actions and feelings.
3. Help the person make sense out of his experience by attempting to conceptualize what happened.
4. Relate the experience to the person's values, goals, behavior and relationships with others.
5. Stabilize the new thought, action and feelings through practice.
6. Internalize the changes.

This teaching strategy is not simply a heuristic device. A considerable amount of support for the validity of these guidelines exists in the theoretical and empirical research literature on personality change.*

---

*The most relevant summaries of this literature can be found in D. C. McClelland, "Toward a Theory of Motive Acquisition," *American Psychologist,* May, 1965; D. C. McClelland and D. G. Winter, *Motivating Economic Achievement,* Free Press, 1969; Campbell, J., Dunnette, M., "Effectiveness of T-Group Experience in Managerial Train-

This strategy indicates a number of ways that Humanistic Education differs from more traditional academic training. The most effective way to proceed through this learning sequence is to set aside a large block of time, often as long as a week or more, in a special location for a concentrated workshop. The atypical setting helps create moderate novelty, reduces distractions and helps focus attention on the new experiences. The concentrated time period is needed to allow the participants to follow new thoughts, to try out new behavior and to stick with their feelings to a natural conclusion. *Emotions,* in contrast to *thoughts,* tend to be non-reversible and difficult to stop quickly at the end of a 45-minute class period. This inhibits the expression of feelings, just as longer time periods encourage the expression of feelings. In this sense, Humanistic Education is experience based and inductive, in contrast to academic learning — which tends to be more abstract, logical and deductive.

A less obvious difference is the integration and simultaneous development of thoughts, feelings and actions. Learning achievement motivation, for example, involves developing a specific cognitive pattern of planning, a special type of excitement and a set of related action strategies. Most normal learning situations differ by rewarding expertise as a "thinker" in academic courses, or as a doer in physical courses like vocational education or athletics. This makes it especially difficult for teachers to be concerned in practice with educating the "whole child." However, there is some justification for the way schooling fragments human functioning into component parts. It does prepare students for adult lives in which separate role performances are played out in many directions. Just as students move from class to class during the day, adults move from role to role. We work in one place, have our intimate, loving relationships in another place, and usually travel to still other places for recreation. In each role adults are known for a narrow set of behaviors, just as students are known by their teachers as a math student, or typing student and rarely as a complex, many-sided individual. Experience-based learning integrates human func-

ing and Development," *Psychological Bulletin,* August, 1968, pp. 73-104.

tioning in the service of balanced maturation.

The art and technology of Humanistic Education, in large part, lies in the creation of productive learning experiences. Only the outlines of this technology are clear at this time. Teachers must be insightful diagnosticians of children's experience, so that moderately novel situations can be created. These situations bridge the gap between where the child is and where he can be. Thus, teachers must know a wide range of Humanistic Education procedures and be knowledgeable about the goals of human development. This expertise allows them to help students conceptualize, relate and apply their new experiential knowledge. Few learning experiences require extensive hardware and materials. Most procedures involve the person in relation to his own body, feelings and imagination or in relation to his environment and other people. A comprehensive source book of humanistic methods would be useful, but ultimately each teacher must adapt and sequence these methods to create the course of learning, i.e., the curriculum. In this sense, curriculum innovation is constant, and Humanistic Educators need to become adept at improvising sequences of learning that lead to internalization.

Compared to typical school goals, Humanistic Education courses aim for long-term internalization, not short-term gains in mastery. More precisely, these courses attempt to increase "operant" behavior as well as respondent behavior. Operant behavior is voluntary, seemingly spontaneous and certainly not required by the situation. What a person does with his leisure time is an indication of his operant behavior. Respondent behavior requires external cues and incentives before it will occur, just as an examination question brings forth respondent knowledge that otherwise probably would not have been demonstrated. In practice, most school learning calls for respondent behavior: multiple choice and true-false questions, reading assigned chapters, solving a given set of mathematics problems correctly, or writing an essay to a prescribed theme. To be most meaningful to a student, Humanistic Education must result in operant, internalized behavior, since after the course is over there will not be anyone to follow him around defining the problems, presenting the alternatives, guiding the response and evaluating the results. Paradoxically, the most important thing to do in helping a person develop long-term operant behavior is to stop doing anything. Support must be gradually transferred from external sources to the person's own inner resources. The problem is to leave on time — not too soon, because guidance is needed in the early phases, and not too late because that retards essential self reliance. At the present time, staging perfectly timed exits is an art in need of becoming a technology.

Humanizing Schools

Educating the "good and honorable man" is a ubiquitous aim of schooling. The problem is not the legitimacy of humanistic goals for public education, but how to translate these goals fully into practice. Specifically, it is unethical to develop students' ability to relate more warmly and directly their achievement motivation, their capacity for creative thinking through Humanistic Education courses, and then send them back into normal classrooms where these processes are not functional. For example, many Humanistic Education courses teach people how to develop collaborative and trusting relationships. Only in schools are there so few structured opportunities for practicing team-work and cooperation. From the humanistic point of view, the way people learn is just as important as what they learn. Ideally, there should be at least as much variety in the teaching-learning process within a single school as exists outside and after school, where students are variously required, ordered, coached, coaxed, persuaded, led, followed, threatened, promised, lectured, questioned, joined, challenged and left alone. Compared to this handsome array of naturally occurring learning processes, the typical range within a school is embarrassingly narrow. As Humanistic Education courses are introduced in schools, corresponding new processes should be available in regular courses in order for students to *practice what they have learned*.

How students learn is determined in large part by the rules of the implicit learning game and the teacher's leadership style. Both rules and leadership styles can be modified easily, although these methods of changing the processes of learning generally are not used. One of the first errors made by teachers who decide to increase the number of alternative learning processes is to decrease the number of rules and amount of teacher leadership, because this seems to decrease authoritarianism while increasing the possibility of many types of student initiative and learning styles. The key to a systematic variation in learning processes, however, is not how many rules and directions, but *what kind*. For example, such highly rule-governed activities as baseball and square dancing are non-authoritarian, and stimulate specific human processes. A variety of desired learning processes can be aroused by changing the rules which govern the nature of the scoring system, the type of obstacles to success and how decisions about strategy and tactics are made.* Implementing a variety of "learning games" requires of teachers great flexibility and repertoire of personal styles; they must have actualized many of the "divine and golden images" within themselves.

Just as it is unethical to develop inner strengths in students and put them into classrooms with a narrow range of legitimate learning styles, so too is it unethical to expect this flexibility within teachers or among a school faculty in a school that does not encourage, support and reward this variety. Ultimately, the administrative style, rules and rewards in a whole school must implement a pluralistic philosophy of education. The task of humanizing schools is, of necessity, multi-leveled.

The technology of planned change in schools is just now emerging. As recently as 1965 there was only one book devoted exclusively to the problem. Since then, the Office of Education and the National Training Laboratories have sponsored a large-scale investigation of how to increase innovation in teaching, learning and human relations at all levels in school systems — The Cooperative Project for Educational Development (COPED). The results of COPED suggest a four-phased strategy for maxi-

---

*For a complete explication of this position see "The Effects of Classroom Structure on Motivation and Performance," A. S. Alschuler, *Educational Technology,* August, 1969, and "Motivation in the Classroom," Chapter 3 in *Teaching Achievement Motivation,* A. Alschuler, D. Tabor, J. McIntyre, Education Ventures, Inc., Middletown, Connecticut, 1970.

mizing the likelihood of effectively introducing Humanistic Education in a school.*

1. *Selection*

    The top administrator and other key decision makers should be committed in principle to innovation in advance of specific training programs. Representatives from all groups within the school should be eligible for the special training programs.

2. *Diagnosis*

    Organizational strengths and weaknesses need to be assessed. This can be done most effectively through interviews with potential participants prior to the major change efforts. Information is obtained on such factors as the reward system, rules, communication patterns, current school issues and individual goals. Often it helps if these data are shared with the school system in a "diagnostic workshop." The purpose of this collaborative meeting is to further clarify the problem and place priorities on the goals of change.

3. *Introductory Training*

    A training program is designed to meet the defined needs. This workshop introduces the members of the school to relevant aspects of Humanistic Education. The workshop follows the six-step sequence described earlier. During the final phase, the school is encouraged to select an on-going "change management team" with representatives from all groups in the school.

4. *Follow Through*

    After the initial training the aim is to build into the school system a permanent team of self sufficient change management experts and well-trained Humanistic Edu-

---

*Based on a private conversation with Dr. Dale G. Lake, Director of COPED and editor of the *COPED, Final Report,* April, 1970, ERIC Files, U.S. Office of Education, Division of Research.

cators. The "change management team" coordinates this development, and conscientiously supports the introduction of Humanistic Education. These changes can be accomplished through internal task forces, additional specialized training or a variety of organizational development services from outside consultants. To start the "follow through," the team is encouraged to implement a high visibility project likely to succeed.

This strategy for change differs markedly from traditional approaches through graduate school teacher education and curriculum reform. It more closely resembles the creation of a Research and Development group within a corporation. This comparison highlights the fact that businesses often spend as much as 10% to 15% of their budget on R & D activities whereas the typical corresponding allocation by schools is less than 1%. The absence of this strong coordinating group in schools vitiates the effectiveness of "new curricula" and restricts the influence of well-trained new teachers. The creation of an effective change management team coordinates and internalizes curriculum innovation within the school.

Although the existence of this coordinating group does facilitate changes in the character of schooling, it does not guarantee perfect guidance towards ultimate human goals. For instance, some teachers make humanistic methods ends in themselves. The use of game simulations and role playing, ipso facto, is considered good. Creativity training courses are endorsed whether or not the problems to be solved are meaningful. Courses in Theater Improvisation are introduced to develop non-verbal behavior independent of significant personal relationships and goals. As a result, these courses and methods often fail precisely in what they are trying to accomplish. Strengthening imagination simply becomes bizarre fantasizing; a narrow focus on feelings leads to misunderstanding; exclusive attention to non-verbal communication stimulates anti-intellectual distrust of rational, goal-directed behavior.

Major advances in Humanistic Education are not likely to come simply from the proliferation of methods, training, teacher-curriculum-developers or the creation of self renewing schools, although each of these tasks are worthy. We need guiding visions of the "good and honorable man" and utopian models for the places where we live. Human abilities are strengthened, integrated, balanced and given meaning only in the pursuit of these goals. The essentially heuristic value of these unattainable ideals is conveyed in the word "Utopia," a pun made by Thomas More on "Eutopia" (good place) and "Outopia" (no place). In the last century, over 200 utopian communities were started — and none has survived. The longest-lived utopian communities are those which face the question of life and death daily (kibbutzem, Synanon) or which surround a single charismatic leader (Ashrams with their gurus) or those which share an ultimate faith (Amish, Oneida). In the United States, most of us no longer face daily life-death issues. We are surrounded by anti-heroes, who command our sympathy by their stand against those public figures who would be our gurus. Ultimate faith is being replaced by immediate action concerns against visible injustice and for personal pleasure. This is reflected in our schools, where pluralistic demands for innovation often mask the loss of an ultimate sense of mission.

The consequences of this value crisis are to leave key ethical questions unanswered for all types of education: What kind of teaching and subject matter is in the best interests of students? Who is to decide? How? How do you know when a teacher is competent? How do you know when teaching is effective, ineffective or negative? Choices about what new curricula to develop, how to train teachers, what kinds of learning outcomes to assess and how best to humanize schooling depend on answers to these ethical questions. Obviously, there is no single set of definitive conclusions; but, instead, there is the opportunity for all educators to engage in a uniquely human search for values. The continuing attempt to discover "divine and golden images" and to draw forth the "good and honorable man" is the mission of Humanistic Education.

23

Administrative
Implications of
Curriculum Reform

Max G. Abbott and Terry L. Eidell

It is assumed, as a point of departure, that there is common
agreement on the proposition that an organization such as a
school functions as a total system and that an alteration of any
part of the system produces alterations, however minute, in all
other parts of the system. Indeed, the very title of this paper
carries such a connotation; that is, modifications in the school
curriculum either require or lead to modifications in the administration of the school. Before proceeding with the discussion,
however, a brief comment on our use of the term *system* is
in order.

MAX G. ABBOTT is director of the Center for the Advanced Study of
Educational Administration and professor of education at the University of Oregon. TERRY L. EIDELL is a research associate in the Center
for the Advanced Study of Educational Administration and associate
professor of education at the University of Oregon.

When an organization is said to function as a system, it is meant that the organization consists of a number of components, with each component differentiated from each other in terms of particular functions to be performed, and that all of those functions contribute in some way to the accomplishment of the organization's purposes. Further, the term *system* implies that the relationships among the various components are characterized by interdependence, regularity, order and predictability.

There are many ways of identifying and describing the components, or sub-systems, of an organization; for analytical purposes it is useful to identify those components in terms of functions to be performed. Thus, for example, Katz and Kahn* have suggested five functional components of any system; the production or technical component, a supportive component, a maintenance component, an adaptive component and a managerial component.

The production component relates to those activities that comprise the major functions of the system. In the case of schools, this consists of the primary activities associated with pupil learning. The supportive component is concerned with the environmental relationships that are necessary to insure the procurement of the system's resources or inputs and the disposal of the system's products or outputs. The maintenance component refers to those activities that sustain and maintain the interdependent behavior necessary for task accomplishment. The adaptive component functions to maintain an awareness of changes occurring in the system's environment and to effect alterations in the system to accommodate those changes. The managerial component consists of the organized activities for controlling, coordinating and directing the other components toward goal achievement. Note that none of the components is described in terms of operating units or specific personnel; rather, they are described in terms of functions or activities that are performed, regardless of the particular units or positions to which those activities or functions are assigned.

---

*Daniel Katz & Robert L. Kahn. *The Social Psychology of Organizations*. New York: John Wiley, 1965.

Although a thorough analysis of an organization requires that all system components be considered simultaneously, for purposes of this paper the primary concern is the production (technical) component and the managerial component. The basic position again is that these components are interactive and interdependent, and that alterations in one necessarily produce alterations in the others.

Because of its pervasiveness and centrality to the total system, the production component is generally the most complex of all of a system's components or sub-systems. As indicated earlier, in the case of a school this component consists of the primary activities associated with pupil learning. In conventional terminology, this component can be viewed as encompassing three major categories or sub-components: instructional materials, instructional processes and instructional arrangements.

Included in instructional materials is the content of the subject matter to be learned and the media used to convey content to pupils. Thus, in addition to well-known subject matter areas, such as mathematics, language and social studies, this category refers to the use of textbooks, programmed materials, movies, television, teaching machines and instructional use of computers.

Instructional processes refer to the methods, tactics, or procedures used for the instruction of students. Included are such strategies as lectures, student recitation, group discussion, field projects, instructional games, and pupil self-directed learning.

Instructional arrangements refer to the means devised for bringing pupils, instructional materials and instructional processes together. This category includes such organizational provisions as the self-contained classroom, departmentalized instruction, team teaching, continuous progress plans, large- and small-group instruction, the dual progress plan and modular scheduling.

It is obvious that in the above categories the materials, processes and arrangements that could have been included in the three categories are merely sampled. It is not the purpose, however, to develop a complete catalog for these categories but rather to illustrate the nature of the interdependence of the components and sub-components of a system and to discuss some of the *implications of this interdependence for the administration of schools as curriculum reform occurs.*

Both the popular mass media and professional literature abound with accounts of innovation in the nation's schools. The impression conveyed by much of the communication on educational innovation is that the forces of society and technological developments are initiating radical and pervasive alterations in the materials, processes and arrangements for instruction in schools. In fact, there are those who argue that the ability of the schools to survive in a rapidly changing society has been due in large measure to the capacity of the schools to change their goals, procedures and organizational arrangements to adapt to shifting environmental forces.

At the same time, however, those who study schools in depth report that the reform movement in education is more illusory than real. Despite the development of new materials and techniques, and in the face of the emergence of a new vocabulary in educational circles, the *practices* employed in most classrooms today are amazingly similar to those employed a generation or more ago. The typical teacher still considers his primary function to be that of presenting information and quizzing students to see if they have ingested that information. And the schools still abound with students who are largely disinterested in what is going on.

A major source of this apparent disagreement about the state of change in the production component of educational organizations is the currently vague and imprecise definition of the term *educational innovation.* This term is commonly applied both to temporary experimental situations and to relatively permanent or institutionalized changes. Yet, available evidence indicates that although temporary experimentation in the production component is rampant, few changes of any magnitude have actually become institutionalized. The few changes in the production component that have been institutionalized are those that disturb minimally other components and sub-components of the organization. On the whole, educational organizations have so far effectively resisted the adoption and institutionalization of radically new instructional materials, processes, or arrangements.

This observation leads to a useful way of categorizing changes. The initial assumption was that a change in any component of the school would create secondary changes in every other component. However, it is apparent that the quality and quantity of the secondary changes produced will vary according to the nature of the primary (initial) change. For example, the adoption of a new textbook will generally create only minor modifications in the processes and arrangements for instruction. On the other hand, the adoption of such an innovation as computer assisted instruction will undoubtedly produce massive and fundamental changes, not only in the production sub-components but also in the other organizational components. To take into account this type of distinction, primary changes that produce minor secondary changes are referred to as *non-reactive* and those that produce massive secondary changes as *reactive* thus, potential changes can be arranged along a reactivity continuum.

The earlier stated conclusion about the resistance of educational organizations to adopting and institutionalizing radical new changes can now be restated. It can now be asserted that schools have effectively resisted the adoption of relatively reactive primary innovations. Although this statement testifies to the stability of the educational organization that has been created, the long-term viability and even the morality of its continued existence must be questioned in light of current social demands for responsiveness in our social institutions.

We are living in an era of social upheaval and personal activism, a time when the nation's citizenry is insisting upon a greater recognition of the rights of the individual, and is demanding that our social institutions be more responsive to those rights. These social pressures are especially relevant for educational organizations because: (1) education is seen by most activist groups as the primary means through which individuals can accomplish their personal goals; (2) educators have long held as an ideology, at least at the verbal level, the uniqueness and importance of the individual; and (3) our developing technology is producing the wherewithal by which meaningful individualization of learning can become a practical reality. Given this set of social, ideological and technological circumstances, it is anticipated that future changes in the production component of educational organizations will be oriented toward instructional flexibility truly sensitive to the needs and demands of individual students.

If this premise is accepted as a reasonably accurate estimation of future directions in education, one fact emerges. Schools in the years ahead must develop the ability and evince a willingness to adopt *reactive* innovations. Serious attention to the needs of the individual student; his goals and aspirations; his social, cultural and educational background; and his interests and learning style demands that new materials, processes and arrangements be developed and implemented which do more than touch the periphery of the production component of the educational organization.

From the best evidence available, and in view of developments under way, it seems likely that the adaptation of instruction in the direction of increased attention to the interests, needs and abilities of individual students will necessitate at least the following: (1) the use of computers and other complex devices; (2) the development of a more rational and explicit division of labor — meaningful task specialization — among instructional and supervisory personnel; (3) some decentralization of authority and responsibility within the organization and a concomitant shift in the focus of many decisions from individuals to groups; (4) the implementation of sophisticated management information systems and planning procedures; (5) the explication of behavioral objectives and the development of materials, processes and arrangements by which those objectives might be achieved; and (6) dependable and meaningful methods of assessing the outcomes of the instructional program.

Although the economic feasibility of utilizing computers and other complex technological devices directly for instructional purposes is still being tested, it is clear that such devices will be indispensable in the management of instruction when individualization becomes common practice. At the classroom level, it will be imperative that vast amounts of information be accumulated regarding each pupil; that this information be retrieved with ease, speed and convenience; and that it be updated regularly and systematically. Otherwise, the provision of learning events and experiences tailored to meet individual learning needs would be impossible.

At the school level, similar quantities of information will be required if the school faculty is to assess with any reasonable degree of confidence the effectiveness of the instructional program as it is being carried out, and if appropriate personnel are to develop new materials and procedures to satisfy unmet needs. Such vast amounts of information can be stored, retrieved and manipulated only with the aid of electronic data processing.

Whether or not computers play a central role in the direct instruction of students in the years immediately ahead, it is becoming clear that human agents can no longer be depended upon as the primary medium for *presenting information* to students or for helping students to develop basic skills. The motivational power inherent in various visual, audio and manipulative media is too great to justify their continued use as mere adjuncts to the central medium of instruction, the "teacher." Moreover, mechanical and electronic aids, with adequate supporting "software," can accomplish what "teachers," who will continue to be in short supply, cannot accomplish; that is, they can present information and skill-developing exercises uniquely suited to a particular student's learning needs at a given point in time. These aids are not confined, as are "teachers" (because of their limited numbers in relation to students), to gearing presentations to the average of a group.

The benefits to be derived from the use of technological devices for presenting information and developing skills are, however, not fully encompassed by those suggested here. Perhaps more importantly, such devices can free humans to perform crucial and distinctly human tasks. These include such things as diagnosing (in a clinical sense) cognitive, social and emotional problems that currently so seriously impede student learning. They also include working with pupils in a social setting to increase their interpersonal skills and to aid them in becoming more effective members of our group-oriented society.

Thus, the increased use of adequate technological aids can lead to a restructuring of the tasks in schools. This restructuring may reduce the degree to which schools are labor-intensive organizations and, in turn, lead to the development of a more rational and explicit division of labor in the schools. The new division of labor would be based upon specialization relevant to performing unique and crucial functions in relation to pupil development rather than a specialization based upon traditional academic disciplines or meaningless status considerations.

A substantial increase in the individualization of instruction will require a shift in the locus of instructional decisions from supervisory and administrative personnel to instructional personnel. This does not mean, however, increased independence for teachers. On the contrary, it implies increased *inter*dependence of specialized personnel as they use vastly increased amounts of information, superior in quality to any that is available today, to plan instructional materials, exercises and events to meet the challenges of a new approach to instruction. Thus, both planning for instruction and instruction itself will call for the cooperative and collaborative efforts of a variety of persons, each possessing specialized competencies, knowledge and skills.

All of this is to say that if schools are to be truly responsive to their individual clients, new processes of educational planning will be required. For example, it will no longer be sufficient to offer a course in American history which requires students to attend a fixed number of classes at specified times throughout a year, and that has as its objective some vague, general statement about good citizenship. Individualization of instruction requires flexibility in the scheduling of instructional events and the creation of meaningful units of instruction which have clear-cut objectives. Without more precise and sophisticated educational planning than now occurs, individualization would precipitate both organizational and instructional chaos.

As we noted above, sound educational processes of the nature required for individualization must be supported by well-designed educational and organizational information systems.

Those who execute the planning of instructional experiences must have detailed information regarding the materials, processes and arrangements for instruction; the behavioral objectives to be achieved; and reports on the evaluation of outcomes. In addition, planners must be aware of the organizational resources being consumed by each instructional program so that realistic allocations can be made in light of a particular program's contribution to the over-all goals of the schools. These systems must also provide the information required to assist students in planning their own educational programs. The traditional cumulative pupil-personnel folder will not provide information in sufficient quantity or detail about a student's activities and performance to support planning for an individualized instructional program.

To summarize, we have contended that curriculum reform in the decade ahead will consist primarily of the development of instructional materials, processes and arrangements that will both allow and encourage students to function largely as independent learners. Such reform will involve reactive innovations and will have far-reaching implications for the administration of schools:

First, administrators will be forced to develop a capacity for understanding the organization as a total functioning system. This includes the ability to identify various components within the system, to understand the interdependencies that exist among these components, and to plan in advance alterations that are required in the supporting components when a deliberate change is made in the production (instructional) component.

Second, administration in schools will become more and more a *supportive* function in contrast to a *controlling* function. Thus, administrators will increasingly be called upon to provide the materials, the personnel resources and the climate that is needed to meet the demands of a rapidly changing curriculum.

Third, administrators will need to develop the skills and provide the tools for more adequate and sophisticated use of information in educational planning. This will involve at least the ability to utilize electronic data processing devices and a knowledge of planning techniques that will make possible the rational use of information.

Fourth, the introduction of new personnel specializations

in schools, with a concomitant increase in the division of labor, will place new demands on administrators for coordination. Specialization inevitably leads to some fractionalization of interests on the part of personnel; unless the activities of specialized personnel are coordinated and focused upon the accomplishment of explicit organizational goals and objectives, such fractionalization can be highly deleterious to the functioning of the organization. With adequate coordination of efforts and activities, however, increased specialization, accompanied by increased personal competence, can enhance greatly the over-all functioning of the organization. Such coordination is by definition an administrative task.

Epilogue
Perspective on Curriculum Design

In concluding this series of papers on *Curriculum Design in a Changing Society,* I write from the perspective of having read the preceding essays. This is both an advantage and a disadvantage. It is a disadvantage because I now feel a certain responsibility toward what the others have written and, as a consequence, am somewhat restrained. It is an advantage because what I have read shapes and gives direction to my thoughts. I am not faced, then, with that familiar nail-biting frustration of being free but despairingly unable to choose among an indeterminate number of enticing alternatives.

There are some difficult choices of inclusion and exclusion to be made, nonetheless. Placing these papers against a background of other writing in the field and my own curricular preoccupations suggests four rather closely related themes. I shall develop only the first but cannot resist writing a few sentences on the others.

347

First, there is the lack of agreement among these and other writers regarding what one talks about under the rubrics, "curriculum," and more specifically, "curriculum design." I shall return to this shortly.

Second, there is the proclivity of students of education to think and write about curriculum as though one large step removed from the realities of students' learning, in the classroom or elsewhere. This complicates even more the problem of little agreement on what constitutes the field. Not being agreed on the realities and their nature, we have little hope, surely, of agreeing on the abstract conceptualization of these unknown realities. A perusal of preceding papers suggests that some writers begin with the assumption that the curriculum is the specific stimulus to which students are responding at any given moment. Others see it as a more general thing — a conglomerate of subjects comprising the program of elementary and secondary schools or colleges, for example.

Third, there is the apparent difficulty of demonstrating clear-cut relationships between data from the several data sources we usually identify as relevant to curriculum development and curricula or curriculum decisions. Presumably, curricula should be designed to reflect rather clearly the "fourteen reasons why our curricula need changing" identified by Burns and Brooks. Similarly, presumably, the curricula of tomorrow's schools should differ from today's, in some way responding to the ten elements in the discernible future predicted by Shane and Shane. But Otto observes that, except in special instances, "the general curriculum of the public schools has never been related directly to current social problems or the community." Why, then, all our concern about the importance of society as a data source in identifying educational objectives? Perhaps, if we studied the matter first-hand, we would discover factors which are far more influential in determining what children and youth learn in school.

Fourth, perhaps accounting for the continued existence of the first three problems, is the matter of conceptualizing curriculum as both real processes and a field of study. And, closely related to it, is the matter of perceiving some useful relationship between abstract conceptualization on one hand and curricular realities on the other. Is the practitioner skeptical of curriculum theory because his background is anti-theoretical or lacking in theoretical perspective? Or is he skeptical because extant theory explains little or nothing about what concerns him? The answer has profoundly different implications for human action.

But now let me return to the first of these four themes, a theme which certainly is enmeshed with the remaining three. The maturity of a field of study is marked, in large measure, by agreement among its students as to what one studies and discusses as a professional sociologist, psychologist, philosopher, or whatever. Each field, then, has its commonplaces, serving to mark rather precisely the points for discourse, whether of agreement or disagreement. Thus, "transfer of training" currently is a commonplace in the field of psychology, with special reference to the sub-field usually referred to as "learning" or "learning and development." The psychologist quickly identifies with transfer of training as a commonplace; may engage in heated argument about conflicting views regarding it, probably citing research to back his position or that of his chosen protagonist; but cannot escape it as a topic about which he must be knowledgeable. A series of internally consistent positions with respect to a number of commonplaces usually is drawn upon in explaining a phenomenon or several phenomena thought to be related. Such a series often is graced with the status of a theory. New research on any commonplace or a fresh interpretation of existing research often calls for reconstruction of a theory and may lead to its rejection and replacement. Occasionally, a new theory leads to the identification of hitherto unrecognized commonplaces. These, in turn, find their way into the specialized discourse of the field as the new theory gains corroborating research and followers.

Very little of this sort of thing has occurred in the field of curriculum, although there has been a formidable amount of discourse *about* theory. There has been a great deal of theorizing but precious little of the necessary, preliminary hard work of identifying and describing the phenomena for which, presumably, theory is to advance explanations and predictions. Scholars in other fields know the futility of bypassing such processes (although many have no compunctions about doing so when they choose to become curriculum experts*). It might be useful even to find out why so many students of curriculum content themselves with talk about theory or with efforts to borrow principles and theories from other fields. Is it because persons addressing themselves to the field of curriculum assume that the commonplaces are obvious and need no systematic identification and justification?

Perusal of the literature suggests the folly of any such assumption. There is not agreement even on what *a* curriculum or *the* curriculum is. This might not be a serious problem (after all, one can define things as one wishes, although this confounds communication) if the implications of a very few alternative definitions were worked through. But working them through immediately confronts the problem of little agreement on commonplaces. With preliminary agreement on what one addresses himself to under the rubric, "curriculum," it becomes possible to discuss the theoretical and practical implications and consequences of markedly differing definitions of curriculum. Lacking such tentative agreement, discourse languishes and is non-cumulative. Partly as a consequence, the practical operations of curriculum-building languish, too. Otto states the problem well, in discussing revision of the elementary school curriculum: "The activities . . . are numerous, diverse, uncoordinated, and frequently in conflict with each other regarding method, content and goals."

It is clear, for example, that the major words in the title of this book, "curriculum design," convey quite different messages to the several authors. Most understand the words in the very general sense of developing entire programs of studies — hence,

---

*After careful study of the literature, Tjerandsen developed a set of rather persistent curricular commonplaces and then examined the writings of persons presumably writing about the social science curriculum. He found that most neglected most of the commonplaces. Whatever they were writing about, they were not writing about the same thing — and not always about curriculum, according to Tjerandsen's definition of the field. See Carl Tjerandsen, "The Adequacy of Current Treatments of General Education in the Social Sciences." Unpublished doctoral dissertation, University of Chicago, 1958.

designing the curriculm. Calfee ties together the *what* and *how* of teaching as the two main questions of curriculum design. Kapfer confines his concerns almost exclusively to ". . . the derivation, specification, selection, mediation and assessment of behavioral objectives." One writer, Sullivan, ties directly and almost exclusively into a much more specialized problem which has been the classic preoccupation with curriculum design of a handful of persons identifying themselves as curriculum specialists. This is the problem of arranging what the learner is to be exposed to (the learning opportunity or learning experience*) in some kind of order. The result of the arranging/ordering process is a curriculum design.

Those of us who have worked in the curriculum vineyard for a generation or more and who have studied the work of an earlier generation of curriculum specialists use a special terminology and conjure up certain generally agreed-upon images of what this terminology represents. We concern ourselves, for example, with *continuity* and *sequence* and with the organizing principle or principles used to justify this or that scheme of ordering stimuli (e.g., chronological or psychological**). We address ourselves to *scope* and to whether different kinds of stimuli are to be *correlated* or *integrated*. The result of choices made is a design of vertical and horizontal relationships, each design identified by a descriptive term such as broad fields, core, discipline-centered and the like. One can readily dismiss such

---

*Tyler uses the term "learning experience" to identify the curricular stimulus. See Ralph W. Tyler, *Basic Principles of Curriculum and Instruction*. Chicago: University of Chicago Press, 1950. I prefer the term "learning opportunity" because it avoids, I think, confusing the stimulus with what happens as a result of it. See John I. Goodlad (with Maurice N. Richter, Jr.), "The Development of a Conceptual System for Dealing with Problems of Curriculum and Instruction." Contract No. SAE-8024, Project No. 454, Office of Education, U. S. Department of Health, Education, and Welfare, 1966.

**The late Virgil E. Herrick made distinguished contributions to questions of curriculum organization and design. See *Strategies of Curriculum Development*. Selected writings of the late Virgil E. Herrick (edited by James B. Macdonald, Don W. Andersen and Frank B. May). Columbus, Ohio: Charles E. Merrill Books, Inc., 1965.

words as jargon, but they facilitate communication — as do the specialized, technical words of all fields. Those in command of them have an immediate basis for discussing mutually compelling problems of curriculum design.

It is interesting that these words and the commonplaces they symbolize rarely appear in the preceding essays. This fact does not diminish the value of any one paper as a discrete entity. But it virtually eliminates the vigorous, comparative analysis by means of which agreements and disagreements regarding a series of curricular commonplaces pertaining to curriculum design might be sorted out and explored. If one were to accept "objectives" as a commonplace of curriculum design — and there would be disagreement on this — then a number of papers could be discussed comparatively, but only by ignoring large sections of each. And then, it would be exceedingly difficult, if not impossible, to discuss the omitted portions of each paper comparatively because each moves off with a differing set of preoccupations. Some overlap not at all. For example, no meaningful comparison of the papers by Bushnell and Sullivan are possible because they address themselves to differing levels of remoteness from the learner, Sullivan being right on top of what the learner might learn when (readiness) and Bushnell concerning himself with general matters of curriculum change (a system approach).

Again, it is interesting to speculate on this lack of agreed-upon curricular commonplaces and an accompanying vocabulary. It could be the result of increasing specialization. The educationist of yesterday was almost certain to gain some introduction to the guilds of the educational psychologist, philosopher and historian, and of the administrative or curriculum specialist. Today, he is much less likely to be exposed formally to this breadth.

More likely, however, it is our failure to take the necessary first steps in establishing a field of inquiry. We simply have no common perceptions of "phenomena curricula." Consequently, we have no common subject matter and no common vocabulary. What are children taught in school? And is all of what they are taught, taken collectively, the curriculum? Are there objectives guiding what is taught? Whose objectives — the teacher's, the student's, the curriculum maker's? Is there a design for what is taught? Whose design? And what difference does it make?

It is long past time to quit assuming that the assumptions about curriculum with which we begin are obvious and commonly held. It is time, also, to quit theorizing or talking *about* theory in general. Curriculum processes are far too many and complex to be encompassed by any general theory. Perhaps, in time, we will have theoretical formulations pertaining to selected commonplaces. Sullivan's rigorous analysis of readiness provides an exemplar treatise.

As stated earlier, however, the road to exploratory and predictive theories regarding specific commonplaces is yet to be mapped and described. In this regard, there is little ambiguity in what Schwab has proposed: "What is wanted is a totally new and extensive pattern of *empirical* study of classroom action and reaction; a study, not a basis for theoretical concerns about the nature of the teaching or learning process, but a basis for beginning to know what we are doing, what we are not doing, and to what effect; what changes are needed, which needed changes can be instituted with what costs or economics, and how they can be effected with minimum tearing of the remaining fabric of educational effort."* Such empirical study should provide the data needed for the practical matter raised succinctly by Oliver: "In short, the key question at this stage in the development of the curriculm field is *not* 'How ought curricular events to be identified, described, analyzed and ordered?' but 'What curricular events ought to be identified, described, analyzed and ordered?' " Let us begin our study, then, with the curricular events that now exist. Finding, quantifying and documenting them is the first order of business.

John I. Goodlad
University of California, Los Angeles and
Institute for Development of Educational Activities, Inc.

---

*Joseph J. Schwab. *The Practical: A Language for Curriculum,* p. 31. Washington: Center for the Study of Instruction, N.E.A., 1970.